Depictions of Home in African American Literature

Depictions of Home in African American Literature

Trudier Harris

LEXINGTON BOOKS
Lanham • Boulder • New York • London

Published by Lexington Books
An imprint of The Rowman & Littlefield Publishing Group, Inc.
4501 Forbes Boulevard, Suite 200, Lanham, Maryland 20706
www.rowman.com

86-90 Paul Street, London EC2A 4NE

Copyright © 2021 by The Rowman & Littlefield Publishing Group, Inc.

All rights reserved. No part of this book may be reproduced in any form or by any electronic or mechanical means, including information storage and retrieval systems, without written permission from the publisher, except by a reviewer who may quote passages in a review.

British Library Cataloguing in Publication Information Available

Library of Congress Cataloging-in-Publication Data

Names: Harris, Trudier, author.
Title: Depictions of home in African American literature / Trudier Harris.
Description: Lanham : Lexington Books, [2021] | Includes bibliographical references and index.
Identifiers: LCCN 2021038125 (print) | LCCN 2021038126 (ebook) | ISBN 9781793649638 (cloth) | ISBN 9781793649652 (paper) | ISBN 9781793649645 (epub)
Subjects: LCSH: American literature—African American authors—History and criticism. | Home in literature. | African Americans in literature. | African American families in literature. | LCGFT: Literary criticism.
Classification: LCC PS153.B53 H37 2021 (print) | LCC PS153.B53 (ebook) | DDC 810.9/356408996073—dc23/eng/20210930
LC record available at https://lccn.loc.gov/2021038125
LC ebook record available at https://lccn.loc.gov/2021038126

In memory of
Jacqueline Miller Carmichael
and
Lovalerie King
Scholars Extraordinaire

Remembering my brother,
Husain Abdul Alim
(14 July 1946 – 7 July 2021),
who searched worldwide
for a home

Remembering my brother,
Peter Harris
(30 July 1949 – 10 September 2021),
who was a long way
from home

Contents

Acknowledgments	ix
Introduction: Home in African American Literature: Difficult to Define, Challenging to Claim	1
Chapter 1: Movement, Migration, and Homelessness: Margaret Walker's *Jubilee* (1966)	21
Chapter 2: Where I Live Is Not Home: James Baldwin, *Go Tell It on the Mountain* (1953); Toni Morrison, *The Bluest Eye* (1970); Suzan-Lori Parks, *Topdog/Underdog* (2001)	39
Chapter 3: Lonely Place, Unwelcoming Space: A. J. Verdelle's *The Good Negress* (1995)	73
Chapter 4: A Mother's Desire, A Son's Hell: Daniel Black's *Perfect Peace* (2010)	95
Chapter 5: A Mother's Domination, A Family's Submission: Dorothy West's *The Living Is Easy* (1940)	127
Chapter 6: Wrapped in Imagination and Desire: Countee Cullen, "Heritage"; Ann Petry, "Mother Africa"; Lorraine Hansberry, *A Raisin in the Sun* (1959); Alice Walker, "Everyday Use" (1973); Toni Morrison, *Song of Solomon* (1977); Phyllis Alesia Perry, *Stigmata* (1998); Yaa Gyasi, *Homegoing* (2016); James Weldon Johnson; Sterling A. Brown	151
Conclusion: While We're in This Place . . .	187
Bibliography	195
Credits	205

Index	207
About the Author	219

Acknowledgments

This project began in a research conference. In April of 2016, Kavon Franklin, who teaches at Alabama State University in Montgomery, Alabama, was in touch to determine my availability to deliver the keynote address for an annual Faculty-Student research gathering. She indicated that the selected speaker also offered suggestions for the scholarly focus of the conference. Of the suggestions I made, committee members elected to focus on home and its representations in African American literature. Focusing my keynote address for October of 2016 on that topic began the journey that has brought me to this point. There are many folks along that pathway who deserve thanks.

In these intervening years, I have made presentations at several universities and at conferences in which I centered upon the topic of home in African American Literature. Dolan Hubbard, now retired from Morgan State University, invited me to deliver the annual "Ruthe T. Sheffey Lecture on African American Literature, Female Studies" at Morgan State University in March of 2017; I was invited to present a Plenary Address at the British Association of American Studies Conference at Canterbury Christ Church University, Kent, England in April of 2017; I presented the Sara and Jess Cloud Distinguished Lecture at The College of William and Mary in September of 2017; I also lectured on home as part of the ceremonies surrounding my receiving The Clarence E. Cason Award in Nonfiction Writing at the University of Alabama in March of 2018.

I am grateful to the University of Alabama for approving my sabbatical proposal for the 2018–2019 academic year and to the National Humanities Center for awarding me the John Hope Franklin Residential Fellowship for 2018–2019 that enabled me to complete a substantial portion of the manuscript.

Laura Wilson, who organized The Southern Writers/Southern Writing Graduate Conference, also provided me with an opportunity to discuss the topic at Ole Miss in July of 2019. Harvey Long, Archivist and Curator at the State Black Archives, Museum and Research Center at Alabama A&M University, invited me to lecture on the topic in Huntsville, Alabama, in September of 2019. Cheylon Woods, Director of the Ernest J. Gaines Center in Lafayette, Louisiana, invited me to deliver the annual Ernest J. Gaines Lecture, where I focused on the topic in October of 2019 specifically in reference to Gaines's *A Lesson Before Dying*.

I thank all the students who were enrolled in my Senior Seminar in African American literature at the University of Alabama during the fall semester of 2019, during which we explored "Ungraspable?: Depictions of Home in African American Literature." I very much appreciate the insights they offered, which in turn led me to think more about the topic.

I also extend thanks to Jim Watkins of Berry College, who invited me to present the McCoy Lecture on Southern Women's Writing in February of 2020, for which I focused on Octavia E. Butler's *Kindred* and the complexities of home that Butler evokes in that text.

For all of these opportunities, I express supreme gratitude.

I also express my gratitude—perennially—to the members of the Wintergreen Women Writers' Collective, who have been aware of this project from the beginning and who offered consistent and unwavering support in the development of this book. Special shoutouts to Janus Adams, Daryl Cumber Dance, Joanne V. Gabbin, Nikki Giovanni, Maryemma Graham, Sandra Y. Govan, Karla F. C. Holloway, Marilyn Mobley, Opal Moore, and Ethel Morgan Smith. I extend additional thanks to Maryemma Graham for research suggestions as well as for allowing her student assistants, especially doctoral candidate Arnab Chakraborty, to conduct searches for me in the archives of the Project on the History of Black Writing, for which Graham is the Founder.

I extend special thanks to Shelby Russell and Alden Perkins for their meticulous work in guiding my book through the intricacies of the publication process at Lexington Books. I thank Cynthia Darling Landeen, my indexer, for yet another fine example of her work. Cynthia has ensured, yet again, that I "love the way [my] book ends."

Throughout this venture, Keith Clark has been most supportive in always offering Godspeed and good wishes. E. Patrick Johnson not only pointed me to various sources, but he added a text of his own for consideration for the project. I thank them both.

Hearty thanks to Lynn Orilla Scott for her meticulous reading of the manuscript as well as for her helpful suggestions for enhancing it.

As always, I am eternally grateful to my sister, Anna Harris McCarthy, for her unqualified support of any endeavor I undertake as well as for her superb critiquing and proofreading skills.

Introduction

Home in African American Literature: Difficult to Define, Challenging to Claim

Home. Ideally in American society it evokes a space that serves as a retreat from the public-faced, faster-paced, work-driven cares of the world. It denotes a space where biologically related occupants of a house, apartment, or other dwelling have transformed that physical structure into the intangible concept of a home, that private domain where family groups go constructively about their lives. In those physical spaces, the occupants thrive in well-kept neighborhoods in modest as well as upscale environments. Home conjures up nuclear families with mothers and fathers who provide emotional, spiritual, and financial support for their offspring. It is imbued with notions of love, harmony, peace, and an overall positive atmosphere. It is, in the traditional American sense, a rendition of one of the physical features of the American Dream. It is a space where all is well and all work together as a group for the unity and success of the whole. In this often-rendered, carefully constructed and mythologized narrative, conflicts—if they exist at all—recede into the background, and the image of successful human interactions takes precedence over everything else. The storybook narrative dominates and covers over any deviation from its established norm. Even if that advocated reality has gaps in it, as it obviously does when race and class are averaged into the formula, those gaps are usually pushed into the background. There is an even larger gap between that touted reality (even reality with gaps) and representation in commercial, visual, and literary arts. Norman Rockwell's painting, *Freedom From Want*, for example, features a glowingly happy nuclear family in a pristine and carefully cultivated homespace that is dramatically different from the kitchenettes and other cramped homespaces in which photographers captured African American families in the WPA images that Richard Wright includes in *12 Million Black Voices: A Folk History of the Negro in the United States*.[1] The movement from the visual to the literary is equally striking. African American literature presents a prime example as a contrast to the American family ideal depicted in a literary source such as Harper Lee's *To Kill a Mockingbird* (1960). The two children in the family in that text—even absent the mother—have a supportive father who listens to them, guides and teaches them, and protects them against tangible forces such as a rabid dog as well as intangible forces such as racism that can be manifested at times in tangible ways. Arguably, the maid as mother figure situates the family in the ideal category.[2]

On the landscape of African American literary representation, home is often not even a distant relative to Americanized, mythologized reality; it is a complete stranger. Throughout African American existence and throughout the history of reflections of African American life in imaginative literary creations, the concept/idea of home has been a complex, plagued, and elusive one. Nonetheless, characters in African American literature identify places and spaces as home. The contours of the representations of those spaces are the subject of this book. What, in African American literature, is a homespace? What forces shape and define it? What external and internal factors influence it? What role has history, especially slavery, played in its shaping? How do characters embrace, react, respond to its shaping and perpetuation? What are the family dynamics operative within such a space? Do family members make homes or do they simply exist in proximity to each other? What are the connections between space and family dynamics?

Home in African American literature is, first of all, a *place* (the geographical location) and a *space* (the finite physical structure within that geographical location). Toni Morrison's *Song of Solomon* (1977), for example, identifies "Not Doctor Street" as the place where the characters in a small Michigan town have labeled their reality despite the efforts of the city and the local post office to force them to identify differently. Residents claim "Not Doctor Street" because the only black doctor in town had lived there—even as the post office persists in labeling it "Mains Avenue" instead of "Doctor Street." Similarly, in Morrison's *Beloved* (1987), 124 Bluestone Road in Cincinnati, Ohio, is the ghost-inhabited specific space, the homespace, for Sethe, her mother-in-law Baby Suggs, her daughter Denver, and her sons Howard and Buglar.[3] Physical location is thus crucial to literary representations of home. How that physical location is shaped and operates in the literature, however, is at times inspired by or has its direct genesis in slavery, as is the case in *Beloved*, which means that the space is fraught with painful memories of a past that threatens at time to consume the present. Sethe and Baby Suggs may have left the chains of slavery in Kentucky, but they take symbolic chains with them to Ohio. They thus show that history and memory directly related to slavery have a tangible impact upon any homespace that could be constructed post-slavery. Slavery's claims upon the construction of homespaces in African American literature extend well into the twentieth and twenty-first centuries and are manifested again and again in the neo-slave narrative tradition of which *Beloved* is a part.[4] The implications of slavery's impact upon representations of home in African American literature both precede and follow *Beloved*, and they make clear the never-ending curse (or creative opportunity) the pre-Emancipation period of American history has had upon African American literary development, particularly in the intimate spaces of home and attempts to construct homes or to label what home is or should be.

To elucidate the point further, I turn to Octavia E. Butler's neo-slave narrative, speculative fiction novel *Kindred* (1979) to illustrate the impact of slavery upon conceptions of home as well as to emphasize the links between antebellum literary representations and twentieth and twenty-first century representations. When Dana Franklin, of late twentieth century California, arrives through yet another of her time travel episodes at the Weylin Plantation in 1838 Maryland, she exclaims, with a mixture of emotions, "Home at last."[5] It is a troublingly curious response for Dana to label the place as home, for she has arrived on a plantation where black people are enslaved, where Dana must encourage her ancestor Alice to consent to plantation owner Rufus Weylin's rape so that Dana can be born, where Dana herself will be whipped, where Rufus will also attempt to rape Dana, and where, every day, Dana witnesses atrocities against black bodies. Yet Dana, with a mission to ensure that her family line will begin, survive, and thrive, is so torn between twentieth century California and nineteenth century Maryland that Maryland holds more immediacy over her person and imagination than California does. After all, she cannot will herself back to California, but, at any given moment, she can—through the sheer desire or need of Rufus—be transported to the Weylin plantation. As the novel develops, and especially after Dana's husband Kevin follows Dana to the past and gets stranded there, more of Dana's life is indeed in the past than it is in the present. A plantation in the nineteenth century thus becomes more home-like than the house into which Dana and Kevin have moved just before her time travels begin—though it certainly does not completely remove identification with twentieth century California as home.

Dana's labeling of a physically violent and psychologically violating space as home captures some of the contradictions and complexities that shape the concept of home throughout African American literature. The place and space are initially significant, for all notions of home have some geographical or physical boundaries. Equally noteworthy is the complex emotional attachment that Dana has toward the place, especially given its location and its enterprise. Dana's response portends that of many characters who find themselves in untenable spaces and yet label them home. There is also a familiarity that leads Dana to label the Weylin plantation as home. Many are the instances in African American literature in which familiarity takes precedent over comfort or caring as characters claim kinship to space and place. I think especially of Delores Phillips's *The Darkest Child* (2004) in the context of slavery looming over African American attempts to construct home. Arguably, Rosie Quinn, the mother in the novel, exhibits some of the traits of a slaveholder as she barters the bodies of her daughters, claims all the proceeds of their labor, and uses violence against them as excessively as she wishes.[6] Though familiarity defines their identification with the space they must call home, Rosie's daughters are just as adrift as is Dana. Overall, Dana's observation has none of the comforts that traditionally and usually get associated with an ideal notion of home. There is no warm cup of milk waiting for Dana, no one to rub her tired feet, no one to comfort her for surviving yet another time travel. Dana is both alien and outcast in this environment, and yet she is central to it, and the forces that work against her, especially Rufus Weylin, are also central to it.

Butler's narrative shows that history, race, power, and economics are central to ideas of home. In the place where nineteenth century slavery is vibrant and perversely healthy, Dana can only be at home as much as Rufus allows. Externally imposed factors impinge upon all those enslaved on the Weylin Plantation (which effectively includes Dana), and there is little that they can do to create homespaces independent of the slaveholders who profess to own them. Even Alice, Dana's so-called "free" ancestor, has her homespace invaded by patrollers who come looking for her husband. They whip him and trample into her cabin as if it were their own private backyards. Echoing Baby Suggs's comment about the children sold away from her, those enslaved on the Weylin Plantation are like chess pieces to be moved, and those who are presumed to be free do not fare any better. In these circumstances where African Americans have little agency in determining what their homes are like, external forces reign. Still, Dana is more at home on the plantation than she would be trying to set up separate housekeeping for herself, as Alice's case makes clear. At least Dana has the "protection" of the Weylins against marauding patrollers or other whites who may accost her, insist that she account for herself, or perpetrate violence against her.

Home for people of African descent on American soil, therefore, is almost always contingent. It could be contingent upon a slave master's whims, such as trading an enslaved person's loved one to repay a gambling debt, or, as Charles W. Chesnutt portrays in *The Conjure Woman* (1899), sending a mother away from her child to gain a race horse, or, as August Wilson depicts in *The Piano Lesson* (1987), exchanging an enslaved person for a musical instrument.[7] After slavery, home could be contingent upon confrontations between blacks and whites in which blacks had literally to run away from home, usually in the South, to a new prospect of home in the North, as Richard Wright dramatizes so vividly in his short story, "Big Boy Leaves Home" (1938).[8] Home could additionally be contingent upon a landowner's reducing wages for sharecroppers and thereby forcing them to abandon the space they consider home and moving to another sharecropping situation, as

Alice Walker depicts in *The Third Life of Grange Copeland* (1970).⁹ Grange's son Brownfield moves his family from one horrible sharecropping shack to another, and Brownfield deliberately sabotages the one instance in which the family is able to move into town and into decent quarters. For Grange as well as for his son Brownfield, what home means or does not mean is tied intricately to economics. Enslaved persons could not control their homespaces in part because they could not take control of themselves; their status as chattel drove the economics of the system and decisions to disrupt their living spaces just as assuredly as, during the days of sharecropping, the same dynamics held true. Neither Grange nor Brownfield is capable of establishing a home without sufficient financial and territorial livelihood to do so, and that livelihood depends upon the goodness—or lack thereof—of the white landowners for whom they work.

Strikingly, in sharecropping, one of the social and historical descendants of slavery, external forces are powerful, but characters do have more agency than those who were enslaved. The white man who owns the plantation on which Grange and his family live in a shack might control Grange's labor and finances, but he does not control Grange's attitude toward his wife. Nor does his white employer control Grange's son Brownfield's responses to his wife and family. The white man for whom Brownfield works does not force him to beat his wife Mem or to blast her into eternity with a shotgun. Grange and Brownfield thus join many of their fellow literary characters in *allowing* those external forces to control them and their actions toward those who should be under their care in their homespaces.

Another descendant of slavery is reflected in the works of Ernest J. Gaines in his representation of the living spaces that remained into the twentieth century. The quarters, as they became universally known and as Gaines charts their continued existence and influence well into the twentieth and twenty-first centuries, were frequently rows of shacks with bare necessities (no windows, doors, or wooden floors, leaky roofs).¹⁰ Their post-slavery depictions present them as livable but not necessarily conducive to thriving. Yet, structures in and of themselves, while crucial, do not ultimately create homes; the people, like Grange, who occupy those spaces have a tremendous impact upon whether or not such structures become homespaces. The Breedlove family in Toni Morrison's *The Bluest Eye* (1970), for example, may live in an abandoned store, a space that was never intended for constant human habitation, but it is what the characters do within that space that determines whether or not it can ever become a home to them.¹¹ In the store-turned-living space that they occupy, self-hatred, anger, and physical fights make any notion of home impossible to grasp. The son, Sammy, responds by running away twenty-seven times, while the daughter, Pecola, tries imaginatively to make herself disappear.

In other instances of representations of home in African American literature, external forces not only prove dominant, but they are excruciatingly violent in disrupting homes or destroying homes that characters create. I think especially of the lynching plays of the 1920s. Every home depicted in those plays gets disrupted by white violence against black characters. Indeed, there is an entire category of snatching away from home in what are referred to as the lynching plays of the 1920s and 1930s. Among such plays are Angelina Weld Grimke's *Rachel* (1916), Mary Powell Burrill's *Aftermath* (1919), Georgia Douglas Johnson's *A Sunday Morning in the South* (1925), *Safe* (1929), and *Blue-Eyed Black Boy* (1930), and Langston Hughes's *Mulatto* (1935).[12] Arguably, any lynching in whatever genre constitutes a snatching away from and instability of home, because home, in these instances, is contingent upon peaceful co-existence with whites, and even that peaceful co-existence might not ensure a person of stability in a homelife.

As these references to lynching plays indicate, and as I mentioned earlier, race exerts a never-ending impact upon African American constructions of home. I suggest that race has a twin in religion and that, together, these two external forces perhaps have greater influences than any other upon homespaces in African American literature. In her essay, "Home," for example, Toni Morrison argues that America is a "racial house" that manifests itself in the very language that is available to describe it or to criticize it. In tying race, language, and home together, she asserts: "I prefer to think of a-world-in-which-race-does-not-matter as something other than a theme park, or a failed and always-failing dream, or as the father's house of many rooms. I am thinking of it as home." She follows by noting that "matters of race and matters of home are priorities in my work."[13] In an effort to try to escape the racial house of language, Morrison composed her short story, "Recitatif," in which she presents two girls turned women of different races and tries to denude the story of racial markers.[14] Race, however, remains just as pervasive as religion, as readers constantly mine the story in efforts to determine which character is black and which character is white.

In her focus on matters of race and home in her first novel, *The Bluest Eye*, Morrison deconstructs the myth of the American nuclear family as far as the Breedlove family is concerned, destroys the possibility of a house/structure being made into a home, and undercuts any positive impact of religion. Movies and an externally imposed and white-based standard of beauty lead Pauline Breedlove to believe that she and her family are ugly and her daughter Pecola to believe that the only way she will be loved and accepted is to acquire the blue eyes that America adores in whiteness. Pauline has absorbed religious ideas and uses them as weapons against her family. In a fight with her husband, for example, she invites Jesus to strike the drunken, wife-beating, and irresponsible Cholly because he is such an affront to everything her Christian teachings have instilled in her. Morrison's foray into race and religion in 1972 is but a dot on a long line of religious portrayals in African American literature that showcase the potentially detrimental effect they can have upon homespaces.

Indeed, the influence of religion upon the creation of African American literary homespaces has pervaded the literature since its beginnings. As Richard Barksdale and Keneth Kinnamon point out in their groundbreaking anthology, *Black Writers of America: A Comprehensive Anthology* (1972), African American literature is built upon "two themes—the appeal of Christianity and the quest for liberty and equality," an assessment that remained valid well into the mid-twentieth century.[15] Readers need but contemplate the poetry of Phillis Wheatley, the short fiction of Frances Ellen Watkins Harper, and numerous texts in the twentieth century to see the validity of Barksdale and Kinnamon's claim. When Lorraine Hansberry's Mama Lena Younger slaps her daughter Beneatha in *A Raisin in the Sun* (1959) and forces the skeptical daughter to assert, "In my mother's house there is still God," she illustrates how physical structure and religion shape each other.[16] That connection between homespace and Christianity extends into the twenty-first century in a novel such as Daniel Black's *Perfect Peace* (2010), in which Christian beliefs and church folks are always looking over the shoulders of the characters portrayed.[17] Arguably, in that novel, the homespace is almost an extension of the church house.

While homespaces in terms of physical structures are crucial to representation in African American literature, home has other dimensions as well. Two of those reside in the realm of imagination. One is portability, and the other is memory. When physical structures are not immediately available to characters, they frequently carry mental images of what home could, should, or ought to be. For example, when Vyry Brown finally leaves the Dutton Plantation in Margaret Walker's seminal neo-slave narrative, *Jubilee* (1966), she is essentially homeless, that is, without a physical space for herself and her family. Yet, she has an idea of what it means to construct a space that she can label home. She carries that intangible possibility with her until she and her husband Innis are able to bring it to fruition. Similarly, when Mama Lena Younger in Hansberry's *A Raisin in the Sun* leaves the South for Chicago, she envisions a space within that concrete geography that she can call home. She is holding on to an idea that she hopes can be transformed into a reality. She carries that idea with her for decades, with its current inadequate manifestation in the kitchenette building providing barely a glimpse of her hoped-for desire. When she is finally able to make a down payment on a house, the possibility of the dream image becoming reality makes it all the more meaningful.

Portability is also relevant for considering how the Great Migration is portrayed in African American literature and how migrants, moving primarily from southern rural areas to northern urban enclaves, brought with them senses of home that enabled them to replicate on northern soil some of what they had known in the South—even as they embraced what newness the North had to offer. From Langston Hughes's poem "One-Way Ticket," to Ralph Ellison's *Invisible Man* (1952), to Albert Murray's *Train Whistle Guitar* (1974), African Americans moving to the North wanted to reconstruct some of the home they had known in the South. As Gwendolyn Brooks showcases in her first collection of poetry, *A Street in Bronzeville* (1945), sometimes those migrants were successful at establishing homes and sometimes they were not. The idea nonetheless guided their hopes and their actions.[18]

Migration, however, does not cancel out some basic similarities in depictions of home on southern and northern territories. To use Zora Neale Hurston as an example, is Janie Crawford Killicks Starks Woods in *Their Eyes Were Watching God* (1937) ever at home with any of the men whom she marries? She despises Logan Killicks and devalues his farm and house, and she eventually grows to hate Jody Starks, in part because the spirit of her marriage to Jody leaves the bedroom and goes to reside in the parlor. Certainly Tea Cake would begin to qualify in establishing a home with Janie, but the home there quickly turns into a nightmare of destruction and bloody death. And when Janie returns home to Eatonville, it is the black community that insinuates to her that she is not welcome, not at home there.[19]

A similar pattern of home not being home holds true for Hurston's first novel, *Jonah's Gourd Vine* (1934).[20] Lucy Potts marries John Buddy Pearson and goes off supposedly to make a home with him. However, the leftover slave quarters space and later the homes they occupy are merely sites on which John creates misery for Lucy with his countless infidelities. The fact that he becomes a minister does not improve his behavior; indeed, his status as a minister simply gives him unlimited access to women who are impressed by his preaching voice and physical stature. Miserable Lucy lives and dies knowing that her husband has never truly committed himself to making a home with her in the spaces that they occupy. Also, in a heartless gesture, her brother removes the bed out from under the pregnant Lucy in repayment for a debt that John owes him; the bed has been a wedding present to the couple. Thus, there are no civilizing or transforming influences either through love or religion that can make the spaces/structures that John and Lucy occupy into a home.

Hurston's versions of the inability to create homes in the rural South of Florida have their counterparts on northern soil. Walter Lee Younger in

Hansberry's *A Raisin in the Sun* feels trapped and stunted by the tiny Chicago kitchenette apartment, with its bathroom down the hall, that he and his family must occupy. Rose Maxson in August Wilson's *Fences* (1986) sees her home crowded out by the personality of her husband Troy, and she is literally pushed into the background in her own space. Indeed, she is forced to become midwife to her husband's bastard child when the woman who gave birth to the child dies.[21] Rose asserts that the child will have a mother but Troy will no longer have a wife, which means that, though they remain together for years before Troy dies, there is little love in the house between the adults, even as Rose works hard to make it a home for Ranelle, the bastard child. Morrison's 124 Bluestone Road in Cincinnati, Ohio in *Beloved* could never be a home to any of its inhabitants, for the presence of the baby ghost makes all of the characters' lives miserable. The women in James Baldwin's *Go Tell It on the Mountain* (1953) do not fare any better given the emotional and psychological abuse they suffer. Deborah, Florence, and Elizabeth in Baldwin's novel are all subjected to the alcoholism, emotional neglect, or religious fanaticism of their husbands.[22] They are unfulfilled, unsupported, and virtually single women in the midst of matrimonial unions, and they live in the spaces they inhabit in constant fear of the men who refuse to allow those spaces to be labeled homes. Perhaps the ultimate violation of the physical space erroneously labeled home occurs in Suzan-Lori Parks's *Topdog/Underdog* (2001). Here, two brothers attempt to co-exist in a one-room space in an urban area. Tensions between them, which are fueled by sexual competition and peculiarly problematic familial, employment, and national histories, result ultimately in one brother shooting the other to death. Even before that death, there has been little between the brothers that would support any healthy definition of home and homespace.[23]

In addition to Hansberry's *A Raisin in the Sun* and Parks's *Topdog/Underdog* in terms of tiny cramped urban spaces labeled as home, the situation of the Thomas family in Richard Wright's *Native Son* (1940) also prevents the possibility of transforming the physical structure in which they reside into a home. Migrants from the South during the Great Migration, Bigger, his mother, his sister, and his brother occupy a single room in the ghetto of the South side of Chicago.[24] They would undoubtedly consider the Youngers' apartment in *A Raisin in the Sun* quite a luxury. As Wright delivers their lives to us, however, the Thomases *exist* rather than *live* in such cramped quarters; for them, privacy is impossible and rodents are constant visitors. Of course I could argue that physical conditions themselves may not necessarily preclude the idea of making a house or apartment into a home. What precludes that possibility is that the outside world of white racism intrudes constantly into their space. Mrs. Thomas is explicit and loud in expressing her displeasure with the twenty-year-old Bigger. She blames him for not finding a job and changing the family's spatial circumstances. She judges Bigger by the yardstick of white American success, which dictates that a man ought to find a job and support his family. If he does not, then he has not only failed them, but he has failed to accept his role in the larger American economy. There can be no peace, therefore, in this space. And while peace is not necessarily the most prominent feature in transforming a physical space into a home, it certainly plays a part. Arguments, physical violence, and psychological cruelty prevail in the Thomas "apartment," which make it impossible, by almost any definition of home, to characterize this space as such.

Memory joins migration and portability in serving as a feature of the creation of homespaces in African American literature. In *Kindred*, Dana maintains her sanity when she transports to the Weylin Plantation in part by remembering her life and her homespace back in twentieth century California. Without such memories to sustain her, Dana may well succumb to the thingafication to which Rufus's father and the other proponents of slavery attempt to reduce her. Memories of home are what sustain Oori in Rivers Solomon's *The Deep* (2019).[25] Having witnessed the destruction of her home world, and being the last descendant of her people, Oori remembers for the sake of those lost, and she performs rituals in their name. For Oori, it is not a matter of recreating her world; it is a matter of remembering what her home was and the cultural and historical value that it must continue to elicit from her. In this mental realm of what home means, therefore, it is an intangible blanket of memory, a spiritual touchstone, an emotional or potentially emotional healing.

Yet another dimension of representing home in African American literature centers upon intangibility and resides solely in the realm of imagination. I am referring here to the ways in which literary treatments mythologize Africa as an ancestral home and the ways in which other such treatments imagine heaven as the ultimate home. During the Harlem Renaissance, many writers and scholars embraced Africa as a source of artistic and creative inspiration. The Africa-inspired works of artist Aaron Douglas, for example, graced anthologies such as Alain Locke's *The New Negro* (1925) as well as the little magazine, *FIRE!!*, that Langston Hughes, Wallace Thurman, Zora Neale Hurston, and Bruce Nugent created in 1926.[26] Poetry by Countee Cullen, Gwendolyn Bennett, and Claude McKay also imagines an Africa of kings, queens, and healthy people of color who are not tainted by the poison of American racism. McKay, a Jamaican who migrated to the United States and earned a reputation as a poet and novelist on American soil, echoes the same sentiment for persons of African descent born in the Caribbean. In "Outcast," McKay asserts, perhaps equally of America and the Caribbean, that he has been "born, far from my native clime,/ Under the white man's menace, out of time."²⁷ The "native clime" to which he alludes is Africa, for he envisions that space as home. Whether it is Cullen's narrator in "Heritage" imagining an Africa of young people caught in unabashed exuberance, or graceful animals, or gods of a different creation, or Douglas's portraits of strikingly regal warriors and maidens, Africa as an imagined ancestral home graces the creations of writers and artists from the 1920s well into the twenty-first century. Ann Petry at mid-twentieth century, Alice Walker in the 1970s, and Yusef Komunyakaa in "Cape Coast Castle" in 2015 are some of the writers who engage the possibility of Africa as ancestral homeland.

The extent to which Africa is considered ancestral homeland is also reflected in African American folk tradition in the legend of the Flying Africans. This group is reputed to have had the ability to fly back to Africa once they found themselves enslaved in the New World. Hints of these Flying Africans or direct reference to them have occurred in any number of African American literary texts. They include, perhaps most strikingly, Toni Morrison's *Song of Solomon*, in which Milkman Dead discovers that his ancestor, Solomon, could fly. Paule Marshall's *Praisesong for the Widow* (1983) also includes portrayals of enslaved Africans who can go back to Africa; in this case, they miraculously walk on water—chains notwithstanding—from the shores of South Carolina to the west coast of Africa. Their contemporary descendant, Avey Johnson, embraces this belief as she reconceptualizes ideas of home. Zora Neale Hurston, in her essay "High John De Conquer," further portrays this belief in Flying Africans. Hurston pictures enslaved people escaping their enslavement by flying away from toil and trouble. While they are unlike the mythical Flying Africans in that they do not escape completely, they nonetheless serve to indicate that people of African descent who were forced to labor in the New World were not content with their forced home and sought refuge in what they viewed as their true home.²⁸

Equally as striking is the recurring representation in the literature of the portrayal of a home after/beyond earth and not in the sense of Octavia E. Butler's notion in *Parable of the Sower* (1993) of the destiny of earthseed (new age believers) taking roots among the stars. Rather, this imagining of a homespace after earth refers to a very traditional conceptualization of heaven. It has its implicit origins in the earliest of African American poetry, in which new believers such as Jupiter Hammon and George Moses Horton expressed their commitment to Christianity. Sterling A. Brown and James Weldon Johnson in the third and fourth decades of the twentieth century composed poems that imagined such a final resting/dwelling place as well. While references to Christianity become less prominent in the literature after the 1970s, the portraiture of heaven as home is significant enough to warrant discussion.

Home as I define it in African American literature, then, is a combination of place, space, character, portability, memory, and imagination. It is a layered concept that adds human interactions to physical structures and then, at times, transcends those structures with the power of imagination about something larger than the world. Scholars have certainly commented passingly on home in any number of African American literary texts, usually while pursuing some other topic. Sustained studies of such portraitures over a significant portion of time, however, have not garnered much attention from scholars. Two notable exceptions are Valerie Sweeney Prince in her study, *Burnin' Down the House: Home in African American Literature* (2005), and Robert B. Stepto in *A Home Elsewhere: Reading African American Classics in the Age of Obama* (2010).[29] Prince focuses her book project on five well-known African American literary texts: Richard Wright's *Native Son* (1940), Ralph Ellison's *Invisible Man* (1952), Toni Morrison's *The Bluest Eye* (1970) and *Song of Solomon* (1977), and Gayl Jones's *Corregidora* (1975).[30] She uses her selected texts to argue that home in African American literature centers upon definitions and redefinitions of the womb, the kitchen, and the city/streets, which she traces over the nearly forty-year publication span of the novels on which she focuses. She undergirds her study with references to Houston A. Baker's discussion of the blues matrix in *Blues, Ideology, and Afro-American Literature: A Vernacular Theory*.[31] Whereas Baker identifies the "hole"—with its sexist overtones—in connection with that matrix, Prince seeks to reclaim his often antifeminist analysis and define a "whole" space for African Americans to conceptualize home.

Prince posits that "the search for justice, opportunity, and liberty that characterized the twentieth century for African Americans can be described as a quest for home," a quest and an objective that have consistently proven elusive, though the blues matrix provides one way home might be articulated.[32] The blues, Prince maintains, "introduces a logic drawn from African American sensibility that makes the notion of home seem possible in a chaotic world."[33] What Prince identifies as "expressive vehicles" or "expressive gestures," often derived from the blues, enable African Americans to sustain themselves in recurringly hostile and chaotic environments as they "chart the journey toward home."[34] The blues emerged from the "troubled past" of African Americans "and works to impose meaning upon the chaos of black experiences" as the quest for home continues.[35] Prince recognizes the complex, unstable, and contested nature of home when she asserts that home in literary representations "is ubiquitous and nowhere at the same time" and in a work such as Morrison's *The Bluest Eye* that "home is at once home and not home."[36] Finally, Prince concludes that the nearly forty years of literature that she treats "reveals that home is somehow beyond place, beyond life, and even beyond death," which anticipates the position I take in identifying heaven as the ultimate home for many persons of African descent on United States soil.[37] While Prince and I both recognize the elusiveness of home, I want to show that that elusiveness is not limited to a few texts (and Prince does mention others), but that it characterizes a tradition in African American literature.

Stepto uses the political era of the early twenty-first century and specifically Barack Obama's *Dreams from My Father: A Story of Race and Inheritance* (1995) to reread Frederick Douglass's *Narrative of the Life of Frederick Douglass* (1845) and to offer comments on Toni Morrison's *Song of Solomon*.[38] Dividing his book in two sections, Part One of which comprises the Du Bois Lectures that Stepto delivered, Stepto mostly uses that first part of the text to deal with notions of home.[39] "Throughout these lectures," he avows, "I return to several subjects: how protagonists raise themselves, often without one or both parents; how black boys invent black manhood, often with no examples or models before them; how protagonists seek and find a home elsewhere; and how protagonists create personalities that can deal with the pain of abandonment."[40] Stepto cites Douglass's comment in response to one of his displacements that he needed to find "a home elsewhere" to elaborate on how that search informs not only Douglass's autobiography but Barack Obama's life narrative and Macon Dead's and his son Milkman's lives in *Song of Solomon*. Stepto applies the idea of "black boys raising themselves" to explore the "self-invention" and "self-creation" that are at the heart of Douglass's and Obama's progressions from troubled boyhoods as mixed-race males to successful manhood as self-identified African American men. Stepto notes that each narrator finds other mothers and fathers to compensate for missing or absent parents. Obama and Douglass are forced to exchange familiar spaces for unfamiliar ones, as the young Obama moved from Indonesia to Hawai'i and as Douglass left the plantation for Baltimore and then New Bedford; he later fled the United States after the passage of the Fugitive Slave Act. In each instance, Obama and Douglass embrace their new, unfamiliar spaces. They thus "invent homes" and form new communities in new geographical and spatial locations. Stepto's focus on life narratives is not commensurate with what I pursue in my study, but I share Stepto's emphasis upon migration, forced and voluntary, and how such movement impacts homespaces. Worthy of note as well is that Stepto features male life narrators and mostly male characters, whereas I treat both male and female protagonists.

Discussing Toni Morrison's *Song of Solomon* in the context of movement, community, and othermothering, Stepto notes that both Macon and Milkman are displaced and without sustaining features of home. Macon is motherless because his mother dies giving birth to his sister Pilate and fatherless because his father is literally blown to death by a shotgun blast. Like Obama and Douglass, therefore, Macon must migrate and "invent" home "as well as the family that composed home."[41] Although both his parents are in place, Milkman is nonetheless alienated from his homespace, due in large part to his dysfunctional family's being unable to turn the imposing physical structure, the house, in which they live into a home. Milkman is thus adrift in determining how to invent manhood and a homespace, and must forge forward in trying to create new communities. To assist in this process, both Pilate and Circe, the woman who hid Macon and Pilate after their father was killed, serve as othermothers to Milkman and guide him to his most significant discovery: that his great-grandfather was a member of the tribe of Flying Africans and flew "home" to Africa. Stepto and I both have reservations about that final action. I am especially skeptical of it in terms of mythologizing Africa as an ancestral or contemporary home for persons of African descent on United States soil.

My purpose in this book, therefore, is to use my articulation of a concept of home to explore texts that are lesser well known in African American literature while providing touchstone references to and commentary on, among others, works of such well-known writers as Toni Morrison, Alice Walker, Zora Neale Hurston, James Baldwin, Richard Wright, and Lorraine Hansberry. I concentrate primarily on fiction, poetry, and drama. As far as I have been able to determine, genre does not have an appreciable impact upon the overall conceptions of home that I have articulated. Whether it is in the lynching plays of the 1920s and 1930s, or Toni Morrison's novels, or Gwendolyn Brooks's poetic depictions of homespaces on the south side of Chicago with her bean eaters, or Rita Dove in her portrait of Thomas and Beulah's courtship and extensive marriage in *Thomas and Beulah* (1986), portrayals of home in African American literature are unwaveringly troubled. I think especially of Brooks poems such as "Sadie and Maud," in which a wayward daughter brings shame to her family, or "Jessie Mitchell's Mother," in which a beautiful and light-skinned black mother is puzzled over how she gave birth to the much-darker Jessie.[42] Several poems in *Thomas and Beulah* convey the tensions between the couple, but I think especially of "Taking in Wash," in which Beulah's drunken, lecherous father seems on the verge of sexually violating his daughter before the mother steps in and declares that, if such an idea does indeed enter his head, she will "*cut* [him] *down/ just like the cedar of Lebanon.*"[43]

My argument in this book, therefore, is that problematic representations of home are so extensive and pervasive in these African American literary genres that few African American writers can resist the urge to follow on a path of troubling depictions. I can compare this phenomenon to the widespread attraction of neo-slave narratives to African American writers from the 1960s to the present or to the current appeal of Afrofuturism to a broad spectrum of African American writers and scholars. Writers influence each other, and a tradition develops. So it is with depictions of home in African American literature. In pursuing my discussions, I select Margaret Walker's

Jubilee to concentrate on how an idea of home that is shaped in reaction to slavery guides protagonist Vyry Brown for years before she can settle into a true homespace. With no role models beyond those she has witnessed during slavery, Vyry sets out to wrest the intangible into the tangible and realize an objective for her family. My exploration of the impact of northern geography upon the creation of homespaces centers upon James Baldwin's *Go Tell It on the Mountain* (1953), Toni Morrison's *The Bluest Eye* (1970), and Suzan-Lori Parks's *Topdog/Underdog* (2001). I assert in these instances that architecture has the potential to determine destiny if the characters allow their cramped spaces to influence them in the ways that Grange and Brownfield Copeland allow their sharecropping circumstances to influence them and lead to their destroying their homespaces.

With A. J. Verdelle's *The Good Negress*, I uncover rich opportunities for exploring the migration of an idea of home from one location to another, in this case from Patuskie, Virginia to Detroit, Michigan in an echo of the Great Migration that influenced so much African American literature. Features of homemaking and homecaring that her grandmother have instilled in Neesey, the primary character, enable her to help her mother, brothers, and stepfather in their apartment in Detroit, but those skills also imprison her as a servant in that space. Memories of what her grandmother has taught her and attempts to bring those memories to reality in Detroit make Neesey especially vulnerable to exploitation by her own family members. Thus the interactions of characters within homespaces, especially the interactions of mothers and daughters, can serve to denigrate or poison the very spaces that they are supposed to enhance. Comparable poisonous interactions between mothers and offspring occur in Daniel Black's *Perfect Peace* (2010) and Dorothy West's *The Living Is Easy* (1940), both of which feature homespaces tightly controlled by women, and both women use their status as mothers to shape the spaces they call home. West's character migrates from South Carolina to Boston while Black's character resides in 1940s Arkansas. In both instances, the imposition of external influences about beauty (especially pigmentocracy), class status, and sexuality lead to disturbing consequences.

Instead of ordering chapters focusing on *The Good Negress*, *Perfect Peace*, and *The Living Is Easy* chronologically, I have arranged them according to the intensity of interactions between mothers and their offspring as well as to the increasing level of psychological, emotional, and financial damage that results. While Neesey recounts several poignant interactions with Margarete in *The Good Negress*, she also captures extensive encounters with her brothers, boyfriend, teachers, and friends. Her family is not as stressed financially as are the Peaces in *Perfect Peace* or the Judsons in *The Living Is Easy*. With the Peace family, the narrative captures many interactions in addition to those between Emma Jean and her family, including those between Perfect and her friends. Emma Jean appropriates funds the family needs so that she can purchase items for Perfect or use those funds to impress neighbors by hosting a large party. Still, her negative impact is primarily upon Paul and the gender-identity crisis that she/he suffers. In terms of portion of the narrative the author gives to her character, Cleo Judson is the center of *The Living Is Easy*; barely is she off a single page in the novel. Her control of her family is absolute, and her financial stresses are more acute than those of Neesey's family or of the Peaces. Not only does she warp her daughter, but she warps just about every character with whom she comes into contact. The chapters move, therefore, in part from the amount of time the mother spends on stage, so to speak, to being commensurate with the amount of damage she causes in compromising or nearly destroying the homespaces over which she has control.

While all of these characters are mired in the troubles of this country (America) and this world (Earth), others envision escapes to find home. Those escapes are prominent in the literary texts that envision Africa as an ancestral home or heaven as the ultimate home. I explore both those possibilities with poetry from the Harlem Renaissance to the mid-twentieth century. I also use Ann Petry's short story, "Mother Africa" (1971), Alice Walker's "Everyday Use" (1973), and Hansberry's *A Raisin in the Sun* to highlight the appeal of Africa as home. It is worthy of note that poetic reflection about Africa as home has a large complement in life narratives, which started being published in the 1970s and 1980s and continue well into the twenty-first century.[44] I use history, music and church traditions to comment on how the literary texts advocating a passageway to heaven are directly reflective of the communities from which such traditions are forged. The conception of heaven provides a place and a space for those who seek it as the ultimate home. Indeed, it perhaps serves more of a psychological boost than many of the in-world manifestations of home.

What becomes clear with all of these examinations is that home in African American literature is a consistently fraught and a consistently incomplete concept to portray in unwaveringly healthy ways. Nonetheless, writers continue to depict homespaces and characters continue to search for and attempt to make such spaces livable and lovable. These characters may not ultimately be successful, but they continue to strive; that striving reflects the essence of African American existence on United States soil, the ever-present will to triumph over adversity, no matter the challenges. Two historical events illustrate that will to triumph: the "Tulsa Race Massacre" of 1921 in Tulsa, Oklahoma and the "Rosewood Massacre" of 1923 in Rosewood, Florida. In both cities, many blacks lost their lives, and home and property damage, primarily by burning, was extensive. Nonetheless, the survivors of these historical atrocities gathered themselves and moved on to building new lives and new homespaces. So too with their literary counterparts. For example, no matter how much loss she and her family suffer, including having one of their homes burned by the Ku Klux Klan, Vyry Brown in Margaret Walker's *Jubilee* gathers herself and tries again. Racist acts against her family are horrific, but she turns her mind ever toward the possibility of success, and her determination ultimately reaps rewards. She joins her literary relatives in grasping any hope that might yield a positive future with a safe and happy home.

NOTES

1. *Freedom From Want* is one of four paintings that Norman Rockwell entitled *Four Freedoms*. To view those and other Rockwell paintings, see https://www.nrm.org/collections-2/art-norman-rockwell/. Richard Wright, *12 Million Black Voices: A Folk History of the Negro in the United States* (1941; Brattleboro, VT: Echo Point Books & Media, 2019).

2. Harper Lee, *To Kill a Mockingbird* (New York: Harper & Row, 1960). Other European American authors who published literary texts that feature mostly well-functioning families and supportive homespaces include Laura Ingalls Wilder in her *Little House on the Prairie* series, Thornton Wilder in *Our Town*, Louisa May Alcott in her Little Women and Little Men series, and Willa Cather in *O Pioneers*. Also, since Toni Morrison specifically unravels the myth of the American nuclear family as it applies to black Americans by using the Dick and Jane primers, I point to that series, for which Random House published sixteen volumes, as idealized representations of European American family life and as a decided contrast to literary representations of African American homespaces and parental and offspring interactions. https://www.penguinrandomhouse.com/series/DNO/dick-and-jane

3. Toni Morrison, *Song of Solomon* (New York: Knopf, 1977); Morrison, *Beloved* (New York: Knopf, 1987). All of Morrison's novels have distinctive locations, such as The Bottom in *Sula* (New York: Knopf, 1973) and Lotus, Georgia in *Home* (New York: Knopf, 2012).

4. There are numerous novels that scholars and readers label neo-slave narratives. This is a short listing: Margaret Walker, *Jubilee* (Boston: First Mariner Books, 1966; 1999); Ernest J. Gaines, *The Autobiography of Miss Jane Pittman* (New York: Bantam, 1972); Ishmael Reed, *Flight to Canada* (New York: Random House, 1976); Charles Johnson, *Oxherding Tale* (Bloomington: Indiana U P, 1982) and *Middle Passage* (New York: Atheneum, 1990); David Bradley, *The Chaneysville Incident* (New York: Harper & Row, 1982); Sherley Anne Williams, *Dessa Rose* (New York: William Morrow and Company, 1986); Caryl Phillips, *Crossing the River* (New York: Knopf, 1994); John Edgar Wideman, *The Cattle Killing* (Boston: Houghton Mifflin, 1996); Edward P. Jones, *The Known World* (New York: Harper Collins, 2003); Toni Morrison, *A Mercy* (New York: Knopf, 2008); Marlon James, *The Book of Night Women* (New York: Riverhead Books, 2009); Dolen Perkins-Valdez, *Wench* (New

York: HarperCollins, 2010); Yaa Gyasi, *Homegoing* (2016); Robert Jones Jr., *The Prophets* (New York: Putnam, 2021).

5. Octavia E. Butler, *Kindred* (Boston: Beacon Press, 1988), 127.

6. Delores Phillips, *The Darkest Child* (2004). Reissued (New York: Soho, 2018) with an Introduction by novelist Tayari Jones.

7. Charles W. Chesnutt, *The Conjure Woman* (Boston: Houghton Mifflin, 1899); August Wilson, *Fences* (New York: Dramatists Play Service/New American Library, 1986).

8. Richard Wright, "Big Boy Leaves Home," in *Uncle Tom's Children* (New York: HarperPerennial, 1993), 17–61.

9. Alice Walker, *The Third Life of Grange Copeland* (New York: Harcourt Brace Jovanovich, 1970).

10. For a sampling of Ernest J. Gaines's works that feature the quarters, see *Catherine Carmier* (Chatham, New Jersey: The Chatham Bookseller, 1964); *Bloodline* (New York: Random House, 1968); *The Autobiography of Miss Jane Pittman*; *A Gathering of Old Men* (New York: Alfred A. Knopf, 1983); and *A Lesson Before Dying* (New York: Alfred A. Knopf, 1994).

11. Toni Morrison, *The Bluest Eye* (New York: Plume, 1994).

12. Angelina Weld Grimke, *Rachel* (Hays, Kansas: McGrath Publishing Company, 1969); Mary Powell Burrill, *Aftermath*, in *Strange Fruit: Plays on Lynching by American Women*, ed. Kathy A. Perkins and Judith L. Stephens (Bloomington: Indiana U P, 1998), 79–91; Georgia Douglas Johnson, *A Sunday Morning in the South, Safe,* and *Blue-Eyed Black Boy*, in *Strange Fruit: Plays on Lynching by American Women*, ed. Kathy A. Perkins and Judith L. Stephens (Bloomington: Indiana U P, 1998), 99–109; 110–15; 116–20; Langston Hughes, *Mulatto*, in *Five Plays*, ed. Webster Smalley (Bloomington: Indiana U P, 1963).

13. Toni Morrison, "Home," in *The House That Race Built*, ed. Wahneema Lubiano (New York: Pantheon Books, 1997), 3. Morrison also titled one of her novels *Home*. It focuses on the small town of Lotus, Georgia and the experiences of a brother and sister who, as children, witnessed whites unceremoniously burying a black man under cover of darkness and who suffer additional traumas during their adulthood, the brother as a result of the Korean War and the sister as a result of medical experimentation.

14. Toni Morrison, "Recitatif," in *Confirmation: An Anthology of African American Women*, ed. Amiri Baraka (LeRoi Jones) & Amina Baraka (New York: Quill, 1983), 243–61.

15. Richard Barksdale and Keneth Kinnamon, *Black Writers of America: A Comprehensive Anthology* (New York: The Macmillan Company, 1972), 2.

16. Lorraine Hansberry, *A Raisin in the Sun* (New York: Random House, 1959), 51.

17. Daniel Black, *Perfect Peace* (New York: St. Martin's, 2010).

18. African Americans who migrated out of the South clearly expected to find better homes in the North, as several scholars have observed. For some of the commentary, see Valerie Sweeney Prince, *Burnin' Down the House: Home in African American Literature* (New York: Columbia U P, 2005), Farah Jasmine Griffin, *"Who Set You Flowin'?": The African-American Migration Narrative* (New York: Oxford

U P, 1995), and Isabel Wilkerson, *The Warmth of Other Suns: The Epic Story of America's Great Migration* (New York: Random House, 2010).

19. Zora Neale Hurston, *Their Eyes Were Watching God* (New York: Perennial, 1990). Scholarship on Hurston's *Their Eyes* and the relationship between Janie and her husbands is extensive. For a few distinctive commentaries, see Jennifer Jordan, "Feminist Fantasies: Zora Neale Hurston's *Their Eyes Were Watching God*," *Tulsa Studies in Women's Literature* 7, no 1 (Spring 1988): 105–17; Lovalerie King, *The Cambridge Introduction to Zora Neale Hurston* (New York: Cambridge, 2008); and John Lowe, *Critical Approaches to Teaching Hurston's Their Eyes Were Watching God and Other Works* (New York: The Modern Language Association of America, 2009).

20. Zora Neale Hurston, *Jonah's Gourd Vine* (Philadelphia: J. B. Lippincott, 1934).

21. August Wilson, *Fences* (New York: Dramatists Play Service, 1986).

22. James Baldwin, *Go Tell It on the Mountain* (New York: Dell, 1980).

23. Suzan-Lori Parks, *Topdog/Underdog* (New York: Theatre Communications Group, 2001).

24. Richard Wright, *Native Son* (New York: Library of America, 1991). Migration also occurred from the South to various western states. That was particularly the case in the 1880s with the Exodusters. For a poignant literary effort sparked by this history, see Pearl Cleage, *Flyin' West* (New York: Dramatists Play Service, Inc., 1995). Cleage's play is especially noteworthy for its depiction of four African American sisters who migrate to Kansas from Memphis, Tennessee and who try to establish and maintain homespaces in the environmentally inhospitable Nicodemus, Kansas, an all-black town. For an historical account of this pattern of migration, see Nell Irvin Painter, *Exodusters: Black Migration to Kansas after Reconstruction* (New York: Alfred A. Knopf, Inc., 1977).

25. Rivers Solomon, *The Deep* (New York: Saga, 2019).

26. Alain Locke, ed., *The New Negro: Voices of the Harlem Renaissance* (New York: Touchstone Books/Simon & Schuster, 1925; 1987); *FIRE!!* (New York: 1926).

27. Claude McKay, *Selected Poems of Claude McKay* (New York: Harcourt, 1953), 41, 13–14. In another poem, "Africa," McKay is less complimentary about Africa. From its former scientific, architectural, and historical glory, Africa has devolved into a "harlot" whose "time is done" (40).

28. Paule Marshall, *Praisesong for the Widow* (New York: E. P. Dutton, 1983); Zora Neale Hurston, "High John De Conquer," in *The Sanctified Church* (Berkeley, CA: Turtle Island, 1981), 69–78.

29. Sweeney, *Burnin' Down the House: Home in African American Literature*; Robert B. Stepto, *A Home Elsewhere: Reading African American Classics in the Age of Obama* (Cambridge: Harvard U P, 2010). Informing Stepto's title is Frederick Douglass's observation in his narrative once he contemplates being separated from his relatives: "I had two sisters and one brother, that lived in the same house with me; but the early separation of us from our mother had well nigh blotted the fact of our relationship from our memories. I looked for home elsewhere, and was confident of finding none which I should relish less than the one which I was leaving." See Frederick Douglass, *Narrative of the Life of Frederick Douglass, An American Slave, Written by Himself* (1845; Cambridge: Harvard U P, 1960), 53. Well-known Morrison

scholar Marilyn Mobley is completing a project on representations of home in the works of Toni Morrison. Her study, *Toni Morrison's Geopoetics of Place, Race and Belonging: Re-imagining Spaces for the Reader*, is scheduled for publication by Temple University Press.

30. Ralph Ellison, *Invisible Man* (New York: Vintage, 1952); Gayl Jones, *Corregidora* (New York: Random House, 1975).

31. Houston A. Baker, *Blues, Ideology, and Afro-American Literature: A Vernacular Theory* (Chicago: U of Chicago P, 1984).

32. Prince, *Burnin,'* 1.

33. Prince, *Burnin,'* 2.

34. Prince, *Burnin,'* 3.

35. Prince, *Burnin,'* 124.

36. Prince, *Burnin,'* 2, 79.

37. Prince, *Burnin,'* 145.

38. Barack Obama, *Dreams from My Father: A Story of Race and Inheritance* (New York: Three Rivers Press, 1995); Douglass, *Narrative*.

39. Part Two of Stepto's study includes four previously published essays and an "Afterword." Among the essays are one commenting on his undergraduate school days and another dealing with correspondence between Harriet Beecher Stowe and Frederick Douglass.

40. Stepto, *Elsewhere*, 5.

41. Stepto, *Elsewhere*, 12.

42. Gwendolyn Brooks, *Selected Poems* (New York: HarperPerennial, 1963; 2006), 8–9, 85–86.

43. Rita Dove, *Thomas and Beulah* (Pittsburgh: Carnegie-Mellon U P, 1986), 47. Italics in original.

44. See, for example, Marita Golden's *Migrations of the Heart* (New York: Anchor Press/Doubleday, 1983); Saidiya Hartman's *Lose Your Mother: A Journey Along the Atlantic Slave Route* (New York: Farrar Straus and Giroux, 2007); and Molefi Kete Asante's *As I Run Toward Africa: A Memoir* (New York: Routledge/Paradigm, 2011).

Chapter 1

Movement, Migration, and Homelessness

Margaret Walker's Jubilee *(1966)*

Holding on to hope for a positive future is the essence of what protagonist Vyry Brown does in Margaret Walker's novel *Jubilee* (1966).[1] Set in the slaveholding and Reconstruction South, the novel chronicles the story of this white-black woman who is the daughter of her master, John Morris Dutton, and sister to the young white woman, Lillian Dutton, to whom she plays a subservient role and for whom she will eventually provide care for an extended period. Walker's narrative depicts/documents the various types of psychological and physical violence that enslaved persons endured, the pain of separation from their families, and their various attempts to locate relatives as well as to claim homespaces in the post-slavery era. Walker also allows her characters to be impressively forgiving of many things that occur during slavery, including Vyry's forgiving her master for punishing her with seventy-five lashes after she tries to escape. In assessing what Walker attempted and/or achieved, there are three things that make the novel especially significant in African American literary history: its subject matter, its year of publication, and, ironically given the first two things, its transformative impact upon African American literary creativity.

Jubilee is a novel about slavery, published in the second half of the twentieth century, long after slavery's end. Not only is it about slavery; it features a protagonist who is the epitome of one of the recurring atrocities of slavery, that is, white male rape of black women. The novel is the result of an exhaustive, thirty-year research project on Walker's part that just happened to be published at a politically volatile time in American history.[2] For an African American writer to focus a nearly five-hundred page novel on slavery in the mid-1960s was perhaps problematic enough to readers, reviewers, and scholars. To have those many pages devoted to a project that does not condemn from the rooftops some of the practices during slavery was even more problematic. Most problematic of all, however, was to limn a heroine who is forgiving of her enslavers, does not believe that all slaveholders are evil, takes care willingly of her white sister, forgives all acts of violence against her and her family, and remains—voluntarily—on the plantation after Emancipation, as if she considers it as much home as any other space she could possibly inhabit. Such a character met mixed reactions across a spectra of readers. Walker scholar Jacqueline Miller Carmichael comments: "Interestingly, initial reviewers of *Jubilee* in both southern and northern publications did not react perceptively or sympathetically to Walker's deconstructive treatment of the legend of the beneficent plantation, the kindly slave owner, and the paternalistic peculiar institution."[3] The novel was, as far as most commentators were concerned, an inexplicable and ill-advised literary venture. Skeptics were not immediately sensitive to the fact that Walker based the novel mostly on the experiences of her great-grandmother or that Walker had been meticulous in researching and composing her novel. Even when reviewers applauded some of Walker's achievement, it still seemed to others a curious anomaly.[4] Thus, in her commentary published in 1998, Carmichael could note that *Jubilee* was "still a relatively unappreciated work."[5]

The linguistic presentation of the subject matter was, to some, as much an area of fault as the actual subject of slavery. Walker's meticulous attempts to create voices, to replicate dialects and speech that might have been appropriate to the period about which she was writing earned as much criticism as it did praise. Carmichael observes: "Walker's use of dialect was a 'thorn in the side' for many blacks who felt that just as they were marching for and achieving true freedom, Walker was reverting to the days of slavery."[6] Reactions such as these hark back to how black writers used dialect at the turn of the twentieth century and into the Harlem Renaissance. James Weldon Johnson lamented in the 1920s the labeling of Paul Laurence Dunbar as exclusively creating dialect poetry at the turn of the twentieth century, for he knew, as Dunbar did, that the poet had been locked into a peculiar jail of creative expectation. Though sympathetic toward Dunbar, Johnson nonetheless, in the Preface to *The Book of American Negro Poetry* (1922, 1931), his edited anthology, looked forward to the day when African American experience could be captured in more expansive ranges:

> What the colored poet in the United States needs to do is something like what Synge did for the Irish; he needs to find a form that will express the racial spirit by symbols from within rather than by symbols from without, such as the mere mutilation of English spelling and pronunciation. He needs a form that is freer and larger than dialect, but which will still hold the racial flavor; a form expressing the imagery, the idioms, the peculiar turns of thought, and the distinctive

humor and pathos, too, of the Negro, but which will also be capable of voicing the deepest and highest emotions and aspirations, and allow of the widest range of subjects and the widest scope of treatment.[7]

I share Johnson's comment to highlight the politics of linguistic representation of characters in African American literature and how long linguistic debates about representation had been going on when Walker published *Jubilee*. Even as Johnson recognized that some things could be captured perfectly well in dialect, his overall position was that something more was needed. If form proved such a distraction to readers, scholars, and reviewers of *Jubilee*, then how effectively could they wade into such a lengthy text and actually appreciate the fact that Vyry worked so long and hard to create a homespace? Instead of demonstrating the historical progress of African Americans as reflected in the 1960s, such skeptics concluded, it seemed as if Walker were embracing too eagerly those bygones days of slavery.

The setting in slavery and Reconstruction brought even more negative attention to the novel given its publication year: 1966. As Carmichael states, African Americans were marching toward what they perceived to be true freedom, and these observers viewed Walker's text as a throwback. The mid-1960s, after all, were only a few years removed from the Montgomery Bus Boycott and the beginnings of the Civil Rights movement, both of which were strong attempts to remove obstacles to civil rights and to negate any traces of subservience to whites, which Vyry's portrait seemed to contradict. Martin Luther King Jr. had led marches all over the South, including the Alabama territory on which Vyry's story is set. Black college students who believed Martin Luther King was moving too slowly had formed the Student Non-Violent Coordinating Committee (SNCC). One militant faction of activism in black communities that did not agree with King's nonviolent tactics had led to the formation of the Black Panthers, and there were a host of other organizations that were intent upon more aggressively and truly transforming America into a place that they could call home. African American writers, especially poets such as Nikki Giovanni, Sonia Sanchez, LeRoi Jones (Amiri Baraka), and others, were using their creative energies to inspire change. Just two years prior to the publication of *Jubilee*, Jones (Baraka) had published *Dutchman* (1964), a play that shook the country for its presentation of a violent encounter between an angry young black man and a young white woman on a subway in New York City.[8] Jones could not remotely begin to imagine the kinds of compromises that are the lifeblood of Vyry's existence. The ostentatious nature of the militancy of these young writers and activists made *Jubilee* seem even more like a throwback to a period that most black folks in the 1960s wanted to forget or at least not think about consciously. As I observed in 1985:

Walker's historical novel, which she had begun many years before, perhaps smacked too much of the social circumstances that the aesthetic of the 1960s worked to push into the background. None of the younger writers had time for a black woman who remained loyal to a slave heritage that blacks were still struggling to overcome in the 1960s. Thus Walker's work, despite its artistic accomplishments, was outdated from the date of its publication. It would be the late 1970s and early 1980s before scholars began to look at the novel for the good things it accomplished and for the solidness of its creations.[9]

Of course a scholar such as Jacqueline Miller Carmichael was the exception to such an observation.

In a curiously developing literary fate, however, the very novel that seemed such a throwback in 1966 would, in a few years, be considered the inaugural novel instituting a new subgenre in African American literature—the neo-slave narrative. As more and more writers turned their attention to the antebellum and Reconstruction periods for their creativity, with Toni Morrison's *Beloved* (1987) being perhaps the most impressive marker of that development, Walker's novel was reconsidered and reappraised. That is not to say that it won universal approval, for the approach to slavery was still considered problematic. Most neo-slave narratives, after all, were designed with the intent of giving enslaved persons more agency than historical records had thus far credited them. Walker, therefore, institutes a landscape of literary creativity rather than the recommended method of cultivating that landscape. Even as Morrison, Charles Johnson, Ishmael Reed, and others were being applauded for their transformative treatments of the antebellum South, Walker languished in the background. Certainly there has been a cadre of scholars, including Carmichael and Maryemma Graham, who consistently focused their scholarly energies on Walker.[10] However, Walker has not garnered the scholarly attention commensurate with her literary productivity. After all, in addition to *Jubilee*, Walker published five volumes of poetry, numerous essays, a book-length conversation with Nikki Giovanni, an account of how she wrote *Jubilee*, and a controversial biography of Richard Wright. It is also of note that Walker, like her character Vyry Brown in *Jubilee*, found home in a place that many believed not to be conducive to African American health and livelihood. After having studied at Northwestern and taught there as well as in North Carolina and West Virginia, Walker returned to Mississippi and joined the faculty at Jackson State University, where she remained for more than fifty years. She commented: "The challenges are greater here than any place. I feel I have the most to give here and it [the South] has the most to offer. It's important that I stay here. My roots are here and, besides, it's my home where I feel I belong."[11] Walker and her character Vyry are decidedly kindred spirits in their assessments of the South and their claiming of that territory as home.

As the ur-text in the neo-slave narrative tradition, Walker's *Jubilee* spans quite an extended amount of time.[12] It begins in slavery and ends long after the Civil War. Along the way, it catalogues practices such as the buying and selling/separation of human beings that those enslaved had to endure. It also marks the end of slavery and the reading of the Emancipation Proclamation. Walker's antebellum period chronicles the cruelty of slaveholders as vividly as slave narratives did. For example, two elderly enslaved men on the Dutton Plantation, who are no longer capable of performing work in the cotton fields, are summarily burned to death under the pretext of tearing down old shacks where those enslaved live and building new spaces. There are scenes of the enslaved being whipped to death as well as shot to death, and, in one instance, Vyry and others from the Dutton plantation are forced to watch the lynchings of two black women who have been accused—merely *accused*—of poisoning their masters. Those enslaved can be sold away at a moment's notice, as is Aunt Sally, with whom the child-turned-adolescent Vyry works in the Dutton plantation kitchen; Aunt Sally is sold because of the climate of suspicion and distrust that the poisonings have created (her sale is announced to her when she arrives in the kitchen one morning, which means she has absolutely no warning of her impending separation from Vyry, who has become as much a daughter to Aunt Sally as any biological child could have). Children are separated from parents both on plantations and between plantations. Vyry, for example, is taken from her biological mother, moved several miles away, and raised by Mammy Sukey, who has responsibility for caring for enslaved children who are too young to work in the fields. Vyry returns to the Dutton plantation only at the request of Hetta, her mother, who is close to death following giving birth to her fifteenth child at the age of twenty-nine; Hetta dies, with Mammy Sukey following soon thereafter. Unsettledness and forced migrations thus reign with Vyry during her early years and obviously contribute to her desire to have her own home after emancipation. With Mammy Sukey and Aunt Sally, Vyry has good women in her life, but they are othermothers. Never does she have a chance to spend time or build a home with Hetta, which is perhaps another reason that she is so committed to the children to whom she gives birth.

Walker thus paints vividly the cruelties that enslaved persons had to endure, including Hetta, Vyry's mother, whom her master favors, whether or not Hetta acquiesces in that favoring; indeed, when she is given to John Dutton when he is a teenager, the much-younger Hetta had been so frightened that she had cried and pleaded to be left alone, but she is ultimately helpless against and has no agency with which to resist Dutton's rapacious sexual advances. Hetta thus experiences the psychological and emotional cruelty attendant upon such relationships, the kind that Harriet E. Jacobs worked so hard to escape in *Incidents in the Life of a Slave Girl* (1861).[13] When Mrs. Salina ("Big Missy") Dutton becomes aware that Hetta is the object of her husband's sexual desire and perhaps even his affection, she "pitched a lovely tantrum then. She threw things at him, called him a beast, cried three days in a row, and even packed to go home to mother."[14] John is simply shocked that his wife could be so naïve about such a "normal" practice in the South. Salina is forced to endure the humiliation until Hetta's death five years later. Having been unable to vent her frustration upon Hetta directly for her straying husband's physical and emotional infidelity, Salina will increasingly take out her frustrations upon Vyry, which makes Vyry's homelessness even clearer.

Walker's representation of enslaved persons and their difficult circumstances highlights powerful forces bolstered by politics and religion. As far as slaveholders are concerned, those enslaved are dehumanized chattel, valued only for the work their bodies can perform, generally considered expendable. In addition to eliminating any remotely possible ambiguity about humanity, slavery also eliminated any ambiguity about who was in charge, and, decidedly, black people were not. Vyry and those enslaved with her thus have no claim to property (not even their own bodies), no claim to land, and obviously no claim to any space that they could identify as home.[15] Feeding enslaved persons religious propaganda about the value of their obeying their masters, as the Duttons emphasized in the few biblical messages allowed on their plantation, served to bolster the power dynamic that the political system had put in place.

For Vyry, therefore, when Big Missy's wrath turns toward her, there is barely a rescue option available to her and little option for rescuing herself. Once Hetta dies, Big Missy calculatedly brings Vyry into the Big House to serve as little Lillian's maid. On one memorable occasion when the seven-year-old Vyry forgets to empty Lillian's chamber pot, Big Missy holds "the pot of stale pee in her hand. Instead of whipping [Vyry], she threw the acrid contents of the pot in Vyry's face and said, 'There, you lazy nigger, that'll teach you to keep your mind on what you're doing. Don't you let me have to tell you another time about this pot or I'll half-kill you, do you hear me?'"[16] On yet another occasion, when the child accidentally breaks a china dish, Big Missy hooks a strap to a nail in a closet, ties Vyry's hands together, and suspends Vyry so that her toes barely touch the floor. It is only because John Dutton returns from a trip that Vyry gets rescued (an unusual pattern given the absence of such rescuers generally). This traumatic maltreatment echoes punishments that Frado received in Harriet E. Wilson's *Our Nig* (1859).[17] Despite these punishments, however, Vyry is expected, indeed required, to perform her assigned chores and respond to the demands of those living in the Big House, no matter how whimsical those demands may be;

thus she, like her historical and literary counterparts, ends up eventually caring for a space in which she might live and work but one that she can never call home. Arguably, however, such placement and caring instill in Vyry what it would mean to have her own space, and that is something she pursues throughout the novel.

Vyry's first conflicted notions of home and homespace occur immediately after news about the Emancipation Proclamation reaches the Dutton Plantation. Faced with the options of leaving what she has known all her life, rejecting her white half-sister's need for her, feeling "duty bound" to wait for Randall Ware (the free black man who is father of her two children), and pursuing her own way in trying to make a home for her family, Vyry chooses morality over revenge when she remains on the Dutton Plantation, serving and helping, until the now mentally ill Lillian's white relatives come to take her away.[18] While readers and scholars may criticize Vyry for remaining on the plantation—even after Innis Brown, a contraband man, helps out and asks her to marry him—her actions are nonetheless understandable. She perhaps exhibits some of the conflict that Dana Franklin experiences when she recognizes that the Weylin Plantation in Maryland is almost more like home than her house in California. It is familiar territory. Given that the Dutton Plantation is all that Vyry has known, and that Randall Ware has promised to return for her, she does not yet have a complete template for imagining something else in terms of a homespace. The novel becomes an account of her attempts to imagine something more, something different, something that is not shaped totally by the conditions of slavery and its aftermath. To say that her path is hard is obviously an understatement, for everywhere that she and her family turn is tainted by the fact and the memories of slavery.

Nonetheless, Vyry does eventually marry Innis and leave the Dutton plantation, for Innis is just as set as Vyry is upon finding a place to call home; he "always had a dream, a daydream, something like a castle in the air. He dreamed of a farm of his own, a place further west with a team of mules, with a house for a family, and a cotton crop of his own. Now as he struggled to tell Vyry his dream, she smiled."[19] For Vyry and Innis, then, their conception of home consists of place and space. They envision a physical structure that will provide safety against natural and human attacks, and they envision a place, a community, in which that physical structure can be erected. Vyry further envisions the kind of security that will enable her family to work together to achieve a financial and moral stability. She wants unity, the kind of togetherness in family that slavery precluded. She adds to that the desire for her children to be educated, since she is illiterate.

These companions on a united quest from Georgia into Alabama suffer again and again as they attempt to realize their dream. Vyry and her family find themselves at the mercy of forces over which they have no control when the first log cabin home they build is washed away by floodwaters (they have foolishly selected low, swampy land on which to build). The loss of animals and crops does not deter them, however, and they again move forward. This time, they unknowingly move into a sharecropper shack and are shocked when the owner shows up (they thought they were negotiating with the tenants who resided in the shack) and coerces them into signing a lease/sharecropping agreement. Cheated and saddled with bills for goods they have not purchased, they escape into another untenable situation, though at first it looks most promising. Helped by soldiers to a new land, they build a home on a solid foundation, only to have the Ku Klux Klan, a newly formed and vicious white supremacist group, burn it to the ground. As Andrea Wolfe observes,

> The burning of Vyry's house, along with many of the other disciplinary actions that the Klan executes against black people, also signifies the collapse of the dichotomy between public and private, a difference central to the presentation of the home as sanctuary in sentimental literature. Readers are expected to sympathize with Vyry because her home, a physical structure that is meant to protect her from the outside world of racism and hate, fails to do so.[20]

Amanda J. Davis comments that the burning reveals "how exposed and susceptible" the Brown home is to "violent disruption given the prejudice and hostility that surrounds them. Images of fire and kerosene oil, so often associated with the warmth and the insular nature of a home, are here remade into weapons of racial terrorism, just as the boundaries of the home as providing protection are rewritten through their vulnerability and incapacity to fully shield their inhabitants from potential harm."[21] Yet the family persists. Movement and migration into other parts of Alabama echo historical and literary patterns as the Brown family tries again and again to locate a place to call home. That concept is potentially realizable enough for Vyry to cling to it in spite of white violence. She is cautious enough on the next move, though, to suggest that Innis not build a house until it is clear that this is indeed a community into which they can settle. She resorts to having her family live in a tent for months.

As she and her constantly traumatized family move from one small Alabama town to another, Vyry carries with her an idea of home, thus portability informs her journey as assuredly as it informs movement of literary black migrants from the South to the North. While she may have internalized some features of what may or may not constitute home, especially from what she has observed in the Big House with the Duttons and in the kitchen with Aunt Sally, she still can only imagine what having safe space for her own family will mean. Vyry is looking for what Amanda J. Davis, drawing upon the work of bell hooks, describes as a space where development as a family and safety from negative external forces can become a reality.[22] Consistently, Vyry is as much other-focused as she is concerned about her own needs and desires. Her family, especially her children, engage her primary attention, and she never deviates from that focus as she tries again and again to find some place to call home.

When I contemplate the arduous journey to find home that Vyry undertakes, I think of heroes in traditional questing narratives and how Vyry shares kinship with them. Vyry has set out on her own quest for a kind of holy grail, which would be the epitome of her idea of a homespace. As with traditional heroic figures, Vyry encounters helpers and hinders on her journey. Whites who discriminate or commit violence against her and her family are obviously hinderers. The white Mr. Porter (Lillian's relative), who assists with securing the legal papers for Vyry's final home, is obviously a helper, as is the family of the young white woman whose child Vyry delivers. If Vyry's heroic quest, therefore, is successful, then Vyry's family will be the beneficiaries, just as various communities benefit from classic heroic actions and successful completions of tasks. Success for the greater familial good situates Vyry's family as its own kind of community, one for which Vyry works tirelessly. Ultimately, that small community seeks to join with other communities in an environment where the individual dwellings within those larger communities, the homespaces, will all serve the greater communal good. This is not to suggest that Vyry is looking for utopia; that would be impossible in this aggressively racist and violent post–Civil War environment. Instead, what she desires is rather modest: her own space, safety for her family, work for Innis and herself, and, dream of dreams, education for her children. It is the smallest scale rendition of the not-yet-articulated American Dream that guides Vyry. Holding on to that idea thus positions her in kinship with several of her literary brothers and sisters.

Strikingly, it is whites who succeed in helping Vyry and her family in getting a stable homespace. In the small Alabama town to which Vyry and her family have retreated during their tent-living episode, she is walking down a street one day when a distressed young white man accosts her. His wife is about to give birth, and he is clearly desperate. Fortunately, Vyry is most capable in this arena, for she has delivered her last child with only Innis's assistance. Delivering the child and returning next day to check on both mother and child enable Vyry to earn a reputation among the young white families in the area. They need a granny, and she needs a home. The arrival of the newly-delivered mother's mother sets this pattern in motion, for she has bought into the stereotype that black grannies can deliver babies much more safely than non-black grannies: "'Why Lawd! Betty-Alice [her daughter], the best grannies in the world is colored grannies. They doesn't never lose they babies and they hardly loses they mothers. They is worth more'n money and you is real lucky to had a colored granny.'"[23] This stamp of approval gets bolstered when Betty-Alice's father learns that Vyry and her family are reluctant to build in the area because of the violence whites have perpetrated against them in the past. He takes it upon himself to poll others in the area and comes up with a plan that he presents to Vyry and Innis:

> 'Well, my wife told us what you said, and we went right out and talked to some of the folks in this settlement. They's a lot of young folks around here, some just married, and a lot of them is raising families, some of them expecting babies right now, and all of them agrees they needs a granny round here, cause they has been losing babies something awful, and we heard how you was fixing to build but you was afraid to, on account of so much ill-will, and we come up here to say if you'll stay here in this here community we'll come up here next week and help you build your house. I'm a contractor myself and I does nothing but build. I built all them new houses round Betty-Alice, and we has the word of the people that if you will stay we guarantee yall won't have nothing to fear, ain't nobody will bother you, do, we'll protect you instead. We'll put you up a house in a day. The women folks'll come too and have a quilting bee, and in a day's time we'll have you under your roof just like you want it. Now, how do that sound to you?'[24]

It is only after this momentous incident that Vyry and her family find themselves in a new homespace, for their white protectors carry out the plan as promised. Having had more than one homespace destroyed, and having suffered the prejudices of whites, Vyry has been hesitant to claim any space as a possible home. Now, with the sanction of those living in the community, she can see a future and the healthy possibilities that it offers for her and her family. Again, worthy of note in this scenario is that folks like the very people who have been responsible for her enslavement up to this point become rescuers of sorts who make possible her family's transition from transiency to stability. And it is younger white couples of child-bearing age who are directly responsible. Perhaps they, the novel suggests, can move from the traditional racist mentality of the previous generations and begin to see black people as human beings instead of property. It is thus fitting that Vyry becomes an agent of life and futures just as her new home suggests new birth for her and her family. While Vyry and her family do not necessarily live happily ever after in a fairytale rendition of fictional possibility, at least her posture at the end of the narrative is one of serenity instead of the uncertainty that has been the dominant tone for most of the narrative. At the close of the novel, in a blend of satisfaction and hopefulness, she is calmly calling her chickens to their evening meal.

Still, *Jubilee* introduces some issues that are relevant for later conceptions of African American homespaces. First, consider how violence has an impact upon or intrudes directly into the space that Vyry is trying to establish and keep pristine enough for her family to grow and thrive. There are dramatic instances of external violence to her various homespaces as well as internal violence within the home. When Vyry and her family watch from a distance as the Ku Klux Klan burn down one of the homes they have built, they can see how the world outside can have a negative and devastating effect upon their efforts to claim sovereignty in this post-slavery environment. This macro-racist aggression has its counterparts in the many small ways that whites convey to Vyry and her family that they are not wanted in various places. The fact that soldiers have to escort the Brown family to one of their potential homesites captures again the negative attitudes that are arrayed against them. Racism is deployed against Vyry and her family in ways that compare to the impact that racist whites have upon black homes and black bodies in the lynching plays of the 1920s.

Threats of violence and actual violence do not only impact Vyry's homespaces from the outside, but Vyry has to deal with the impact of violence *within* the homespace that she has tried so desperately to set up as a shield against such intrusions. The relationship between Vyry's husband Innis and her son Jim is the case in point. Innis resents Jim's refusal to work as hard as he does on their newly acquired farm. Jim, whose father is Randall Ware, the free black man with whom Vyry fell in love while she was enslaved, has a different notion of how black people should exist in the post-Emancipation world than his stepfather has. Thus the clash. Innis Brown's model for parent/child interactions is the master/enslaved person interactions that he has witnessed during slavery. That is, if someone does not do what the person in charge tells them, then the person in charge should punish them physically. Even more is that the case when a person destroys property, as Jim inadvertently does when he allows the pregnant and very valuable sow that Innis is nurturing to drown in mud. The only punishment from Innis's perspective is a caning. Innis has thus bought into a hierarchy of power that brokers no resistance. His beating of Jim dramatizes how external forces creep into African American homespaces and lead the people living in those spaces to replicate the dynamics of violence and domination that define the larger society. Indeed, this is a point that Vyry herself makes:

> It [the beating] brought back all the violence and killing on the plantation when Grimes was driving and beating the field hands to death. It brought back the horror of the deaths of Mammy Sukey, and Grandpa Tom, the branding of Lucy, and burning the old men to death, the plague, and the hanging, murder, and fire, when the slaves all knew their lives were not worth a copper cent with a hole

in it. It went back to the war and all the bloody fighting and killing and dying, the death of all her master's family one by one, and the final assault on Lillian that had left her mind wounded for life. It was part of all the turbulence of the Ku Klux Klan and the fire and all the evil hatred she had felt before the house was built here. Now this awful hatred and violence was threatening to destroy her happy home and her loving family. It was in her own brand-new house.[25]

In beating Jim, Innis thus has no healthy role model for how to respond to his stepson's reluctance to complete manual labor and other farm chores (Jim clearly has some of Randall Ware's desire to imagine a life beyond slavery and servitude). In his beating Jim, who resents being driven "like a mule," Innis brings into his own home the toxic quality of relationships that defined so much of slavery.[26] He cannot be a *man*, in his estimation, unless he is in total, indisputable control, unless he subdues Jim into doing what he wants, and the only way he can do that is by domination through violence. It is a domination that anticipates other toxic literary African American homes stretching from slavery through Alice Walker's *The Third Life of Grange Copeland* (1970) into Suzan-Lori Parks's *Topdog/Underdog* (2001).[27] Keeping African American homes inviolate against societally inspired violence will be a consistent challenge in literary representations of such spaces.

The violence that Innis introduces into his home links with white community responsibility for the building of the house for Vyry and her family (as well as for their peace of mind following the building) and takes the novel in a different direction. Among the relatives who have taken Lillian away to Georgiana, Alabama, is Mr. Porter, who has knowledge of how deeds and property ownership work. When, after arriving in Alabama, Vyry visits Lillian at Mr. Porter's house and shares some of the difficulties her family has had previously, Mr. Porter offers to come to the Greenville area, deal with the local records office, and ensure that Vyry and Innis's property will indeed remain theirs once they have settled in. The altruistic nature of Mr. Porter's visit several weeks later has two important consequences for Vyry and her family. On the one hand, he is as good as his word in taking all the legal steps to ensure that the illiterate Browns are secure in their claim to the land, that their homespace will be safe. On the other hand, he disrupts that home when he inadvertently sees the results of Innis's beating of Jim. This leads him, on his next trip to Georgia, to relate to Randall Ware what he has seen. Randall Ware's arrival, therefore, begins another phase—though a happy one—for Jim. Ware takes Jim with him to put him in school at Selma, where he can study to become a teacher. Through this specific action, combined with Vyry's unwavering desire to have her children learn how to "read and write and cipher," Walker thus recognizes the upward mobility through education that defined so many people of African descent on United States soil.[28] Jim's departure will alleviate the conflict between him and Innis, and it will secure Jim's future even as it changes family dynamics for Vyry, Innis, Jim's sister Minna, and Jim's little brother Harry. Jim's departure is bittersweet in its disruption but ultimately necessary in terms of historical and familial progression. Important, too, is that Vyry's contentment at the end of the text signals to readers that Vyry is accepting of and hopeful about what Jim can accomplish as well as about the general state of her family's future.

This upward mobility through education is but one of the historical patterns that undergirds Walker's fictional representations. As noted, Walker spent the better part of thirty years researching and writing her historical novel. It thus has an impressive historical credibility, and many of the episodes in it can be verified through the experiences of historical figures. Mulatto enslaved female and slave mistress interaction is one such experience, as is illustrated by Vyry's mother Hetta and Vyry herself in relation to Big Missy. No better historical example of these interactions exists than Harriet E. Jacobs's *Incidents in the Life of a Slave Girl*. Like Hetta, Linda Brent, the stand-in for the historical Jacobs, earned attention—most unwanted—from her master. When the mistress gains knowledge of her husband's pursuits, she immediately turns to blaming Linda. Given the intensity of the situation, of the fact that Linda must encounter both master and mistress every day during her enslavement, there is absolutely no way that she can be comfortable in this home environment. She therefore devises the well-known plan to escape but not to escape, to remain in her grandmother's attic for seven years, during which Dr. Flint, her tormentor, is led to believe that she has escaped to the North. Home to Linda is not the Big House; nor is it the space with her parents and her brother, a space that Dr. Flint disrupted easily. Home for Linda is a cramped, damp, unhealthy attic space, from which she suffers lifelong debilitation.

While in that space, one of her greatest concerns is for the welfare of her children. She envisions, as Vyry does, a time and a place where she can gather them to her in a space that she will be able to identify as home. It is the same kind of claiming of motherhood that drove Sethe to commit the acts she does in *Beloved*, for both Sethe and Linda refuse to allow slaveholders to dictate their claiming of their children and their embracing of motherhood. For Linda, it will take years and more extensive separation from her children before she can accomplish the feat of gathering them unto herself. What is striking here is the determination and persistence with which she sets about achieving freedom, her refusal to allow the dark forces to prevail, and her ultimate location of a space where she can be relatively safe with the remnants of her family, for, just as Vyry loses family members, especially Hetta and Aunt Sally, so does Linda. Her brother disappears when he has the opportunity to do so, and her only comfort in the void of his absence is the knowledge that he is no longer enslaved.

Both Linda and Vyry echo Frederick Douglass's notion of a home elsewhere. Vyry especially suffers the physical if not spiritual abandonment that forces her to seek homes outside the biological circle into which she is born. Having been separated from Hetta at birth, Vyry lives with Mammy Sukey before she is whisked back to say goodbye to Hetta and to move into the Big House. In that space, abandonment is rendered sharply in that there is no othermother to whom Vyry can turn. When she finds that othermother in Aunt Sally, she is better able to navigate the inhospitable waters of the Dutton plantation home. Aunt Sally's cabin thus becomes the home elsewhere, the only space on the plantation that Vyry can see as a true respite. When Aunt Sally is sold away, she inadvertently bequeaths her kitchen and her cabin to Vyry, and this elsewhere space serves Vyry well until she leaves the plantation for a series of other homes elsewhere in mostly hostile communities. When she and her family receive assistance from white supporters, the final home elsewhere becomes Vyry's true home. It is a home, in kinship with some other literary representations, in which she hopes that a Christian ethic will prevail. That ethic may serve Vyry, but it receives challenges and anticipates later problematic literary representations.

Forgiveness is at the center of Vyry's faith, a faith that Vyry has embraced as a result of attending church meetings with Aunt Sally and listening to Uncle Zeke's sermons. That faith, however, is tested sorely when Vyry's family's home is burned and especially when Innis beats Jim. Instead of becoming angry and bitter in these instances—and in many others—Vyry resorts to prayer and forgiveness. She may question God, but she prays her way through questioning into renewed belief. That progression shows a woman whose hope is based in something larger than herself and who is willing to be transformed by that something larger. Though Vyry may rail at God in her prayers and question why her family is so violently targeted by nameless white folks toward whom she has expressed no ill will and done no harm, she never allows destructive deeds to deter her from her ultimate objective of securing a homespace. After their home is burned, she and Innis simply resolve to move forward to another town and try yet again. When Innis beats Jim, she is more deeply troubled, because the discord is within her homespace. The prayer she prays after that incident makes clear the impact of Christianity upon Vyry, its transformative nature, and the possibility for its transforming the relationships in her homespace.

> 'I come down here, Lord, cause I ain't got no where else to go . . . . We can't go on like this no longer, Lord. We can't keep on a-fighting, and a-fussing, and a-cussing, and a-hating like this, Lord . . . . Let your peace come in our hearts

again, Lord, and we's gwine try to stay on our knees and follow the road You is laid before us, if You only will.

'Come by here, Lord, come by here, if you please. And Lord, I wants to thank You, Jesus, for moving the stone!'

Now with the morning rocking around her like a storm shaking through the earth beneath her, she waited till the thundering sound of crashing trees and trembling worlds had ceased, and she got up from her knees. She looked around, startled and almost amazed that the day was still so hushed and still. The sunlight dappled through the trees and she put her hands out to touch the absolutely motionless leaves. In wonder she looked again at the blue sky, and then in a sudden lightness of movement, feeling that once again she was a feather, she began to pick her way out of the woods.[29]

Perhaps in this best instance of what Christianity is designed to do, that is, enable believers to keep the faith and to keep on keeping on under extremely trying and difficult circumstances, Vyry showcases the very best of literary representations of the tradition. Her transformation at the end of the prayer incorporates bountiful nature, a tangible example of God's handiwork that, in its peaceful presentation, signals that all will be well. Even when Randall Ware returns and is critical of Vyry's belief and demeans her faithfulness, Vyry remains steadfast. Indeed, Randall's return because he has heard of Innis's beating of Jim enables Vyry to put the finishing touch on her claiming of home.

To illustrate that she has no ill will against the former slaveholders or whites in general against whom Randall rails, Vyry recounts that she has herself been beaten but is not bitter. To both Randall's and Innis's shock, Vyry bares her scarred back, which shocks them even more. She then declares to Randall:

> I wants you to bear me witness and God knows I tells the truth, I couldn't tell you the name of the man what whipped me, and if I could it wouldn't make no difference. I honestly believes that if airy one of them peoples what treated me like dirt when I was a slave would come to my door in the morning hungry, I would feed em. God knows I ain't got no hate in my heart for nobody. If I is and doesn't know it, I prays to God to take it out. I ain't got no time to be hating. I believes in God and I believes in trying to love and help everybody, and I knows that humble is the way.[30]

Andrea Wolfe comments that, "during this scene, Vyry uses her back to represent the potential that she sees for her future and that of her family. She believes that, although they may retain scars, she, and Randall and Innis, can heal. Vyry presents her scars as proof of her ability to survive and to continue to love despite her experiences of material brutality and emotional horror."[31]

By exposing her back and shedding cleansing tears, almost in a ritualized religious conversion, Vyry conveys that there are no longer any secrets, any barriers between her and Innis, and no longer a possibility for Randall to have any role in her life other than as father to Jim. By baring her back, in her homespace, and avowing that slavery and slaveholders have no hold over her, Vyry executes the last step in separating herself from slavery and in defining how she wants her family to move forward in freedom. Her stance ensures that her homespace will be saturated with and guided by the best tendencies of humanistic interactions. It does not matter that the man she once loved is derisive, or that racism still reigns, because she is secure in her own skin, secure in her own belief, and secure in the knowledge that the direction she has chosen for her family is indeed best for them.

Walker is thus able to end this narrative of an African American female character's quest for home on the best possible note. There are no screaming hallelujahs. There is simply the reassurance that Vyry has arrived at the objective for which she traveled and for which she searched for so long, that her homespace in this moment is surrounded by the perfect pause of serenity and peace. The fact that she can engage in the mundane action of calling her chickens signifies that her quest has put her in a positive space and that it has benefited her entire family. What may or may not happen after this moment is irrelevant. What is noteworthy here is that Vyry and her family have achieved what many formerly enslaved persons went seeking and never found: a homespace to call their own. Indeed, her success presents one of the rare occasions in African American literature in which there is a relatively happy ending in a healthy homespace.

NOTES

1. Margaret Walker, *Jubilee* (Boston: First Mariner Books, 1999).

2. For an account of the thirty-year research and writing process that resulted in *Jubilee*, see Margaret Walker, *How I Wrote Jubilee* (Chicago: Third World P, 1972).

3. Jacqueline Miller Carmichael, *Trumpeting a Fiery Sound: History and Folklore in Margaret Walker's Jubilee* (Athens: U of Georgia P, 1998), 39.

4. For a superb accounting of the reception of Walker's *Jubilee,* see Carmichael, *Trumpeting*, Chapter One.

5. Carmichael, *Trumpeting*, 70.

6. Carmichael, *Trumpeting*, 20.

7. James Weldon Johnson, ed., *The Book of American Negro Poetry* (1922; New York: Harvest, 1959), 41–42.

8. LeRoi Jones (Amiri Baraka), *Dutchman and The Slave* (New York: Morrow, 1964).

9. Trudier Harris, "Black Writers in a Changed Landscape, Since 1950," in *The History of Southern Literature*, ed. Louis D. Rubin, Jr. et al. (Baton Rouge: LSU P, 1985), 567.

10. I have already cited Carmichael's volume. Maryemma Graham edited and published *On Being Female, Black, and Free: Essays by Margaret Walker, 1932–1992* (Knoxville: U of Tennessee P, 1997), *Fields Watered With Blood: Critical Essays on Margaret Walker* (Athens: U of Georgia P, 2001), and *Conversations with Margaret Walker* (Jackson: U P of Mississippi, 2002). She also edited Walker's *How I Wrote Jubilee and Other Essays on Life and Literature* (New York: Feminist P, 1990). In addition, Graham is completing the definitive biography of Walker, which is scheduled to appear from Oxford University Press in 2022.

11. Quoted in Carmichael, *Trumpeting*, 101.

12. In *How I Wrote Jubilee* (1972), Walker details the research that went into the conception and writing of the novel.

13. Harriet Jacobs, *Incidents in the Life of a Slave Girl* (Cambridge: Harvard U P, 1987).

14. Walker, *Jubilee*, 10.

15. There is at least one notable literary exception to these general tenets. I am thinking specifically of Edward P. Jones's *The Known World* (New York: Harper Collins, 2003), a neo-slave narrative in which black people own other black people during slavery. Those who experience such ownership are able to do so in part because of land, property, and financial resources that have accrued to them. They, therefore, can be just as abusive toward their "property" or just as settled into their homes as are the whites they often emulate.

16. Walker, *Jubilee*, 31.

17. Harriet E. Wilson, *Our Nig* (New York: Vintage, 2002).

18. Walker *Jubilee*, 285.

19. Walker, *Jubilee*, 296. As Valerie Sweeney Prince points out in *Burnin' Down the House: Home in African American Literature* (New York: Columbia U P, 2005), African American female authors, in contrast to many male writers, are more inclined to emphasize the "built physical structure" as the embodiment of home (60). This is certainly true of the quest in which Vyry and Innis engage in Walker's *Jubilee*.

20. Andrea Wolfe, "The Narrative Power of the Black Maternal body: Resisting and Exceeding Visual Economics of Discipline in Margaret Walker's *Jubilee*," *Interdisciplinary Literary Studies* 20, no. 4 (2018), 418.

21. Amanda J. Davis, "Shatterings: Violent Disruptions of Homeplace in *Jubilee* and *The Street*," *MELUS* 30, no. 4 (Winter 2005): 32.

22. Davis, "Shatterings," 25–51; bell hooks, *Yearning: Race, Gender and Cultural Politics* (Boston: South End P, 1990).

23. Walker, *Jubilee*, 432.

24. Walker, *Jubilee*, 434.

25. Walker, Jubilee, 453.

26. Walker, *Jubilee*, 444.

27. Alice Walker, *The Third Life of Grange Copeland* (New York: Harcourt Brace Jovanovich, 1970); Suzan-Lori Parks, *Topdog/Underdog* (New York: Theatre Communications Group, 2001).

28. Walker, *Jubilee*, 370.

29. Walker, *Jubilee*, 454, 455.

30. Walker, *Jubilee*, 485.

31. Wolfe, "Maternal," 422.

Chapter 2

Where I Live Is Not Home
James Baldwin, Go Tell It on the Mountain *(1953); Toni Morrison,* The Bluest Eye *(1970); Suzan-Lori Parks,* Topdog/Underdog *(2001)*

The end of *Jubilee* presents a Vyry Brown who has migrated time and time again and who has settled into a homespace where Christian values guide her life. Although her son Jim has left with his father Randall Ware to pursue an education, the basic nuclear family is in place. That basic configuration invites comparison to James Baldwin's *Go Tell It on the Mountain* (1953), which is a narrative about migrants from the South who find themselves in Harlem during the Great Migration.[1] The novel features characters who have sought refuge in homes and communities beyond the ones into which they were born. It also focuses upon a stepson and his relationship with his stepfather. Most important, it showcases the Christianity that defines literary families in many works following and preceding Walker's *Jubilee*. The impact that Christianity has upon the Grimes family, the central characters in the novel, is detrimental to the formation of their homespace and has negative influences upon the interactions that occur in that space. Implicitly, Baldwin suggests that migration from the South to the North ultimately fails in a variety of ways. While there might be more job opportunities in the North and perhaps even more of the freedoms that characters did not have in the South, the stunting of healthy identity far outweighs those positive factors.

In this chapter, I use Baldwin's *Go Tell It on the Mountain*, together with Toni Morrison's *The Bluest Eye* (1970) and Suzan-Lori Parks's *Topdog/Underdog* (2001), to explore how migration and Christianity are relevant to the creation of homespaces in the first two works and how the spatial dynamics of homespaces is a factor in all three. While Morrison's characters also migrate from the South to the North, Parks does not make the immediate origin of her characters clear. What is clear is that they, like the Grimes family in *Go Tell It on the Mountain* and the Breedlove family in *The Bluest Eye*, are smothered by the spaces in which they live. Psychological and emotional alienation from family and space is prominent in all three narratives. Equally relevant is that all three are located in northern urban areas, which means that the writers implicitly draw conclusions about the successes and failures of migration, and they consistently make statements about how spatial configurations can influence human interactions.

WHEN CHRISTIANITY CAN'T HELP—THE DIRTY HOME IN *GO TELL IT ON THE MOUNTAIN*

James Baldwin's *Go Tell It on the Mountain* develops in an urban space in Harlem and is a tale of family dysfunctionality that includes emotional spousal abuse, the beating of children, and the suppression of adolescent identity formation. The irony of the text is that it is undergirded with religious traditions that should suggest tolerance and unity instead of strife. The husband, Gabriel Grimes, is a migrant from the South who, after extreme sinfulness that included drunkenness, gambling, and whoremongering, converted to Christianity and began to follow the path of apparent righteousness for which his mother had always prayed. He becomes, to non-family observers at least, a model Christian and progresses to becoming a minister. As is the case with a lot of new converts, the intensity of his fanaticism is obvious when, during a revival, he chastises other ministers for their loose—and to them humorous—remarks about Deborah, the gang-raped woman whom he decides to "lift up" by making her his wife. His current wife Elizabeth (whom he has similarly "lifted up" after she has given birth to an illegitimate child), Elizabeth's son John, Gabriel's son Roy, and Gabriel's sister Florence are all witnesses to and participants in the problematic family dynamics that make Gabriel's trek to the North almost as ineffectual as that of the Breedloves in *The Bluest Eye*.

Baldwin is certainly interested in the physical space of the apartment in which the Grimeses reside, but he is equally intent upon showcasing the ugliness of the lives they lead, most of which is the direct result of Gabriel's sharply misguided and physically and emotionally destructive self-righteousness. Indeed, the physical space in many ways reflects the spiritual and emotional state of the family. The apartment space is subject to invasion by vermin and echoes the depiction of the opening scene in Richard Wright's *Native Son* (1940) in which a huge rat disrupts the Thomas family early one morning in their one-room "apartment."[2] Fourteen-year-old John, a central character in *Go Tell It on the Mountain*, has heard, over the noise of his parents engaging in sex, "the sound of rats' feet, and rat screams, and the music and cursing from the harlot's house downstairs."[3] The lack of privacy echoes lack of privacy in other literary renditions of urban homespaces, but it is not as blatant as the Breedlove children sharing the same room with their parents. Indeed, the Grimes apartment, despite the vermin, is fairly sizeable; there is a living room, a dining room, a kitchen, and at least two bedrooms, one of which John shares with his brother Roy. The striking thing about the space is less its size than, echoing the Youngers' apartment in Lorraine Hansberry's *A Raisin in the Sun* (1959), its weariness.[4] There are blotches on the ceiling, the furnishings are worn, and there is constant dirt everywhere. That dirt is the central metaphor for the problematic lives the characters lead. On the morning the novel opens, which is John's fourteenth birthday, the family goes about its usual Saturday ritual of attempting to clean the space. It is, as John points out, a Sisyphean task. Dust covers everything, just as the dirt of Gabriel's life prior to his arrival in Harlem covers all of his interactions with his family.

A late convert to Christianity—at least by Southern standards, since he does not profess belief until he is twenty-one—Gabriel has risen through the short ranks of preaching in the South before he migrated to the North. What he keeps hidden from everyone, but about which his first wife Deborah had written to her sister-in-law Florence, is that the newly-minted minister had not only fallen from his moral throne down South, but he had fathered a child in the process. That child, born to Esther, a young woman who worked in the same white home as Gabriel and with whom he had lustful sex on the kitchen floor of that house, survived his mother's death in childbirth in the North, returned to the South for a short period as a teenager, and ended up being stabbed to death in a tavern in Chicago. The point is that Gabriel talks himself into believing that God would replace the dead son named Royal with a new beginning of a royal line, thus the name Roy for the son in Harlem. Gabriel's sins in this sequence of events are legendary: he mistreats Esther by buying her off and sending her north to save his reputation; he gets the money for that payoff by stealing from Deborah; he never acknowledges until after Royal's death that Royal was his son; he blames Deborah for his actions even as he finally confesses his paternity to her; he keeps his sinful previous life hidden and lords his righteousness over Elizabeth, who has given birth to John out of wedlock, a fact that John never learns; and he repeats his earlier uplift campaign by marrying Elizabeth—a soiled and tainted woman sharing kinship with Deborah, he believes—under the pretext that he is infinitely morally superior to her. When Deborah asserts that she would have taken Royal and raised him as her own son, Gabriel's arrogant and judgmental response is: "'But I didn't want no harlot's son.'"[5] As Deborah declares, "'Esther weren't no harlot,'" Gabriel still cannot see the beam in his own eye for focusing on the speck in the eyes of others.⁶ The remotest designation of the harlot label could only come from the misguided and deluded regions of Gabriel's mind. Believing that Esther would have dragged him "'right on down to Hell with her,'" because her "'mind weren't on the Lord,'" Gabriel is strikingly blind to his own actions and conclusions as well as to the sufferings of others.⁷

Gabriel's ugliness and the dirt of the life that Gabriel has concealed are reflected in the dirt of the apartment, which will not be made clean no matter the effort that John and others exert. It is as if the very walls know Gabriel's history and reflect it every day. Baldwin describes the kitchen thusly, a description that is echoed when John later tries to clean the living room:

> The room was narrow and dirty; nothing could alter its dimensions, no labor could ever make it clean. Dirt was in the walls and the floorboards, and triumphed beneath the sink where roaches spawned; was in the fine ridges of the pots and pans, scoured daily, burnt black on the bottom, hanging above the store; was in the wall against which they hung, and revealed itself where the paint had cracked and leaned outward in stiff squares and fragments, the paper-thin underside webbed with black. Dirt was in every corner, angle, crevice of the monstrous stove, and lived behind it in delirious communion with the corrupted wall. Dirt was in the baseboard that John scrubbed every Saturday, and roughened the cupboard shelves that held the cracked and gleaming dishes.⁸

It is fitting that John links the dirt he observes to a biblical text: "*He who is filthy, let him be filthy still*" (italics in original).⁹ Later, when John is sweeping the carpet in the living room, the narrative remarks: "John hated sweeping this carpet, for dust rose, clogging his nose and sticking to his sweaty skin, and he felt that should he sweep it forever, the clouds of dust would not diminish."¹⁰ The cloying, inescapable dust is just as pervasive as the sinful state in which Gabriel believes his wife and children exist. As John cannot escape the dust in the apartment, so he cannot escape his father's judgment, constant disapproval, and insults. Like the dust, Gabriel is on a mission to get everyone around him to recognize his power even if they are resistant to submitting to his authority. What Elizabeth and her children call home, therefore, can never be a healthy place as long as Gabriel is head of the household.

Ironically, Gabriel seems unaware that the dirt that saturates his home and that represents sinful states is most applicable to him. Gabriel is "dirty" in his many sins and is as "filthy" as is implied in the sermon text that John remembers. Biblical interpretations posit the state of lack of grace, that is, not being saved, as one in which the dirtiness of sin dominates. Conversion to Christianity is viewed in traditional, fundamentalist African American churches as being "washed whiter than snow," which means that the unconverted state has implicit in it a condition of impurity, dirt, lack of clean communion with God. That tainted condition ends when one enters the fold of belief and marks that entry with membership in a Christian church. Gabriel's total embracing of patterns and practices in traditional Christianity means that Gabriel is subsumed under the same views about dirt and cleanliness, thus readers can view him as the dirtiest of all the characters, even as he tries repeatedly to shunt his own sins off onto others.

Gabriel is an unflinching disciplinarian who believes that both his wife and his children should obey him. He rules with verbal commands and insults, and, if those should fail, he resorts easily and readily to corporeal punishment. Without knowledge of his true relationship to Gabriel, John is mystified as to why Gabriel treats him as he does. At this point, when John is most needful of forming a healthy identity, Gabriel shortcuts any possibility for that outcome. On the morning of his birthday, John recalls that Gabriel has beaten him for being wicked (whatever that means, since John is a mere adolescent). Not knowing his origins, John is nonetheless clear that he "would not be like his father, or his father's fathers. He would have another life" and thus be away from "the darkness of his father's house."[11] Already John is planning to replicate a pattern of migration that the adults in his family carried out by migrating from the South to the North, for he is alienated from and feels as if he is an outcast in his own homespace. Marc Dudley agrees that John has effectively been "cast out of his father's house" and that he is "alienated from a homely space."[12] Csaba Csapo adds:

> In John's mind, the objects of his fear are ultimately inseparable. In terms of their threat to his existence, there is no significant difference between God, Gabriel, and the racist and heterosexist society that emerges as a threat to destroy him . . . . Gabriel is to some extent equivalent to the God of the black church, so he can be identified with the white homophobic society. He thinks that he is immaculate, so to say 'white,' without any stain. If he is the saintly, the saved, the elected, then logically there must be the evil, which is the black. He would rather the illegitimate child pays for the price of his sin.[13]

It is Gabriel's actions, Gabriel's iron-fisted rule over his family, that have led John to the conclusion that he should leave his father's house and create another home, an option that is more readily available to him than it is to Vyry's son Jim in response to his conflict with his stepfather. Gabriel consistently makes his family feel as if they are aligned with the forces of Satan, against which Gabriel, the only righteous and true man of God, must do combat. So, he insults John by tying him to "the evil one." Not only has Gabriel called John "ugly," but he has expanded that to the Satanic: "His father had always said that his face was the face of Satan" (and how would Gabriel know unless he has communed with Satan?), which leads John to examine his physical features for some truth in that accusation.[14] The cleft that John has in his chin "was, his father said, the mark of the devil's little finger."[15] Even when John is in the throes of the religious experience that will transform him into a believing Christian, he still has internalized his father's scathing assessment of him sufficiently to have a vision of Gabriel in which Gabriel refers to John as "the Devil's son."[16] In that same scene, from Gabriel's point of view, readers see the same reference: "Gabriel had never seen such a look on John's face before; Satan, at that moment, stared out of John's eyes."[17] In church, in what should be a most sacred moment, Gabriel is unable to resist a negative judgment of John, who has done absolutely nothing to earn such condemnation. Gabriel's brand and practice of Christianity, therefore, are a long way from the altruistic and transformative belief system that sustains Vyry Brown.[18]

It takes no child psychologist to articulate the extensive psychological damage that a child can experience as a result of such labeling and implicit rejection. Yet, this ugliness comes from a man who professes to serve God, which means that Gabriel, as the undisputed ruler of his home, creates an environment in which his family can never feel at home. That is clear in comments related to John as well in statements that Roy makes in conversation with Elizabeth. When Elizabeth comments that Roy is lucky to have a father like Gabriel who is concerned about his children and wants them to grow up in the right way, Roy responds with a list of the strictures that Gabriel places on Roy and John: "'Yeah,' said Roy, 'we don't know how lucky we *is* to have a father what don't want you to go to movies, and don't want you to play in the streets, and don't want you to have no friends, and he don't want this and he don't want that, and he don't want you to do *nothing*" (italics in original).[19] Even making allowances for parental caring and concern, the picture that Roy and John paint of Gabriel is one of an un-understanding, spiritually flawed and aggressively focused man who works to ensure that his family will land in heaven instead of hell (or so he professes anyway). In the meantime, however, there is the current reality, and that reality reveals Gabriel as a humorless, demanding, shortsighted, and insulting husband and father whose single-minded approach to Christianity has alienated him from everyone in his life—even though they may be too afraid to show it in his presence.

Of note as well is that Gabriel's current behavior provides a sharp contrast to what Gabriel promised during the period that he courted Elizabeth. He had been attentive to her, and he had "become her strength."[20] He also asserted that he viewed Elizabeth and John as God's restoration to him of what he had lost—presumably in Deborah and Royal. He had not, at that point, "stood in judgment on her."[21] Equally important, he had been attentive to and protective of the toddler John. When he proposes to Elizabeth, he promises her: "'And I'll love your son, your little boy,' he said at last, 'just like he was my own.

He won't never have to fret or worry about nothing; he won't never be cold or hungry as long as I'm alive and I got my two hands to work with. I swear this before my God,' he said, 'because He done give me back something I thought was lost.'"[22] In this moment, Elizabeth obviously responds to Gabriel with visions of a happy home. Given her backstory, it must seem to Elizabeth that she has arrived at a stable port after a series of hurricanes on rough sea waters.[23] In that moment—and in his pride—Gabriel perhaps believes what he says. However, there is a huge gap between the letter and the substance of his words. He may provide food and shelter for John, but he decidedly does not love him, and he only inspires hate in John. Then, once Roy is born, any altruistic feeling about John disappears completely. Gabriel is jealous of the fact that John is the acquiescent, studious, good son that Roy will never be. He thinks when he sees John on the threshing floor of the church preparing to become a believer that "neither of his sons was here tonight, had ever cried on the threshing-floor . . . . Only the son of the bondswoman stood where the rightful heir should stand."[24] Likening himself to Abraham in the Old Testament, who fathers Ishmael by the bondswoman Hagar, Gabriel is even more arrogantly egotistical. Whatever his original intentions, Gabriel would like to blot John from his very existence. He constantly spews venom on the white teachers who have affirmed John's intelligence, and he heaps blame upon John's shoulders for any and every little thing that might go wrong in the Grimes household. John becomes the scapegoat for the void in Gabriel's life that his legitimate son Roy will never fill. Gabriel thus becomes a bitter, vengeful, judgmental, hypocritical, deluded, and ultimately unhappy man who is locked in his own deep, dark, funky dungeon of sin and secrets. The homespace over which he presides, therefore, will never allow any of his family to relax fully and feel truly at home. Marc Dudley remarks that Baldwin suggests "that the human act of living is an incessant movement toward communion, toward a shared homely space. Loneliness and alienation are thus a kind of homelessness."[25]

In this unhealthy space, John knows the kind of familiarity that informs Dana Franklin's response to the Weylin plantation as she arrives and refers to it as home. By virtue of adolescence and dependency, John cannot escape from his homespace, though his familiarity with it comes with the psychological and physical violence that compares to Dana's. John can be whipped, just as Dana is. He can be directed, chastised, and blamed for things that are not his fault. Dana, for example, is blamed for one of the enslaved men being sold away from the Weylin plantation merely because she speaks to him, just as John can be blamed for Roy's stabbing even though he was not on the scene and did not participate in the fight. John, like Dana, is subject to the total authority of the person who owns the space in which he resides. He must, like Dana, develop strategies for tiptoeing around that authority and saving himself as best he can. It is thus perhaps not too farfetched to assert that, in this confined space, Gabriel is as brutal, ruthless, and unsympathetic as any slaveholder. Indeed, there are instances in which slaveholder Rufus Weylin, in his interactions with Dana, is ultimately more humane than Gabriel is in his interactions with John.

Gabriel's un-Christian behavior and detrimental impact upon his family are no more clear than in the scene following a fight in which Roy has been stabbed. It occurs on John's birthday while John has been at the movies (his mother encouraged him to go out before his father came home, and that in itself might be an indication of Gabriel's ability to spoil everything, including John's birthday, which Gabriel never mentions). As John enters the apartment, Gabriel is tending to Roy's wound, Elizabeth is nearby, and Florence is also present. Gabriel blames everyone except Roy for the incident. If Elizabeth had been more careful as a mother, then Roy would not have been injured. If John had been in place with his brother, the injury similarly would not have occurred. Even as Florence and Elizabeth try to get Gabriel to understand that Roy is nearly uncontrollable and went out and got into a fight with white boys without the assistance of anyone present in the room, Gabriel is still on a mission to find fault. "'You ain't got but one child,'" Elizabeth tells him, "'that's liable to go out and break his neck, and that's Roy, and you know it . . . . You just better pray God to stop him before somebody puts another knife in him and puts him in his grave.'"[26] That echoes too closely with what has happened to Royal, Gabriel's first son, so Gabriel, "with all his might . . . slapped her across the face."[27] Insult and injury lead to more chaos as Roy yells out: "'Don't you slap my mother. That's my *mother*. You slap her again, you black bastard, and I swear to God I'll kill you'" (italics in original).[28] Obviously, the authoritarian Gabriel will not tolerate such a rebuke, so he takes off his belt, "and it fell with a whistling sound on Roy, who shivered, and fell back, his face to the wall. But he did not cry out. And the belt was raised again, and again. The air rang with the whistling, and the *crack!* against Roy's flesh" (italics in original).[29] Elizabeth falls upon Roy and cries, and general confusion reigns until Florence catches and holds the belt.[30] Worthy of note in terms of the state of Gabriel's relationship to Roy is that Roy defiantly refuses to give Gabriel the satisfaction of tears during what must have been an excruciatingly painful ordeal for him.

Without in any way attempting to justify Roy's cursing of Gabriel, it is nonetheless clear that Gabriel is as guilty in this scenario as is Roy. If Gabriel had not been so intent upon assigning blame, upon protecting his precious Roy (who mostly does not want the protection) from his family as well as from the streets, then he might have been able to step back emotionally and judge the situation with less heat. However, given his portrayal, along with his wrongheaded belief that God has forgiven him for the death of his first Royal and given him another royal heir in Roy, it is impossible for Gabriel to detach himself from the situation. The result is that a father and husband, who in the abstract should be the protector of his home and family, turns into a vengeful, wrathful demon who wreaks havoc on that family. Given his response in this scene, it is easy to understand why John whispers to his baby sister when his mother sends him out of the room to quiet her crying: "'Now, you let your big brother tell you something, baby. Just as soon as you's able to stand on your feet, you run away from *this* house, run far away'" (italics in original).[31] The figurative dirt and darkness of the house are of Gabriel's creation, and no one who wants to be healthy, John surmises, can survive there for long. In a Gothic reading of the novel, Sherry R. Truffin offers: "Conceptualizing the novel as Gothic also helps to account for its claustrophobic effect: historical and familial legacies trap John physically (in a small house), geographically (in a northern ghetto), and culturally (in a fundamentalist church). John feels incarcerated and suffocated, and his avenues of escape are limited."[32]

Immediately after this horrific scene, an unrepentant Gabriel goes to his church for the Saturday night tarry service, a service at which John will "go through," that is, experience a conversion, and himself embrace Christianity. Arguably, Gabriel demands total control in his home because he is not able to secure an impressive enough position in his church. Instead of being the minister, Gabriel is the head deacon in the church in Harlem, perhaps a demotion in his mind from his touted sermons in the South. In his desire for some kind of mastery, he becomes lord over his wife and children. Unfortunately, none of them has information that would give them some kind of equalizing power with Gabriel: Elizabeth does not know about Royal, and neither John nor Roy knows that Gabriel is not John's father. From his house of secrets, Gabriel can rule over his family with the ugliness of a tyrant and still—in his own mind, at least—claim righteousness (and the saints around him, that is, church members, who know nothing of his home life, view him as righteous as well). Gabriel adds to the toxic masculinity that defines so many African American literary homes by defiling his further with a perverted and toxic version of Christianity, one that makes it impossible for Elizabeth, John, Roy, and the two younger children ever to be truly healthy or happy in that space. As Csapo comments, "Gabriel's sanctimonious self-image about his life seems to be a moral evasion; his family and his friends exist for him merely as a contrastive basis for his pretentious sanctimoniousness."[33]

In writing about his title character in "Sonny's Blues," Baldwin comments that young black men in Harlem of Sonny's age "were growing up with a rush and their heads bumped abruptly against the low ceiling of their actual possibilities."[34] John and his family share Harlem with Sonny, whose friends end up on drugs (as Sonny does), in jail, or dead. The low ceiling of possibility has been put in place by the forces that created the ghetto, a ghetto in which John and his family reside. Instead of desiring that John escape from the limitations that the low ceiling maintains, Gabriel is the force that presses the ceiling down upon John's head. Gabriel has no altruistic desire for John to get an education and escape from the ghetto, or even to find success within the ghetto. Indeed, Gabriel probably would not shed tears if John simply disappeared or died. Once Roy is born, there is no concern at all for John; Gabriel simply views him as a problem, an interloper. Gabriel is determined to squelch John's spirit and render John incapable of resilience or resistance. The hatred that he feels for his stepson mirrors the hatred that the larger society implicitly expresses by locking African Americans into ghettos. Those forces declare that young black men will never be "native sons." Gabriel joins them in declaring that John will never be a native son in the Grimes household. Outsider, alien, outcast—only some form of such rejection will satisfy Gabriel as far as John is concerned.

Despite her best efforts, Elizabeth is ultimately not successful at being a mediating force between Gabriel and her children, which means that she cannot protect either John or Roy from Gabriel's wrath. In terms of parental authority, therefore, Gabriel rules supreme—in his approximation of what an Old Testament household might have looked like. Gabriel's domination is facilitated in part by Elizabeth's continuing guilt for having borne a child out of wedlock. In a society where the female always seems to be judged more harshly than the male in such out-of-wedlock births, Elizabeth has absorbed thoroughly the sense of sinfulness and guilt that the communities in which she lives assign to such actions. That guilt can only lead her to "take low" from Gabriel, defend him as a good provider for her children, and ill equip her for challenging Gabriel on anything. Her position and actions as mother, therefore, do not provide her with the resources to counter the ugliness of the homespace that Gabriel creates, for she is as much a victim as are the children. While she is the only family member to remember John's birthday, that small island in a sea of mistreatment and negativism is insufficient to make the space a healthy one, for even the pleasure that John has experienced in going to the movies is nullified by the scene that occurs after Roy is stabbed.

Homespace on earth is thus emotionally unhealthy and spiritually vacuous for John, his mother, and his siblings. Gabriel wants to ensure that John—since he is the focus of the conversion—experiences the same sense of discomfort and loss when he contemplates a heavenly home. By denying the validity of John's all-night conversion experience, and by refusing to interact positively with John the morning after, Gabriel essentially assigns John to a space of spiritual homelessness. Since the illegitimate son, so Gabriel believes, cannot carry his royal line forward and ensure a space in heaven, then he has no business being in heaven at all. Gabriel therefore consigns John to a homelessness that positions him outside the "house" of

God. Converts such as John are usually welcomed and guided spiritually by the elders in fundamentalist churches, whether those elders are deacons or ministers. Gabriel, the head deacon, refuses that role as spiritual elder and as presumed biological elder. As far as he is concerned, John may well be cast onto an island of forgetfulness, for there is nothing in Gabriel's mind, demeanor, or actions that would suggest that John could have a home in the same spiritual space that Gabriel identifies self-righteously as his birthright, and, in this scenario, his birthright only.[35]

UGLY SPACE, UGLY PEOPLE, UGLY LIVES

Like Baldwin's *Go Tell It on the Mountain*, Toni Morrison's *The Bluest Eye* (1970) portrays migrants who leave the South with the hope of making new homes in the North.[36] Cholly and Pauline Breedlove arrive in Ohio from Kentucky with high hopes for their futures on northern soil. They locate a house and begin lives that would seem to suggest that dreams can indeed be realized. Those expectations, however, devolve into nightmare; the new territory does not yield the paradise for which these migrants had hoped. Instead, the space they inhabit imprisons them physically, psychologically, emotionally, and economically just as effectively as southern laws, customs, and general racism cut them off from opportunities. They apparently live in several places in Lorain, Ohio before moving into the storefront-turned-house in which readers get a thorough look at them. This space in which Cholly and his family reside for a short time is ugly and at odds with the desires of the characters—Pauline wants to be with her white family, Sammy wants to run away, Pecola wants to escape into blue eyes, and Cholly just does not give a damn. The transiency and short-circuited expectations of the Breedloves thus illustrate the unsettledness and inversions of many of those who migrated to the North.

Physical spaces may not have any intrinsic, innate ability to impact the characters that reside in them, but they clearly influence the behavior, actions, and psychological and emotional states of those characters. There is nothing about the physical structure of the storefront that evokes anything warm from the Breedloves—and certainly not a sense of pride. Their alienation from the space is made more apparent when Cholly is forced to accept and pay for damaged furniture. More important, there is nothing in their biological group that approximates a sense of family that could claim that storefront space and domesticate it into a home. Forced into this habitation, the characters depicted are, to borrow a phrase from scholar James A. Crank, "disposable people."[37] The larger society does not care about them, and the employers for whom they work and to whom they are usually indebted similarly do not care—at least not beyond concern about the capacity of such persons to complete the work that the employers desire. Spaces certainly do not speak, but they can—quite effectively—convey a sense of the inertia and the lackluster nature of existence that accompany characters whom the society has almost used up and about whom they have no regrets when they are ultimately thrown away. It is perhaps ironic, therefore, that many African Americans who left the South in the wave of the Great Migration of the early twentieth century and expected to find something different in the North, to re-shape their identities and claim new spaces that would not destroy them psychologically, only found themselves living in southern territory on northern soil.

History and literature document that many of the black people who were newly arrived from the South into northern urban spaces found little relief in the spaces that they could call home. Conditions, in many instances, may have been worse than in the South. At least the South had open spaces in the yards and fields that surrounded those sharecropper shacks. In the North, in the concrete jungles that existed in almost every large northern space into which African Americans migrated, pavement and multiple-storied housing dominated the landscape, and overcrowded conditions were the norm rather than the exception. Diseases, especially tuberculosis and heart trouble, were constants. In African American literary works that portray such spaces, black characters endure cramped, crowded, rat-infested conditions that are incubators for crime and that offer constant challenges to any prospect of upward mobility. Richard Wright provides cogent commentary on the impact of such spaces:

> The kitchenette blights the personalities of our growing children, disorganizes them, blinds them to hope, creates problems whose effects can be traced in the characters of its child victims for years afterward . . . . The kitchenette fills our black boys with longing and restlessness, urging them to run off from home . . . . The kitchenette throws desperate and unhappy people into an unbearable closeness of association, thereby increasing latent friction, giving birth to never-ending quarrels of recrimination, accusation, and vindictiveness, producing warped personalities.[38]

Practically everything that Wright observes about the cramped kitchenette apartments that cluttered the northern, urban landscapes to which African American migrants from the South trekked in hopes of better lives is applicable to the Breedloves. Unlike the glamorous couple that James Van Der Zee depicts in "Couple in Raccoon Coats," most migrants never achieved any stable level of financial security.[39] Struggling day by day as they had done in the South, they nonetheless clung to the (perhaps tainted or destroyed completely?) myth that the North was better than the racist conditions, with their attendant severe economic and social ramifications, that had inspired them to leave the South. They were now "upSouth," and their living conditions were frequently no better than the southern shacks or other spaces from which they had fled.

Initially, Pauline is hopeful and is equally as meticulous about housekeeping in the North as she was in the South, down in Kentucky, and she strives to be a good wife. Cholly's drinking and her escape into movies, however, bring a brutal reality into their home. Pauline had perhaps thought early on that she could make up for her slight limp by pressing her hair after the manner of movie stars and escaping from her own life into the lives of the white women whose middle-classness draws her again and again into their screen lives. Then, she loses a tooth, and she resigns herself to being black and unattractive.[40] Though Cholly has courted her tenderly in Kentucky, once they arrive in Ohio, his drinking and her increasing inadequacy as she measures herself against the black women around her ensure that unhealthiness will prevail in this relationship.

It is fitting that Morrison begins her novel, a narrative that explodes the myth of the American (white) nuclear family and its applicability to black Americans, with a house. "Here is the house" is the first sentence of the Dick and Jane primer that features Mother, Father, Dick, and Jane.[41] Just as that idealistic image disintegrates in Morrison's introductory presentation, one in which she moves beyond English capitalization, sentence construction, and sentence division until the first part of that primer is nothing more than gibberish, so too does the possibility for domestic bliss with Cholly and Pauline. They enter the narrative as inhabitants of an "abandoned store"; it is only later that we learn the backstory of how they have arrived in this predicament.[42] Once a pizza parlor, the store is now one of the many kinds of spaces in which migrants from the South could end up. It is sterile, unattractive, literally a blot upon the landscape. The narrative indicates that "it foists itself on the eye of the passerby in a manner that is both irritating and melancholy."[43] With this introduction, readers quickly deduce that little good can thrive within or come from this space. It is here that we find the Breedlove family—Cholly and Pauline, with their son Sammy and their daughter Pecola—all sharing a space that is more psychologically than physically cramping. Morrison is detailed in describing the living quarters generally and the bedroom space specifically.

> The large 'store' area was partitioned into two rooms by beaverboard planks that did not reach to the ceiling. There was a living room, which the family called the front room, and the bedroom, where all the living was done. In the front room were two sofas, an upright piano, and a tiny artificial Christmas tree which had been there, decorated and dust-laden, for two years. The bedroom had three beds: a narrow iron bed for Sammy, fourteen years old, another for

Pecola, eleven years old, and a double bed for Cholly and Mrs. Breedlove. In the center of the bedroom, for the even distribution of heat, stood a coal stove. Trunks, chairs, a small end table, and a cardboard 'wardrobe' closet were placed around the walls. The kitchen was in the back of this apartment, a separate room. There were no bath facilities. Only a toilet bowl, inaccessible to the eye, if not the ear, of the tenants.[44]

The few furnishings that are in place, Morrison notes, led to there being "no memories among those pieces. Certainly no memories to be cherished."[45] The family merely inhabits the space, and its inability to thrive there is apparent in the violence that Cholly and Pauline bring into that space. Neither parent has a vested interest in the space as space. Neither aspires to attempt to make it into a home. They merely exist in these quarters, marking time until they are again out of doors or until the vicissitudes of fate disrupt their lives in other ways.[46] In their corpus-based, linguistic approach to *The Bluest Eye*, Alcina Pereia de Sousa and Alda Maria Correia note that "in Morrison's narrative the house/home contexts (different houses and abodes), of more violent and contradictory kind, reflect class, race and differences in the same community; home is mostly perceived, not as a safe place, but rather as a space of decadence and poverty."[47]

An overall tone of somberness surrounds the Breedloves and the space in which they live. The narrative notes that "they lived there because they were poor and black, and they stayed there because they believed they were ugly."[48] Self-esteem issues, combined with poverty, form lethal psychological weapons in this narrative. Sammy is so disgusted with his home life that, by the time he turns fourteen, he has run away twenty-seven times. Even more detrimental is the homespace life to Pecola. Having witnessed her parents fight for years, Pecola wants escape, and the escape she settles upon forms the crux of the novel. Pecola, who has been labeled "ugly" by her own mother, wishes for beautiful blue eyes with which to view the world, another indication of how external values and racist formulations can enter black psyches and homespaces.[49] Her mother might have inadvertently passed on to Pecola her own preference for cinematic representations of life or Pecola might have reached these conclusions on her own. What is apparent is that Pecola is not nurtured sufficiently by her parents or by her community to grow into a healthy human being. That lack of growth and development is surely influenced by the physical ugliness of the space in which Pecola lives as well as the ugliness that her parents manifest toward each other in almost all of their interactions. All of the verbal and other messages that Pecola receives in this homespace are negative ones, and she internalizes that negativity to the point of wanting to escape from her body. Because negation and ugliness surround her, she hopes desperately that perception through blue eyes will transform her world.

The physical space of the Breedlove storefront home ensures that there will never be psychological safety for Pecola or Sammy, and the poisonous family dynamic that operates in that space ensures that there will never be emotional safety. The proximity of beds makes it impossible for Pecola and Sammy not to hear their parents having sex (they stopped "making love" a long time ago). The claustrophobic quarters also ensure that Pecola cannot escape when Pauline begins to goad Cholly into a fight. Pecola's silent pleas to Pauline are just that—silent and ineffectual. Pecola cannot remove herself from the situation even by going into another room, for there is no other walled-in room to enter. The ugliness of family disagreements and fights is therefore on display for all to see. There is no security or comfort in this homespace that might signal to Pecola and Sammy that all can be well in their world. Dissatisfaction with the space (especially Pauline probably comparing it to the Fisher household and Cholly's memory of being forced to accept damaged furniture for it) hangs in the very air of these tight quarters to deny Pecola and Sammy not only privacy but any kind of stable haven. Absence of psychological safety will combine with the absence of physical safety later to create a fatal combination for Pecola—from her mother's rejection of her to her father's rape of her.

Seldom in African American literature do we witness extended psychological disintegration in characters. Pecola fits that mold, and her fitting into it is a direct consequence of her living space and her mother's rejection. In the often-noted scene in which Pecola goes to the white home in which Pauline serves as cook, nursemaid, and all-around ideal colored servant, Pauline rejects her daughter in favor of the little blond girl to whom she tends. When Pecola accidentally spills a berry cobbler, Pauline is swift in punishment and rejection:

> In one gallop she was on Pecola, and with the back of her hand knocked her to the floor. Pecola slid in the pie juice, one leg folding under her. Mrs. Breedlove yanked her up by the arm, slapped her again, and in a voice thin with anger, abused Pecola directly and Frieda and [Claudia] by implication.
> 'Crazy fool . . . *my* floor, mess . . . look what you . . . work . . . get on out . . . now that . . . crazy . . . *my* floor, *my* floor . . . *my* floor.' . . . She went to the sink and turned tap water on a fresh towel. Over her shoulder she spit out words to us like rotten pieces of apple. 'Pick up that wash and get on out of here, so I can get this mess cleaned up.'[50] (italics added)

Having transferred any inkling of nurturing from her own home and children to the white home and the little blond girl for whom she cares, Pauline claims the home of the whites as her own, and she protects it fiercely from "invaders" such as Pecola and the MacTeer sisters, who have gone in search of Pecola in a folklore-inspired effort to get whiskey to prevent Frieda from being ruined as a result of Mr. Henry's touching her breasts (they know Cholly drinks and are hoping that Pecola knows where his stash might be). As Pecola internalizes this rejection and witnesses how tenderly her mother cares for this white child and this white space in comparison to her fighting rampages with Cholly in the storefront apartment, there is no way that she can grow up to be a healthy child. Unlike Vyry, who is left alone because of her mother Hetta's death, Pecola is spiritually and emotionally orphaned and abandoned by a mother who hates herself and her offspring.[51] It is no wonder, therefore, that Pecola sinks into madness near the end of the narrative, a madness that is immediately precipitated by the violence that her father commits against her.

Pauline wounds Pecola by scarring her physically and mentally. Cholly Breedlove does the same. Having married Pauline but not having a clue as to what fatherhood meant, Cholly is baffled by his children. Drunken memories of Pauline when he met her in Kentucky combine with alcohol and lust to lead Cholly to rape his daughter. He does so in the kitchen area of the storefront apartment when he comes upon Pecola washing dishes and rubbing the back of one leg with the toe of the other as he had seen Pauline do.[52] Rape is horror enough, but even more horrific is the fact that Pauline is not the least bit sympathetic to her daughter's accounting of what has happened to her. In fact, Susmita Roye argues that Pecola "is raped by both her parents," with one rape being physical and the other psychological.[53] It is ambiguous if Cholly rapes Pecola a second time (her imaginary blue-eyed friend hints at that), but the first is sufficient to complete the horror of disidentification with either parent. Pauline has abandoned her homespace for one inhabited by whites, and Cholly has made the space that Pecola calls home psychologically uninhabitable for her. She may continue to reside in the space physically, but she is totally alienated from it, thus she can never find any comfort or solace in it. It was bad enough that Pauline and Cholly fought like prize fighters in the storefront and made it impossible for Sammy and Pecola to ever feel relaxed and "at home," but it is even more de-familiarizing when Cholly ensures that every wall in the storefront, but especially the space of the kitchen, will reflect back to Pecola that her father did not value her enough to protect her, indeed that he was the source of violence against her. Even more painful is the fact that Pauline may or may not believe Pecola's account of what her father has done to her and that a pregnancy results from the rape.[54] The space is now saturated with shame, a shame that is much more intense than the occasion on which Pecola and Cholly witnessed their parents fighting while Cholly was nude. As Susmita Roye observes in her discussion of several girls in *The*

Bluest Eye and *A Mercy*, "the starkest example of a miserable family's woeful influence in disrupting girlhoods is seen in Pecola's case."[55]

From the introduction of the Breedloves that culminates with one of the recurring fights between Cholly and Pauline, to Pauline's coming home and finding Pecola raped on the kitchen floor, there is not an iota of acceptability, love, caring, or nurturing in the Breedlove home.[56] And while that certainly has as much to do with the personalities of the husband and wife as it does with the physical space, that space is certainly a factor. For example, when Cholly and Pauline fight, they fail to consider—and apparently do not care about—the impact that it has upon their children. When Pauline awakes one morning to a cold storefront, she provokes Cholly into a fight about his having forgotten to bring in coal by throwing a pan of cold water into his face. He jumps up naked, knocks Pauline down, and strikes her in the face several times before she takes a stove lid and knocks him "right back into the senselessness out of which she had provoked him. Panting, she threw a quilt over him and let him lie."[57] During the fight, Sammy has struck his father several blows and referred to him as a "'naked fuck!'" But when Sammy screams, "'Kill him! Kill him!,'" Pauline calmly tells him to "'cut out that noise, boy'" and directs him to get the coal that she needs.[58] After this episode, Pecola asks God yet again to let her disappear, and she prays fervently every night for blue eyes. Thus the "nurturing" that Pauline and Cholly inspire is antisocial behavior and self-negation. The space of the storefront therefore breeds a dysfunctionality that is intensified by the antisocial behavior of the parents and the splitting of family ties that result in Sammy's physical running away and Pecola's mental running away. Pecola thus uses her mind in a powerful negative way to get away from her parents as well as away from the space that can never be separated from her father's violent sexual violation of her.

But the Breedlove storefront is not the only African American home represented in the text. There is the space above the Breedlove storefront where the prostitutes, China, Poland, and Miss Marie ply their trade, there is the MacTeer home in which Pecola spends a brief period after Cholly burns down their living space, and there is Geraldine's home. The only remotely healthy space is the MacTeer home, and even that has its challenges when a man to whom the MacTeers rent a room fondles Frieda's breasts. While Mrs. MacTeer might exhibit a form of harsh love, especially during the episode in which Pecola has a cold, or when she fusses at the girls and even spanks them without getting sufficient information about the episode in which Pecola starts menstruating, she is fundamentally a caring mother who endeavors, along with her husband, to protect their two daughters. She is of the traditional school of thought that children should be seen and not heard, but she is nonetheless as nurturing and as supportive of her daughters as the times allow. This caveat is necessary because, seldom in African American literature, as Morrison illustrates so vividly in *Sula* (1973), do black mothers have time in their bread-winning schedules to pause and play games with or to entertain their children.[59] Caregiving and economic security come first, and that is the case with Mrs. MacTeer. Even when she is frustrated, she turns her frustration to song (the blues) and monologues instead of taking it out on Claudia and Frieda. She is not the storybook mother of the Dick and Jane primer, but she is nonetheless an admirable one.

At the opposite end of the scale in terms of dysfunctionality and negative homespaces, the prostitutes and Geraldine share kinship with the Breedloves. Prostitution in and of itself is considered generally to be antithetical to family life, a disrupter of homes, and suspect morally. Yet, ironically, it is the "three merry gargoyles" who practice this profession in *The Bluest Eye* who are among the few sympathetic responders to Pecola.[60] They, like the Breedloves, have no attachment to the space they inhabit beyond its practicality in hosting their johns. As outsiders to the so-called Christian community surrounding them, they share a stigma with Pecola. They are thus far less judgmental of her than most of her community turns out to be. Pecola is more vocal when she visits them than she is in almost any other scene, and they in turn are tolerant of her. Clearly, they are not nurturing in the traditional sense of mothering, but they at least allow Pecola the space to be—and then they simply ignore her. While Pecola may escape to their space for short periods of time, it offers no long-term solution to her outcast status—even if they invited her to remain. No matter how merry those who live there may be, the space is still a house of ill-repute, one against which Mrs. MacTeer has warned Claudia and Frieda. And, thoroughly aware of how the community feels about them, the prostitutes have no qualms about violating space (Mr. Henry, Claudia's violator, invites them into the MacTeer home when the parents are away) or about potentially harming children (China throws a root-beer bottle onto the street near Claudia and Frieda when Frieda asserts that their mother will not allow them to go into the space above the storefront because the women there are "ruined").[61]

While there might be some humor in the appearance of the whores in the text, there is none—*absolutely none*—with Geraldine. The narrative documents her as a migrant from one of various cities in the South who used arrival in the North as a way to cement disconnection from all things black and funky. Such women wanted everything the North had to offer, but they wanted it in a way that was totally under their control—even against their husbands and children. In Geraldine's case, this control positions Geraldine as comparable to Pauline Breedlove in the home of the white family for whom she works. Pauline claims the space as hers even though she has not built it. Geraldine has constructed her concept of home in a space that she has gotten a sailor to underwrite (he is as noticeably invisible in the narrative as is his relevance to Geraldine beyond paying for the home and sperm donation for her one and only child). Geraldine's house is a space that the Thomas family in Wright's *Native Son* or the Younger family in Hansberry's *A Raisin in the Sun* would have celebrated owning. It is not cramped, not vermin-infested, and certainly not at the mercy of bank takeover. Rather, it is spacious and, unlike the Breedlove home, tastefully decorated. Yet, for all its prettiness, it remains as sterile and as un-nurturing as the Breedlove storefront.

As Morrison makes clear, there is a kind of mythology of creation that undergirds Geraldine's dream of a home. She knows precisely what will separate her from the hordes of black migrants to the North, and she knows how to achieve what she wants. Geraldine is intent upon erasing the "Funk" from her existence, that is, the range of human emotions that signify complex relationships and willful engagement in those relationships.[62] Geraldine wants the funk out of her home and out of her life, which leads to a sterility that might be even more poisonous than the brand that Cholly and Pauline practice. She therefore, Morrison writes, "will build her nest stick by stick, make it her own inviolable world, and stand guard over its every plant, weed, and doily, even against" her husband.[63] Geraldine's one son, Junior, is encouraged to play with white children: "his mother did not like him to play with niggers. She had explained to him the difference between colored people and niggers. They were easily identifiable. Colored people were neat and quiet; niggers were dirty and loud."[64] Thus Junior, like Pecola, grows up unsure of his place in the world. What is available to him and not to Pecola, however, is a self-confidence and power that derive from his mother's building her house and articulating clearly to him what his status should mean in the world. When he entices Pecola into that space, ostensibly to see some kittens, he then uses his mother's cat to bully her. His mother's arrival is unfortunately timely, for Geraldine enters to see in Pecola everything she has tried to escape by leaving the South and moving north. Detachedly assessing Pecola as one of those monstrosities, she can only respond: "'Get out, . . . You nasty little black bitch. Get out of my house.'"[65] Pecola is thrust into ambiguity, as she observes "the pretty milk-brown lady in the pretty gold-and-green house who was talking to her through the cat's fur."[66] The image of Geraldine and the house might be comparable to Pecola's desire for blues eyes. Seemingly, this lady has everything, and yet she is incredibly mean to Pecola. Geraldine thus protects her home in a way that conveys to Pecola that even the designation of such a space as "pretty" cannot counter the poison that spews from the person occupying it.

Geraldine's home is like a painting. The image is the perfect thing. In that painting, everything is in place, and everything is pretty. What the image does not show is that Geraldine is a haughty, snobbish excuse for a human being and mother who has no real relationship with either her husband or her child. They have been mere boxes that she has checked off on her way to building the house that she wanted and acquiring the pet that she wanted. It is only in private moments with the cat, when it seems to arouse her sexually but without the funky connotations of having to deal with fluids that could result in other instances of sexual arousal, that Geraldine seems to be at peace. In this sterile environment, Junior cannot grow into a healthy young man. He wants to play with the other black boys at school, but he does not know how. It is only through trickery that he gets Pecola to enter his house, and he becomes jealous when the cat seems to like her. Since it is his mother's cat, and since he cannot take out his frustrations on his mother, he snatches the cat from Pecola and hurls it into a window, which is the point at which his mother enters and picks up the seemingly unconscious cat. Junior thus sees clearly that things (the house and its decorations) and non-humans (the cat) occupy his mother's emotional life. There is no room left for him or his father. They can be the backstory of the painting, but they can never be featured in it. Thus, Geraldine's cultivated superficiality and the artificiality of her home are just as detrimental to securing a healthy homespace as are the fighting rituals in which the Breedloves engage.

NOT ENOUGH SPACE, AND CERTAINLY NOT A HOME—PERVERSIONS IN *TOPDOG/UNDERDOG*

In *Topdog/Underdog*, Pulitzer-Prize-winning playwright Suzan-Lori Parks echoes the spatial dynamics of earlier African American literary homes in her presentation of a single room in an urban area in which two ironically named brothers, Lincoln and Booth, try to co-exist. However, this space is unusual in its layout, in the spatial, familial, and national history that is brought to bear upon it, and in the controlled as well as unleashed animosity that reigns within it. Still, this space evokes other literary ones in terms of the ideas that are brought to bear upon it. For example, memory and portability are crucial to how the brothers interact with each other in the their cramped homespace. They inherit from their parents distorted notions of parental/child interactions and perverse notions of sexuality, and they remember and carry those ideas from their previous homespaces into their current one. The men's father, who has cheated on his wife, has taught Lincoln, the older brother, a pattern of infidelity and disloyalty that ultimately guides his interactions with his brother Booth. On the other hand, the brothers' mother is a cheating wife who has taught Booth about sexual excess, which he brings into and brags about in the current homespace. In addition, Lincoln brings a brief memory of a destroyed myth of homespace into this single room when he tries to overlay the past with an image of the happy American nuclear family. Booth's and Lincoln's childhoods were obviously filled with little parental love and affection, yet, at a crucial moment, Lincoln chooses to remember otherwise. Of utmost importance is the fact that the parents abandoned the brothers, and they have not yet succeeded in making a home elsewhere.

Parks describes the single room in which Booth lives and where his brother Lincoln comes to live with him as "a seedily furnished rooming house room. A bed, a reclining chair, a small wooden chair, some other stuff but not much else."[67] The last couple of phrases and lack of more detailed description evince a detachment from the physical place that points readers and viewers more toward the dynamics of the characters within that space. This space is almost worse than such a room in a kitchenette building would be, for those at least had a sink and, at times, a small stove or hot plate. There is no toilet, no sink, and obviously no running water in this room. Late in the play, a drunken Lincoln, missing a toilet, urinates in a plastic cup.[68] Booth sleeps in the bed, under which he has stacks and stacks of girlie magazines, and Lincoln sleeps—uncomfortably but mostly without complaint—in the reclining chair. Their actions throughout the play indicate that neither brother is particularly interested in nor particularly bothered by the space they share. Neither has realistic expectations for how they might transform that space or move to another; indeed, change is too great a thought to move either of them out of their states of inertia. Booth is stuck on trying to become a 3-card monte hustler (at which Lincoln is an expert) and getting his invisible girlfriend, Grace, to return to him, and Lincoln is in a holding pattern, waiting to see if he will be able to retain his job as an historical Abraham Lincoln impersonator at a local arcade.[69]

The room thus becomes a space in which whatever is real gets overshadowed by unrealistic expectations. Grace, if she exists (when Lincoln states that he has met her, he might simply be humoring the unpredictable Booth), will never give Booth the chance to exercise his hypersexuality with her, and he certainly will not be able to have the children he maintains he will produce with her, one of which he asserts he will name after Lincoln. Booth is too awkward, too emotionally volatile, too prone to violence, and completely without the manual dexterity or mental skills needed to become a 3-card monte hustler, so that fantasy dies in this space as well. Lincoln is caught in the throes of trying to forestall technology and fiscal expediency when he hopes that the arcade will retain him as the Lincoln impersonator instead of setting up a dummy to be assassinated by the overly-eager customers who try to put their mark on history. Booth's dream is antisocial and criminal, and Lincoln's is pervertedly ahistorical. Both characters share a penchant for criminality, and both seem unconcerned about where they might be from day to day. For example, in a fit of anger, Booth asks Lincoln to move, which he agrees to do. Yet, the next scene moves forward as if neither brother has mentioned the subject of moving.

As James Baldwin observed about the characters in the kitchenette apartment in Lorraine Hansberry's *A Raisin in the Sun*, Lincoln and Booth exist in "a kind of claustrophobic terror," informed by what goes on inside their room as well as outside.[70] The potential for disaster lurks just beneath the surface of all their interactions. That violent potential is reinforced in Parks's use of "Rests" and "Spells," during which neither character speaks. Silence with the possibility of doom builds each time the characters reach an impasse in their conversations. Those silences echo what Pecola is increasingly forced into as well as what John Grimes experiences in the presence of his father. In all these instances, silence covers over emotions and conflicts that could erupt into violence or that could destroy characters psychologically and emotionally. If John were to speak up with Gabriel, he would probably be beaten unmercifully. If Pecola were to say anything during that epic battle between her mother and father, she would probably be shouted back into silence just as quickly as Sammy is. If Lincoln were to insist that Booth cross the room and get the Chinese food, violence would probably occur sooner than it does. The very walls of the room, therefore, seem to press down on the brooding possibilities for destructiveness that make it impossible for the brothers to shape a healthy homespace.

The cramped quarters of the room thus mirror the constant tensions between the two brothers. Booth, a high-strung shoplifter who is seldom without his gun, threatens Lincoln on several occasions. He knows he has the upper hand because his name is on the lease for the room, so he can make demands that Lincoln finds it hard to resist, such as insisting that Lincoln walk a few steps to get the Chinese food that he has brought home one evening. The spatial dynamics of the room are key in this instance. Given that rooms are usually in the range of twelve feet or so, and given that Booth's and Lincoln's meagre furnishings take up part of their room, it becomes apparent that the challenge Booth offers to Lincoln is almost an eyeball-to-eyeball one. In such proximity, Lincoln cannot escape whatever facial gestures or bodily postures of intimidation Booth might exhibit. Thus, Lincoln acquiesces—only to have Booth insist that he prefers the shrimp that Lincoln has bought for himself to the meat that Lincoln has bought for Booth. Control of space and control of food choice thus dominate the scene. As the title suggests, a constant one-upmanship persists between the two brothers. Booth, as the younger brother and the unskilled 3-card monte player, is always pushing against Lincoln, the older brother and 3-card monte expert. Booth therefore uses the space of the room, which is the only space in which he could possibly become topdog, to advantage whenever he can for power plays against Lincoln. Thus tension reigns even when motivation might be questionable.

For example, there are recurring verbalizations of sexual prowess or lack thereof between the two brothers. Booth usually offers the more extreme insults in these exchanges. For example, when Lincoln observes that he has seen "like 100 fuck books" under Booth's bed, Booth's response is:

> When I don't got a woman, I gotta make do. Not like you, Link. When you dont got a woman you just sit there. Letting yr shit fester. Yr dick, if it aint falled off yet, is hanging there between yr legs, little whiteface shriveled-up blank-shooting grub worm. As goes thuh man so goes thus mans dick. Thats what I say. Least my shits intact . . . . You a limp dick jealous whiteface motherfucker whose wife dumped him cause he couldnt get it up and she told me so. Came crawling to me cause she needed a man.[71]

I posit that Booth inherits his sexual excess in part from what he witnessed between his mother and her lovers (there were apparently several. He identifies one as her "Thursday man," with the implication that there are other men for other days). The mother was not concerned about public exposure as she gave in to sexual desire—in her own homespace with the possibility of any family member returning unexpectedly—and neither is Booth.

Later in the play, when Lincoln is finally truthful in assessing Booth's skills as a 3-card monte player, his comment is not sexually based but it is equally insulting. He tells Booth, who has recently renamed himself 3-Card: "You a double left-handed motherfucker who don't stand a chance in all get out out there throwing no cards."[72] Lincoln also disparages Booth's claim that he has spent a night with Grace. This level of tension and insult is nearly constant in the play, as the one-upmanship continues. It is again a part of parental inheritance, the general disrespect for the family unit, that the brothers acquired from their dysfunctional parents. They have thus moved unhealthy memories into the space with them. Unable to escape each other because of the glaring lack of privacy in the single room, each brother is left to deal with insults as best he can. Again, there is talk of leaving but no departure, which means there is a kind of perverted satisfaction that the brothers derive from these exchanges.

What ties the brothers together through the insults and the problematic living space is the history that they bring into Booth's room. That history is one of a loss of parents and a loss of homes. Lincoln and Booth's mother and father abandoned them when Lincoln was a teenager and Booth was an adolescent. While abandonment is certainly horrific, the life they led with their parents was perhaps equally horrific. They moved from a "nasty apartment into a house" that was little improvement, for it had a "cement backyard and a frontyard full of trash."[73] It was a family situation in which neither parent was ultimately committed to the other and in which unhealthy behavior patterns dominated. Not only did the father have extramarital affairs, but he inadvertently shared at least one of his women with the young Lincoln. "One of his ladies liked me," recalls Lincoln, "so I would do her after he'd done her. On thuh sly though. He'd be laying there, spent and sleeping and snoring and her and me would be sneaking it."[74] On the other hand, Booth witnesses his mother's infidelity with her infamous "Thursday man": "He had her bent over. They both had all they clothes on like they was about to do something like go out dancing cause they was dressed to thuh 9s but at thuh last minute his pants had fallen down and her dress had flown up and theyd ended up doing something else."[75] The Thursday man eventually impregnates the mother. That leads to her giving Booth five hundred dollars, his "inheritance," and leaving. Two years later, the father gives Lincoln five hundred dollars and makes his departure. Left to fend for themselves, the brothers rely on each other in spite of their parents' efforts to pit them against each other (the mother had admonished Booth to take care of Lincoln, but the father had advised Lincoln not to share his inheritance with Booth).[76]

Yet Lincoln tries briefly to overwrite this ugly history with a myth of family unity and childhood entrepreneurship. After a family move from an apartment to a house, Lincoln recalls to Booth that "We all thought it was the best fucking house in the world."[77] Booth reminds Lincoln of the cement back yard and the trash in the front yard and chides Lincoln, "don't be going down memory lane man," to which Lincoln offers this gem: "We had some great times in that house, bro. Selling lemonade on thuh corner, thuh treehouse out back, summers spent lying in thuh grass and looking at thuh stars," with Booth responding, "We never did none of that shit."[78] Memory and imagination thus become weak links to the past as the brothers try to envision a formula for creating a current homespace. Lincoln's middle-class, suburban image of home and kids' activities is matched somewhat in Booth's efforts to create a photo album, which he picks up occasionally during the play. These symbols of stable homelife and documentation usually suggest pride in what is being achieved and in what is being documented. However, Lincoln and Booth have little of which they can be proud, thus the creation of the photo album is just as fanciful an effort as the created memory of a seemingly well-functioning nuclear family. Instead, the parents have splintered the family in a way that portends disaster for the brothers even if their historically determined names did not do that equally as well.

The brothers thus inherit the possibility for distrust of each other from their parents. They are also taught that relationships are fluid; one can maintain a certain fidelity if it is convenient to do so, but there is no guiding principle that demands it. In addition, they inherit from their parents, especially their father, a penchant for abusing alcohol. If they are not alcoholics in the text, the distance between that state and what they are is minimal. It is a ritual with the brothers that Lincoln brings home a bottle of "med-sin" each Friday night when he turns over the majority of his pay to Booth (the brothers do a Ma/Pa skit as Lincoln transfers the money), and Booth budgets for additional alcohol purchases during the course of the week.[79] The Ma/Pa skit indicates again the extent to which memories of the parents continue to live with the brothers. Jochen Achilles suggests as well that "both brothers seem to have settled into the semblance of a husband-and-wife arrangement, with Booth in the feminine role."[80] Viewers and readers learn that the father, from whom Lincoln and Booth have inherited the drinking habit, was financially as well as morally reckless: "What he didnt spend on booze he spent on women. What he didnt spend on them two he spent on clothes."[81] The drinking inheritance is manifested in the brothers' Friday night toasting ritual as well as during the week, and the clothes habit is manifested in Booth's shoplifting of suits for himself as well as for Lincoln. Thus their arrival at their current states has been set in motion by the actions of their parents and the circumstances resulting from their having spent several years parentless as an adolescent and a teenager, then young adults.

Adrift in a world where they dodged social workers and managed to survive, the brothers have only each other and, for the longest time, that interdependence sustains them. Booth remarks to Lincoln as he tries to convince him to take up the 3-card monte hustling life again that he did not regret their parents' abandoning them: "I didnt mind them leaving cause you was there. Thats why Im hooked on us working together. If we could work together it would be like old times. They split and we got that room downtown. You was done with school and I stopped going. And we had to run around doing odd jobs just to keep the lights on and the heat going and thuh child protection bitch off our backs. It was you and me against thuh world, Link. It could be like that again."[82] But Booth is unable to convince Lincoln, who gave up hustling after his partner Lonny was killed ("One day I was throwing the cards. Next day Lonny died. Somebody shot him. I knew I was next, so I quit. I saved my life").[83] Being there for each other in the past becomes a distant memory in the face of the current action and Lincoln's refusal to get involved in the card hustling scam again. Thus, in these cramped quarters, when Booth pushes Lincoln to play the 3-card monte game and, when he does, believes that Lincoln has conned him and wrongfully won the money-filled nylon stocking that his mother gave him, their shared history of surviving neglect and abandonment comes unglued.

That ungluing is tied in part to the ironic names with which their father has saddled them. Thus national history enters the play to foreshadow Booth's killing of Lincoln. Readers and viewers suspect from the beginning that, unless Parks is undertaking a complete re-writing of history, this will be the outcome. That history is realized when the personal history gets subsumed into the national history. Booth wants to believe that Lincoln is truly teaching him how to play the 3-card monte game when he allows Booth to win a couple of hands near the end of the play. That, however, is merely the set-up for Lincoln's teaching Booth that he can never win at the game; he is merely a "mark" to be taken.[84] Lincoln realizes too late that Booth is so invested in the money-filled stocking, his inheritance, and so upset about having been conned that he is prepared to kill Lincoln—after he announces that he has killed Grace, ostensibly for rejecting him. The space of the arcade thus invades the space of Booth's room, and the real-life execution of Lincoln mirrors, tragically and ironically, what happened to Lincoln the Abraham Lincoln impersonator in the arcade as well as what happened to the historical Abraham Lincoln. As Parks scholar Jennifer Larson comments, "Booth now sees his brother just as Booth-the-actor saw Lincoln-the-President—as a ruthless demagogue poised and determined to destroy his identity and way of life. So now he is Booth, killer of Lincoln. He is the assassin."[85] By showcasing an historical assassination that has division as its basis, Parks brings the historical division in the house of America into the sibling division within the house of Booth. To lose his inheritance and to be gipped at the same time is just too much for Booth to bear, so he obliterates the remainder of his family. His explanation for committing fratricide, at least as he explains it in speaking to the dead Lincoln, is figuratively tied to money, property, and history, all features of the historical as well as the individual family circumstance.

> Think you can take my shit? My shit. That shit was mines. I kept it. Saved it. All this while. Through thick and through thin. Through fucking thick and through fucking thin, motherfucker. And you just gonna come up in here and mock my shit and call me two lefthanded talking bout how she [their mother] coulda been jiving me then go steal from me? My *inheritance*. You stole my *inheritance*, man. That aint right. That aint right and you know it. You had yr own. And you blew it. You *blew it*, motherfucker! I saved mines and you blew yrs. Thinking you all that and blew yr shit. And I *saved* mines . . . . You aint gonna be needing yr fucking money-roll no more, dead motherfucker, so I will pocket it thank you . . . . Ima take back my inheritance too. It was mines anyhow. Even when you stole it from me it was still mines cause she gave it to me. She didnt give it to you. And I been saving it all this while.[86] (italics in original)

Booth's howling remorse at the end of the play comes, as Toni Morrison might say, much, much too late. The consequences of perverted family life in cramped or emotionally unhealthy spaces have led to an irreversible conclusion, one that tempts readers and viewers to return to the invitation that Parks extends at the beginning of the play. She states in an introductory note that "This is a play about family wounds and healing. Welcome to the family."[87] Readers and viewers are left to contemplate the histories and interactions that have brought about this result, none of which had the potential for a healthy outcome. In contrast to what Parks states, there can be no welcome in this family, though viewers might indeed welcome the chance to view the play. As Christine Woodworth notes, "Booth and Lincoln are metaphorically and literally destroyed by their inability to break free from the cycles of poverty and betrayal inherited from their parents." She observes further that *Topdog/Underdog* is one of Parks's plays where the characters' "childhoods emerge as ghosts that haunt their adult lives."[88]

Instead of what readers and viewers might usually expect in family interactions, *Topdog/Underdog* is saturated with a poisonous family history, a tainted national history, hypermasculine competition, verbal abuse, and a strange kind of sharing (when Booth asserts that he has slept with Lincoln's ex-wife Cookie because Lincoln has not satisfied her sexually).[89] Ultimately, violence dominates, whether it is the psychological and emotional violence that the parents heap upon their children, the impending violence in the exchanges between the brothers throughout the play, or the final act of violence that ends Lincoln's life and ensures that Booth's is essentially ended as well. Booth and Lincoln have been assured that no healthy identity formation could occur once their parents abandoned them, thus this outcome is along the pathway of negativity that that abandonment projected. From the "nasty apartment," to the cemented back yard and trash-filled front yard of the house into which they moved, to the room they shared as youngsters intent upon avoiding being taken into the system, to the single room they share in which their story comes to such a tragic end, Lincoln and Booth have not lived in or shared with their parents any space that could have led to a happy outcome for them. Their homes have been a series of perverted violations and aggressively violent spaces, whether that violence was apparent mentally or physically. As a representative urban space that contains "the family," Parks's homespace, like the dirty space the Grimeses inhabit or the storefront that solidifies Pecola's mental deterioration, challenges reader and viewers to wonder if it is ever possible for African American characters in urban areas to find spaces that are conducive to their existences and turn them into homes.[90]

One of the most striking things about the homespace and characters in *Topdog/Underdog* is the seeming vacuum in which they exist. There is no community or mention of interaction with a community. Lincoln comments on his encounter with the boy on the bus, and there are references to the crowds that gathered when Lincoln was actively engaged in executing the 3-card monte scam and when he enters the bar once he starts throwing the cards again, but those are fleeting rather than sustained interactions. The same is true for Booth. He turns stealing into an art form, and though he may encounter other people in the process of stealing from them, there is no relationship. His "relationship" to Grace is questionable at best. For both the brothers, there are no friends, no church folk acquaintances, no next-door neighbors, no frequently-visited local bar. There are just the two men isolated on an island of a room that does not matter to anyone, anywhere. Their situation is thus dramatically different from the community that surrounds John Grimes, or the community that engages with—or at least watches—Pecola Breedlove, or the community of responsive citizens among whom Vyry Brown and her family establish their final homespace. Lincoln and Booth's isolation, therefore, is another commentary on the inability to create a healthy homespace, for there are seemingly no models against which such a construction could be compared/evaluated. Locked in memories of the past and unable to function in healthy economic or emotional ways in the present, the brothers are ultimately as insignificant to the larger society as are the Grimeses and perhaps even more disposable than the Breedloves.

The seeming isolation of the homespace, however, does not negate the fact of its porous walls. As with Gabriel Grimes, who holds his family hostage to his ideas of the racism that governs all their lives as well as to the Christianity that he believes should govern them, Lincoln and Booth allow external forces to define how they operate within their homespace. Just as Pauline Breedlove allowed externally imposed notions of beauty to guide her judging of her family's physical attractiveness—or lack thereof—so Lincoln and Booth allow the external world to guide their interactions with each other. That world has reduced them to hustling black men by preventing them from living up to their full potential as black males. Like Bigger Thomas who dreams of flying, so Lincoln and Booth could possibly have dreamed of lives that did not involve hustling. Now, as outsiders/aliens, they can only react in negative ways toward the society around them instead of being incorporated into it. That larger society, which has established notions of manhood, has also infiltrated their living space, so that competition surrounding virility is dominant in their lives. Equally so, the national narrative about the place of brown-skinned native sons in a land that judges true citizenship by whiteness has penetrated the walls of Lincoln and Booth's room, and they act out scenarios of enslavement tied to the Lincoln impersonator and what Abraham Lincoln presumably meant to people of African descent on United States soil. Just as Lincoln and Booth cannot clear their homespace and their minds and memories of their parents, neither can they clear their space of local and national narratives that position them as lesser in the society. There is no final cleansing scene for them comparable to the one that Vyry executes; there is only the bloody conclusion to a story of brothers lost in an American wilderness of diminished manhood, self-hatred, and parental abandonment and who can never find their way safely to any home except the finality of the grave.

NOTES

1. James Baldwin, *Go Tell It on the Mountain* (New York: Dell, 1980).
2. Richard Wright, *Native Son* (New York: Library of America, 1940; 1991).
3. Baldwin, *Go Tell*, 5.
4. Lorraine Hansberry, *A Raisin in the Sun* (New York: Random House, 1959).
5. Baldwin, *Go Tell*, 173.
6. Baldwin, *Go Tell*, 173.
7. Baldwin, *Go Tell*, 173. Keith Clark comments that Gabriel "disposes of Esther and their son in the same way that many slaveowners ridded themselves of their unwanted slave mistresses and their illegitimate offspring." See "Baldwin, Communitas, and the Black Masculinist Tradition," in *New Essays on Go Tell It on the Mountain*, ed. Trudier Harris (New York: Cambridge U P, 1996), 142.
8. Baldwin, *Go Tell*, 16.
9. Baldwin, *Go Tell*, 17.
10. Baldwin, *Go Tell*, 22.
11. Baldwin, *Go Tell*, 13.
12. Marc Dudley, *Understanding James Baldwin* (Columbia: U of South Carolina P, 2019), 23, 24.
13. Csaba Csapo, "Race, Religion and Sexuality in *Go Tell It on the Mountain*," in *James Baldwin's Go Tell It on the Mountain: Historical and Critical Essays*, ed. Carol E. Henderson (New York: Peter Lang, 2006), 69–70, 70–71.
14. Baldwin, *Go Tell*, 14, 23.
15. Baldwin, *Go Tell*, 23.
16. Baldwin, *Go Tell*, 233, 234.
17. Baldwin, *Go Tell*, 175.
18. Andrew Connolly evaluates Gabriel in the context of his religious beliefs and practices and is much more sympathetic to his character. He argues—against most previously published critical commentary—that "*Go Tell It on the Mountain* does not portray Gabriel simply as a villainous character who commits emotional and physical violence against his family but as a committed participant in a religious system that fails him." While Connolly recognizes that Gabriel does some pretty indecent things, he still posits his explanation for Gabriel's behavior as a systemic problem rather than an individual one. For Connolly's rather involved discussion, see "Shame, Rage, and Endless Battle: Systemic Pressure and Individual Violence in James Baldwin's *Go Tell It on the Mountain*," *The CEA Critic* 77, no. 1 (March 2015): 120–42.
19. Baldwin, *Go Tell*, 19.
20. Baldwin, *Go Tell*, 220.
21. Baldwin, *Go Tell*, 221.
22. Baldwin, *Go Tell*, 223.
23. Elizabeth was raised by an aunt in the South after her mother died and the aunt prevented her father, who owned brothels, from raising her. After having met Richard, she followed him to the North, began a passionate romance with him, and became pregnant. Falsely accused of a robbery, Richard was freed from jail, but the experience of having been wrongfully accused and beaten while in jail led him to

commit suicide, thus leaving the pregnant young Elizabeth to fend for herself. After John's birth, Elizabeth met Florence at her job, they formed a friendship, and, through Florence, Elizabeth met and married Gabriel—over Florence's *vehement* objections. Elizabeth's seeking after stability and safety thus lands Elizabeth in the untenable position of being Gabriel's wife, giving birth to three children with him, and sharing the space and the relationships that must pass as their home.

24. Baldwin, *Go Tell*, 129.
25. Dudley, *Understanding*, 26.
26. Baldwin, *Go Tell*, 49.
27. Baldwin, *Go Tell*, 49.
28. Baldwin, *Go Tell*, 49.
29. Baldwin, *Go Tell*, 50.
30. The commendable role that Florence takes in this scene in trying to talk sense into Gabriel and trying to help him bring peace into his home is a striking contrast to her behavior earlier as a young wife. Married to a fiscally irresponsible man whose sex appeal she could not resist, Florence browbeat him with complaints about his behavior as well as about his friends. Determined to escape from the ranks of the "dirty niggers" and the "common niggers" (95) among whom she and her husband Frank were forced to live, and intent upon lightening her dark skin with chemicals as further denunciation of her origins, Florence nagged her husband Frank until, ten years after they were married, he walked out and never returned. Unlike Gabriel, however, she takes responsibility for the dissolution of her marriage and her home.
31. Baldwin, *Go Tell*, 43–44.
32. Sherry R. Truffin, "'Terrors of the Night': Salvation, Gender, and the Gothic in *Go Tell It on the Mountain*," in *James Baldwin's Go Tell It on the Mountain: Historical and Critical Essays*, ed. Carol E. Henderson (New York: Peter Lang, 2006), 135.
33. Csapo, "Race," 70.
34. James Baldwin, "Sonny's Blues," in *Going to Meet the Man* (New York: Vintage, 1995), 104.
35. It is worth noting that Baldwin readers and scholars can trace a trajectory of progression in Baldwin's works in terms of his treatment of families in their home-spaces. I am thinking especially of the almost idealized portrayal in *If Beale Street Could Talk* (1974), in which Tish's family works as a unit to try to get Fonny out of jail when he is falsely accused of rape. Hers is a sharp contrast to Fonny's family, where, though the father is sympathetic toward Tish and Fonny, the mother and sisters are arrogantly condescending. I discuss this problematic family dynamic in *Black Women in the Fiction of James Baldwin* (Knoxville: U of Tennessee P, 1985).
36. Toni Morrison, *The Bluest Eye* (New York: Plume, 1970; 1994). Morrison has commented on many occasions that she wrote *The Bluest Eye* because it was the kind of novel that she wanted to read.
37. James A. Crank, "Down N' Dirty." *south: an interdisciplinary journal* vol 48, no 2 (Spring 2016): 157–69.
38. Richard Wright, *12 Million Black Voices: A Folk History of the Negro in the United States* (1941; Brattleboro, VT: Echo Point Books & Media, 2019), 110–111,

108. For a contrasting take on the impact of kitchenette buildings, with direct evocation of Richard Wright, see Lynn Orilla Scott, "At Home on the South Side: Chicago in Gwendolyn Brooks's *Maud Martha* and *Report from Part One*," *Midwestern Miscellany*, vol 43 (Spring/Fall 2015): 34–51.

39. For Van Der Zee photographs, see http://100photos.time.com/photos/james-vanderzee-couple-in-raccoon-coats.

40. Jess E. Jelsma comments that "figurative tooth loss and decay symbolize the humiliating and anger-inducing impotence experienced by the entire Breedlove family. This powerlessness, implanted by instances of white oppression, is deep rooted and infectious, spreading from Cholly to contaminate the Breedlove household and family." See "Decay and Symbolic Impotence in Toni Morrison's *The Bluest Eye*," *The Explicator* 75, no. 3 (2017): 200.

41. Morrison, *Bluest*, 3. There are obviously a plethora of scholarly works that treat *The Bluest Eye*. For a couple that discuss the idea of home, see Prince, *Burnin' Down the House* (2005) and Marc C. Conner, "From the Sublime to the Beautiful: The Aesthetic Progression of Toni Morrison, " in *The Aesthetics of Toni Morrison: Speaking the Unspeakable*, ed. Marc C. Conner, Jackson: U P of Mississippi, 2000, 49–76.

42. Morrison, *Bluest*, 33.

43. Morrison, *Bluest*, 33.

44. Morrison, *Bluest*, 34–35.

45. Morrison, *Bluest*, 36.

46. Cholly has caused his family to be put outdoors because he set fire to their home.

47. Alcina Pereira de Sousa, "Living in Between a House and a Home: Where's the Comfort Zone Anyway? Dislocated Identities in Morrison's *The Bluest Eye* and Cisneros' *The House on Mango Street*," *Oceanide* 12 (2020): 19. I am indebted to Professor Maria Frias of the University of La Coruna, Spain, for providing a copy of this article.

48. Morrison, *Bluest*, 38.

49. Morrison shared on many occasions the impetus for her centering the novel around a young black girl's desire for blue eyes. Here is one account: "I began to write that book as a short story based on a conversation I had with a friend when I was a little girl. The conversation was about whether God existed; she said no and I said yes. She explained her reason for knowing that He did not: she had prayed every night for two years for blue eyes and didn't get them, and therefore He did not exist. What I later recollected was that I looked at her and imagined her having them and thought how awful that would be if she had gotten her prayer answered. I always thought she was beautiful. I began to write about a girl who wanted blue eyes and the horror of having that wish fulfilled; and also about the whole business of what is physical beauty and the pain of that yearning and wanting to be somebody else, and how devastating that was and yet part of all females who were peripheral in other people's lives." See Charles Ruas, "Toni Morrison," in *Conversations with Toni Morrison*, ed. Danille Taylor-Guthrie (Jackson: U P of Mississippi, 1994), 95–96.

50. Morrison, *Bluest*, 109.

51. Sarah E. Wright presents a sharp contrast to Pauline Breedlove in her character Mariah Upshur, who appears in *This Child's Gonna Live* (New York: Dell, 1969). Published a year before *The Bluest Eye*, the novel focuses on a self-sacrificing mother on the eastern shore of Maryland whose dirt-poor existence serves to underscore her dedication to the welfare of her children. Christin Marie Taylor argues that Wright published *This Child's Gonna Live* specifically to counter national narratives about black mothers and black families that became prominent after the appearance of the famed Moynihan Report in 1965; the Report posited that the genesis for most issues in black families centered around black mothers and their domination of their families, especially the males in their lives. See "Feeling Rejected: National Denial of Black Working Mothers in Sarah E. Wright's *This Child's Gonna Live*," in *Labor Pains: New Deal Fictions of Race, Work, and Sex in the South* (Jackson: U P of Mississippi).

52. Morrison, *Bluest*, 162. Prince asserts in *Burnin' Down the House* that "the tragedy of home for Pecola is described best in this scene. The space of home has become so compressed that she is left to maneuver psychologically within the confined space of the kitchen floor" (90).

53. Susmita Roye, "Toni Morrison's Disrupted Girls and Their Disturbed Girlhoods: *The Bluest Eye* and *A Mercy*," *Callaloo* 35, no 1 (2012), 219. Lynn Orilla Scott adds another dimension to the rape analogy when she asserts that "Metaphorically speaking, Pecola has been raped by 'whiteness,' long before her father enters her"; see "Revising the Incest Story: Toni Morrison's *The Bluest Eye* and James Baldwin's *Just Above my Head*," in *James Baldwin and Toni Morrison: Comparative Critical and Theoretical Essays*, ed. Lovalerie King and Lynn Orilla Scott (New York: Palgrave, 2006), 89. Denise Heinze not only blames Cholly and Pauline for raping Pecola; she adds Geraldine into the mix: "Even though Cholly, Pauline, and Geraldine are victims of a repressive system, they are all in part responsible for Pecola's rape and subsequent loss of sanity." See *The Dilemma of 'Double-Consciousness': Toni Morrison's Novels* (Athens: U of Georgia P, 1993), 74.

54. Pecola's pregnancy echoes that of Mattie Sue in Ellison's *Invisible Man* (1952), whose father, Jim Trueblood, impregnates her and her mother so that both are large with child at the same time. The element of shame is a factor for both girls, as well as for Trueblood's wife. The incestuous sexual violence that these girls experience is mirrored, without the pregnancy, in James Baldwin's *Just Above My Head* (1979), where Julia's father rapes Julia into her teenage years, and Daniel Black's *Perfect Peace* (2010), where Caroline, a childhood friend of one of the main characters, is the daughter of a father who rapes her repeatedly. Given these circumstances, it is impossible for any sense of a livable—let alone happy—home to reign in any of these works.

55. Roye, "Disrupted," 219.

56. Morrison comments in the "Afterword" to the 1994 Plume edition of the novel that "The extremity of Pecola's case stemmed largely from a crippled and crippling family—unlike the average black family and unlike the narrator's." *The Bluest Eye* (1970; New York: Plume, 1994), 210.

57. Morrison, *Bluest*, 44.

58. Morrison, *Bluest*, 44.

59. Toni Morrison, *Sula* (New York: Knopf, 1973).
60. Morrison, *Bluest*, 55.
61. Morrison, *Bluest*, 104.
62. Morrison, *Bluest*, 83. For a discussion of the various ways in which funk erupts in *The Bluest Eye* as well as in other Morrison novels, see Susan Willis, "Eruptions of Funk: Historicizing Toni Morrison," *Black American Literature Forum* 16, no.1 (Spring 1982): 34–42.
63. Morrison, *Bluest*, 84.
64. Morrison, *Bluest*, 87.
65. Morrison, *Bluest*, 92.
66. Morrison, *Bluest*, 92. Heinze remarks in connection with the cat imagery that Geraldine has become "little more than an innocuous feline at the feet of an exacting social code" (70). Heinze also comments that "When she orders Pecola out, Geraldine also dismisses her history, culture, passions, and love. There is no love for Pecola in Geraldine's house because the woman has no love for herself" (71).
67. Suzan-Lori Parks, *Topdog/Underdog* (New York: Theatre Communications Groups, 2001), 7.
68. Parks, *Topdog*, 54.
69. For a discussion of the appeal of Abraham Lincoln to Parks and how she uses him in her plays, see Jennifer Larson, *Understanding Suzan-Lori Parks* (Columbia: U of South Carolina P, 2012).
70. James Baldwin, "Sweet Lorraine," in *To Be Young, Gifted and Black: Lorraine Hansberry in Her Own Words*, adopted by Robert Nemiroff (New York: Signet, 1969), xii.
71. Parks, *Topdog*, 45.
72. Parks, *Topdog*, 94.
73. Parks, *Topdog*, 67, 65.
74. Parks, *Topdog*, 90.
75. Parks, *Topdog*, 100. Larson offers extended discussion on the significance of clothing and costumes in the play; see *Understanding*.
76. Laura Dawkins argues that "the brothers' loss of their parents links them with a slave past marked by familial loss and separation, and their inability to gain access to that past (and come to terms with it) implicitly leads to their final disastrous confrontation." See Dawkins's "Family Acts: History, Memory, and Performance in Suzan-Lori Parks's *The America Play* and *Topdog/Underdog*," *South Atlantic Review* 74, no. 3 (Summer 2009), 95.
77. Parks, *Topdog*, 64.
78. Parks, *Topdog*, 65.
79. Parks, *Topdog*, 32.
80. Jochen Achilles, "Does Reshuffling the Cards Change the Game? Structures of Play in Parks's *Topdog/Underdog*," in *Suzan-Lori Parks. Essays on the Plays and Other Works*, ed. Philip C. Kolin (Jefferson, N.C.: McFarland, 2010), 107.
81. Parks, *Topdog*, 29.
82. Parks, *Topdog,* 70.
83. Parks, *Topdog*, 35.

84. Michael LeMahieu provides a detailed discussion of conning in the play in "The Theater of Hustle and the Hustle of Theater: Play, Player, and Played in Suzan-Lori Parks's *Topdog/Underdog*," *African American Review* 45, no. 1,2 (Spring/Summer 2012): 33–47. LeMahieu offers especially convincing points to suggest that Booth is much more of a con artist and hustler, is much more aware of what is going on in his exchanges with Lincoln, than previous scholars have been inclined to acknowledge.

85. Larson, *Understanding*, 80.

86. Parks, *Topdog*, 110.

87. Parks, *Topdog*, np.

88. Christine Woodworth, "Parks and the Traumas of Childhood," in *Suzan-Lori Parks: Essays on the Plays and Other Works*, ed. Philip C. Kolin (Jefferson, N.C.: McFarland, 2010), 144.

89. We might also read the play as a commentary on the house of America. In this scenario, Booth's room is indicative of the lack of commitment America has shown toward persons of African descent, especially in placing them in cramped quarters without ready resources within the limits of the law. Protest of such conditions can only end in violence.

90. There are obviously many other African American literary texts that could be included in this discussion. Ann Petry's *The Street* (1946), for example, provides an especially attractive possibility for considering the impact of homespace upon character. See Trudier Harris-Lopez, "Architecture as Destiny? Women and Survival Strategies in Ann Petry's *The Street*," in Harris-Lopez, *South of Tradition: Essays on African American Literature* (Athens: U of Georgia P, 2002), 68–90.

Chapter 3

Lonely Place, Unwelcoming Space
A. J. Verdelle's The Good Negress (1995)

Warring or estranged spouses, such as the Grimeses or the Breedloves or Lincoln's and Booth's mother and father, can certainly make African American literary homespaces difficult—or at least problematic—to navigate. But what happens when one of the spouses or parents is missing from the home? What happens when, even if there is a father or father figure present, he has minimal or no influence over the dynamic that operates between mothers and their children? In A. J. Verdelle's *The Good Negress* (1995), there is a stepfather who has little influence—and no desire to exert any—upon the relationship between the put-upon adolescent daughter and her increasingly demanding mother.[1] The impact of space upon the mother/daughter relationship is apparent in this narrative in which a girl turned adolescent measures her self-worth in the cooking and cleaning she does for a family that mostly takes her for granted. The young girl has her life defined in part by the apartment space she occupies and by the at-times poisonous relationship that she develops with her mother in what should be a supportive environment. What Verdelle portrays in the novel is taken from a long-standing African American cultural practice.

    There is a well-recognized pattern in historical African American communities in which girls of adolescent age are put in charge of their younger siblings. While their mothers work or are otherwise preoccupied, these girls are forced to give up their youthful status to become surrogate parents. They ensure that they and their younger siblings get off to school on time, they cook, they clean, and they generally become "little mamas." Instead of enjoying the carefree existences of twelve and thirteen year-olds (some even younger), they assume adult responsibilities. They become proficient in running households and providing the caregiving that they themselves should be receiving. Events that lead to these circumstances may be varied and may involve a departed or absent father or irresponsible or not-to-be-trusted older male siblings. Whatever gives rise to these young girls becoming adults before their time, they do so. If they object to their new statuses, there is little redress that they have. Many resort to feeling a source of pride in the fact that someone so young can take care of so much, while others feel burdened by their circumstances. Issues of justice and morality that might inform the taking of adolescence away from these girls and forcing them to take care of themselves and the households in which they reside get pushed into the background as expediency triumphs over fairness. Indeed, there is little consideration on the parts of the mothers assigning their daughters to such roles that the daughters might have any voice in the matter. The girls are simply told what to do, and they do it in a strange mixture of childhood (being told what to do) and budding adulthood (authority to tell those younger what to do). Their status could amount to a contemporary form of indentured servitude, for, as long as they are under the roofs of their mothers and there are younger siblings around, they will be forced to serve in these nurturing capacities. Since African American literature draws heavily upon historical patterns of existence in African American communities, it is not surprising that literary texts would portray such relationships.[2]

Verdelle's *The Good Negress* draws heavily upon this historical pattern in African American communities by presenting an interesting case of forced and voluntary servitude with an adolescent black female. Before that status evolves, the novel showcases a mother's abandonment of her daughter, an abandonment that eventually leads to return and servitude. Her abandonment echoes that of Lincoln's and Booth's but is much more poignant because of the age at which it occurs as well as the circumstances under which it occurs. Denise (also spelled "Deneese") nicknamed "Neesey" Palms, who lives in Detroit with her mother Margarete, her two brothers, and her father, finds herself at age seven in tiny Patuskie, Virginia with her grandmother when her father dies suddenly. That unexpected uprooting mirrors another pattern in African American culture, the one in which southern migrant parents who moved to the North routinely sent their offspring to the South to live with grandparents during the summer. The problem with Neesey's removal is that the short term becomes extended. A temporary homespace becomes a quasi-permanent one as her mother leaves Neesey with her grandmother. It is especially egregious because Margarete gives Neesey the impression that they are simply going South for a visit, and, to avoid resistant confrontation, Margarete sneaks away in the early hours one morning before Neesey wakes up. The temper tantrum that Neesey throws in response to this sneaky abandonment yields no change of venue for her; she is stuck—as she believes initially—with her grandmother. Neesey, evoking Frederick Douglass, is thus forced to find a home elsewhere.

The thread stretching from mother to daughter to grandmother is the major one in the novel, but the narrative entails several other issues, including conflicts between Margarete and her new husband over her favored and spoiled younger son, a traumatic encounter between that grandson and the grandmother, and a folk-based account of the father's death (belief that he died from eating ham when he really died from the complications of a stroke). In episodic presentations, the narrative progresses in a mostly nonlinear fashion that challenges readers to stay abreast of chronology and overall sequencing. The major event is waiting for the birth of Margarete's child, of whom Neesey is expected to take care, but that gets interspersed with scenes of Neesey's time with her grandmother, her early educational experiences, her later educational experiences, and her getting to know the young man who, like herself, becomes a migrant to the North. In one early sequence, for example, the baby may be born, while, a few pages later, the birth is still anticipated. In another sequence, Neesey may be with her grandmother and then back in Detroit. Page breaks offer a bit of control and tips to chronological sequencing but not much. Alternations of reporting of incidents combined with a lack of adherence to chronological progression and a liberal use of flashbacks and flash-forwards ensure that readers must give their fullest attentions to the novel to keep time and events progressing logically in their own minds. In allowing Neesey first-person narrative privilege, Verdelle puts the text in the hands of a character who is intrinsically engaging but who lacks an overall masterful control. Thus the narrative wanders where it will, through associative and other connections, and finally just pauses, with significant issues unresolved and with Neesey's relationship to her mother still defined by a dominant-subordinate pattern, though Neesey is a young adult at that point.

TRAINING TO BE ENSLAVED

The narrative begins, however, with Neesey in a home elsewhere, and she has to learn to adapt to that new environment. First, Neesey must accept the fact that she will not be allowed to return to Detroit, then she has to be acclimated thoroughly to her grandmother's home. In achieving both objectives, Neesey's grandmother resorts to tough love. In a detached though firm way, Neesey's grandmother guides Neesey through the troubled waters of her mother's seeming rejection and into a path that serves her well when she returns to Detroit five years later at the age of twelve. Certainly the skills that her grandmother teaches her, such as cooking, cleaning, and washing, are valuable ones, but they also serve as the basis for Neesey's servitude once she returns to Detroit. Through painstaking detail that she initially uses to keep Neesey's mind off the fact that Margarete has run out on Neesey, Granma'am teaches her young granddaughter to be an artful and creative cook and to be uncompromising in keeping a clean house. These superficially virtuous qualities get tangled up in the mother/daughter dynamic that will dominate Neesey's life for years in a chain of events that will essentially turn Neesey into an indentured servant if not an outright slave.

Granma'am is silent on the topic of why Margarete has left Neesey in her care; indeed, if Granma'am had anything objectionable to say about Margarete's leaving Neesey with her, that is never apparent. That silence is in effect acquiescence. It suggests that Granma'am either approves of Margarete's action or that she has insufficient influence over Margarete to advocate for a daughter's needing her mother. It might also be the case that Granma'am herself wanted/needed company and was perfectly content to have Neesey left with her. She responds to Neesey's declarations that she wants to go home with quiet, unbending assertions: "'You cain't go home'" and "'I done told you, you home right here.'"[3] Neesey's being forced to remain in the South and learning the skills that she does from her grandmother inadvertently lead to Neesey's being trained for future degradation. The training is a matter of body and mind, and her time in Detroit will reveal the extent to which muscle memory is ingrained in her very psyche in terms of the chores she performs and her acquiescent attitude in those performances.

Also relevant to her return to Detroit is Neesey's Christian training under her grandmother's guidance. While the grandmother is not a fanatic, she has made sure that Neesey attended church, and church people and church activities are integral parts of their lives. Inherent in Christianity is the directive to turn the other cheek, which implies an endurance under difficult circumstances. By any measure, Neesey turns the other cheek time and again in Detroit when her labor is exploited as her family uses her for all the dirty work that other family members do not wish to undertake. Christian instructions do not hang constantly over Neesey, but such instructions are implicit in her interactions with her family. While she is not an expressively devout believer and does not spend much time in church in Detroit, she is nonetheless heir to the traditions her grandmother has instilled in her.

The five years that Neesey spends with Granma'am cover only a few pages of the novel, but they make clear the differences in southern and northern homes as well as educational practices and achievement levels. For example, Neesey learns the art of cooking the greens that grow readily in her grandmother's garden. This labor-intensive cooking joins the making of pies, gravies, and biscuits as some of the talents that Neesey will bring to Detroit. She also brings the old-fashioned ways Granma'am has of dressing and house cleaning into an environment where they can easily evoke negative commentary or become the subject of jokes. When, as a twelve-year-old, she ties up her head in a rag in old-lady fashion to clean house, her brother Luke edward is polite but derisive in condemnation of her old-fashioned ways: "'Well, you look a sight. You got on more rag than you got hair, don't you? I think you should quit scrubbing and put on some clothes.'"[4] Later, Neesey notes that Luke edward invites her out because "he thought it would be better for [Neesey] than being in the house cleaning and cooking all the time like a maid" (though he never offers to do any of that himself).[5] She says of herself: "I wake up early, especially in Detroit. I am like a old person, I cain't sleep late."[6] The generational gap between Neesey and her grandmother has been closed by leading the child to become an "old soul," so to speak, in the midst of folks who are much less strictured and less structured. Another detrimental way in which the old-fashioned informs Neesey's return to the North is in her speech. As a well-intentioned but illiterate woman, Granma'am has put Neesey's education in the hands of the folks she thought could serve Neesey best. Unfortunately, they are less able to manage standard, non-vernacular English or to provide the lessons of education to which Neesey will be held accountable when she returns to Detroit. She therefore arrives as a smart young woman (as a helper to her teacher in Virginia, she has taught the younger students in their one-room classroom) whose tendency to drop endings in her speech and whose non-prestige, accent-laden southern dialect mark her as the epitome of the southern hick who usually ends up being put back in grades upon arrival in the North. Though Neesey's innate skills come through to her teachers and though she is not put back, she is still an outsider whose very vocalizations draw snickers from her fellow students and reprimands from her teachers. To the careful observer, that southern dialect might also suggest an illiteracy that is associated with slavery.

Neesey's stint in the South, therefore, may have served her mother well and may have provided her grandmother with company, but it has handicapped Neesey for dealing with the northern educational system. She will spend most of the narrative trying to make up for the inadequacy of her southern education and the embarrassment of her vernacular-defined speech, which means that Margarete has inadvertently handicapped Neesey in ways that she did not anticipate or about which she was not necessarily concerned, and the latter seems to be the case. Expediency on Margarete's part is ultimately acceptable to Granma'am, as the advice she gives Neesey to follow upon her return to Detroit brings to the fore the servitude theme that dominates the text. Neesey reflects at one point: "Things fly through my mind like thrown hardballs. I am remembering Granma'am's rhythm: 'You be sure and he'p y'mother, now; be sure and he'p y'mother.'"[7] Granma'am also tells Neesey: "'You just be a worker bee, like I taught you.'"[8] This analogy means that Margarete will be the queen whom Neesey will serve, and that turns out to be the case. Neesey returns to Detroit not because Margarete has come to miss her. Nor does Margarete allow her to come back in order for Neesey to achieve some goal of her own. Instead, Neesey is brought back to serve. After years of being alone following her first husband's death, Margarete is now not only remarried but she is pregnant. She directs Neesey to return to help her with the baby when it arrives.[9] Neesey becomes, therefore, a ready-made babysitter for a mother who prefers her work as a hairdresser and her socializing as a card-playing, smoking and drinking good timer to anything that her daughter might wish. Granma'am supports the role that Neesey is brought back to play when she advises her to do everything she can to make herself useful, indispensable, to become a part of what will be the "good team" of Neesey and Margarete. In offering such advice, Granma'am joins with Margarete in seeing Neesey as a commodity, a resource to be expended for the comfort of others. In the power dynamic that exists between mothers and daughters or grandmothers and granddaughters, therefore, Neesey—especially as a twelve-year old—has no recourse but to serve.

Neesey's memories of her grandmother's directives also indicate that she has an image of a homespace somewhere in her imagination that she is trying to bring to reality within the confines of her mother's apartment, thus the element of portability applies to her as well, no matter how destructive that application turns out to be. It is the memory of the time at her grandmother's house that guides—morally and physically—almost everything that Neesey does in Detroit. Her grandmother is a constant touchstone against the less than pleasant realities that she encounters again and again in Margarete's house and some of what she encounters at school. Neesey bows to the impact of memory when she declares about trying to remember the position of a baby in its mother's stomach that suggests sex: "My memory does come back sometimes, bold and unannounced, intact."[10] Neesey might not remember prenatal positioning immediately, but she always remembers her grandmother's advice, and she follows it down the long lane of servitude that defines her status in Margarete's apartment.

USE VALUE; OR, ENJOYING SLAVERY

What is fascinating about the path of servitude that she embarks upon is that, though Neesey might express occasional objections, she embraces it thoroughly. An indication of her willingness to serve, especially in terms of cooking, is obvious from her admiration for Margarete's kitchen:

> The kitchen is big with appliances soldiered all around. A big electric Frigidaire. A nice white gas stove backed right up to the wall. No griddle. Plenty cabinets

up and down, pine, stained brown. Nice, big table, flecked linoleum top, six chairs to go with. Look like Margarete and her new husband doin good; you can tell by the ease a the kitchen.[11]

Home back in Detroit, therefore, becomes for Neesey a space in which she sleeps on a cot in the living/front room, cooks every meal for her expectant mother, stepfather, and two brothers, and cleans the apartment like a nineteenth century char woman. A careful reader could compile a cookbook—or at least a substantial set of menus—from the numerous recipes and meal plannings that Neesey executes in the novel. From the minute she arrives in Detroit and Big Jim, Margarete's new husband, discovers that Neesey can cook, she is subject to Big Jim's leaving money for her to purchase items to cook for the family dinners. Though Big Jim might object initially to meat being undeviatingly smothered in gravy, that is minimal in comparison to his praise of Neesey's skill and his overall appreciation for Neesey's cooking. Neesey, in turn, uses cooking as a way to get to know her reconstituted family and to position herself—hopefully—as an integral part of it. Neesey assesses her role in this way:

> Big Jim—Margarete's new husband—was a big house of a man . . . . He was brand new to me, and for a much longer time than I was new to him. He got to know me pretty quick, mostly through the food I cooked. Ain't much food cain't show you bout people. In three or four weeks time, I had made enough meals to index. So, me and Big Jim got to the place where he might say when he left the house, 'Neesey, I put three dollars on the table for you to go down and get some neckbones and whatever you want to cook alongside.' He would close the door behind that remark, and that was how I would know what he wanted to have for dinner. I might ask Margarete what else I should fix, and in the beginning she would tell me. Later, after she finds out how good a cook I am, she just says, 'Neesey, you the one like to cook, just get what you want. It'll be good, Jim'll be happy.' So that's how I got to the place where when I left for school in the morning, I would take whatever money Big Jim left on the table, and then on the way home, I would stop at the butcher and get what I thought best. I made all the meals.[12]

Lest readers forget, these remarks are coming from a twelve-year old whose pregnant mother has thoroughly abdicated her role as wife even before she will abdicate her role as mother. Neesey becomes, therefore, a titular co-wife to Big Jim and a surrogate mother to the entire family. The comment that Neesey "likes" to cook may be true, but it is also an imposition of responsibility upon the adolescent. She becomes, in effect, enslaved to the household that her mother has created.[13] And the primary recipient of her largesse, Big Jim, has the audacity, after Neesey has been in the apartment and cooking for a while, to demand special consideration on occasions. When Neesey makes "a few scrambled eggs, some toast from the loaf, some slab bacon," which she considers "a real good breakfast" for a Saturday or Sunday, she encounters additional requests and implicitly more expectations:

> But Big Jim has learned that I can make biscuits and that I know how to keep the lumps out a hominy grits. So he wants biscuits and grits, and for a while, while I was still confused about refusin to be cookin all this breakfast, he took to bringin the breakfast meat he wanted home with him from work on Friday nights. He would bring enough meat for both Saturday and Sunday, and I would make sure to add enough—fried potatoes, stewed apples, biscuits or breakfast cake—so that it fed everybody.[14]

Although Neesey believes that Margarete should prepare breakfast for Big Jim, she is not in a position to voice that assessment. She just keeps cooking humungous meals until the baby is born, at which time the baby becomes her excuse for cutting back on cooking.

These scenes are but two of *the many* in which Neesey documents her cooking for her family; she asserts that she "would spend all day on a meal in a heartbeat."[15] She is equally zealous in her cleaning and equally detailed in documenting the instances in which she practically takes the entire apartment apart and puts it back together. That is especially true just after her arrival in Detroit. In a chapter entitled "Once I Start to Cleanin, It's Hard for Me to Stop," she recounts spending her first two weeks in Detroit cleaning and sleeping. As Lisa B. Day observes, Neesey "plays the role of a black mammy and a kitchen slave," adding: "Indeed, the most problematic element in Deneese's characterization as a slave is her obsessive joy in housework."[16] Neesey gives the apartment a thorough cleaning, scrubbing, and washing once everyone leaves for their activities of the day. She cleans Margarete and Big Jim's bedroom as well as the bedroom that David and Luke edward share. She straightens closets, rolls up and cleans under rugs, washes baseboards, bleaches everything, uses ammonia liberally, and reorganizes closets. There is no mention of how her brothers respond to her cleaning, but Margarete does appreciate Neesey's efforts, primarily because it relieves her. Margarete is "ecstatic" after Neesey's thorough cleaning of her bedroom. Neesey also notes that Big Jim comments to Margarete that Neesey is "gone make somebody a good wife."[17] An exchange between Margarete and Neesey highlights the role that Neesey has assigned to herself by working her way into it.

> She [Margarete] notices my progress [in cleaning]. 'Oh, Neesey, you wouldn't believe what a time I have keepin this house clean.'
> I don't answer, because anybody got eyes would believe.

> Margarete goes on. 'I can get help with the heavy work. I can get David or Jim or Luke edward to get up on a ladder for me. But by the time I pick up all these cups and glasses and socks and things and wash them up, and dust and wipe all the furniture, and sweep the rugs and floors, too, I'm tired, and I still have to go to work. Lord have mercy, I'm so glad you here to help me.' . . . She pulls my head up so she can look directly at me. She smiles. She says again: 'You are such a help.'[18]

This is one of the rare pleasant exchanges between Margarete and Neesey, and it highlights one of the major currents of the novel, that is, the gender dynamic. Verdelle shows how that gender dynamic informs what occurs once Neesey returns to Detroit as well as how it informed Margarete's initial abandonment of Neesey. Neesey has two older brothers, David and Luke edward, whom Margarete keeps with her in Detroit when she leaves Neesey in Virginia. It is never explicitly clear in the text why the mother gave up her daughter instead of one or both of the sons, but the choice yields an estrangement between mother and daughter that cannot be repaired with Margarete's superficial approval of Neesey's housekeeping skills. The usual respect that daughters might grant to their mothers, and especially in their addressing them as "mama," "mother," or "mom," gets negated. Over the years Neesey has resorted to calling her mother by her first name. She has planned a response when Margarete questions her:

> 'I don't mean no disrespect, Margarete,' I rushed. Now, this first part was a lie. 'I haven't been round you in so long, sometimes I called Granma'am Mama. And, well, when I talked about you down home, I just called you Margarete,' I said. Another lie. I only called Granma'am Granma'am. And I only called Margarete Margarete when I was listenin to other people talk about her. But what could she know about how true it was or wasn't. There was no way she could know what I knew, and I knew I did not want to call Margarete Mama anymore, not unless I had to, not unless she made me . . . .
> She never said anything else about the Margarete business. And so that is how I came to call my mother Margarete, and that is how I knew that we agreed on a few things: the power of changing subjects, the serious significance of the wearing of clothes, the control we have over the naming of names, and how in truth the change of name can change the person, even if the change is done in secret, or is done by somebody else. And how in the light of day nothing can be done to change the person back, there is no return to the prior name.[19]

Inherent in Neesey's calling her mother by her first name is definitely a lack of respect, perhaps some resentment, and assuredly the ever-present signifier that the mother has failed the daughter in some way. The fact that Neesey is prepared to lie to justify her new practice is an additional indication of lack of respect. The relationship with the mother thus becomes even more troubled, and home in Detroit is therefore alienated and alienating while home in Patuskie, Virginia, though initially rejected, becomes the source of the training and the instilling of values that will guide Neesey for the remainder of the narrative.

As noted earlier, some young girls caught in the cycle of cooking, cleaning, and caregiving for their families took a measure of pride in doing so. There is no doubt that Neesey experiences such. However, there is equally no doubt that her family, including her mother, exploits her for years. Once Margarete gets into the habit of expecting excellent cooking from Neesey, for example, she slides into the authoritarian role of demanding no less. After all, this is still a mother/daughter relationship, and the mother still wields the power. That is abundantly clear on the occasion when one of Neesey's teachers, concerned that Neesey not slow down in her studies once the baby arrives, comes to the apartment to request that Margarete support Neesey's educational pursuit. Margarete, like Granma'am, is vehemently opposed to outsiders interfering in family business. Unable to vent her frustrations on the teacher, she takes them out on Neesey instead, and she uses cooking to show that that is the realm in which she expects Neesey to perform, not education. She is "hot as white coal" about the teacher's visit, confronts Neesey, and moves from smiling appreciation of something Neesey has done to refusing to allow her to use the bathroom as punishment for what she perceives to be Neesey's urging the teacher to visit.[20] Despite Neesey's thinking that she "would pee on the floor," Margarete is deliberately and viciously insensitive to the urgency of her predicament and makes her stand and stand,[21] then:

> After I don't know how long, Margarete said, 'It's a chicken in there need to be fried for dinner. Jim'll be home in forty-five minutes.'
>
> 'OK, Margarete,' I answered and turned toward the bathroom.
>
> Margarete raised her voice, 'GO IN THAT KITCHEN AND FRY THAT CHICKEN I SAID.' I turned around and stood still again, trying to check on her face.
>
> 'Go in that kitchen and fry that chicken, Deneese. I'm not gone tell you again.'
>
> There were two chickens, not one . . . . Now, here I stand: in Detroit, frying chicken, looking out the window trying to decide what I hate. I like to cook, still. I like the changing of food from one state to another. So it's not the cooking I hate. It's the bawling threat of the baby I don't like. It follows me everywhere. It is responsible for my having to leave Granma'am. Now that I have moved, and I know there are other worlds, the baby is forcing me to lose again . . . .
>
> I had the chicken browned on the second side and was peeling the potatoes when Margarete called in that I should go to the bathroom and get out of my school dress.[22]

Power and resentment. Margarete wields both in her reaction to Neesey after the teacher's request. Lisa B. Day comments that Margarete operates "much like a slave mistress."[23] She is calculatingly cruel in denying Neesey bladder release and perhaps resentful of an opportunity that Neesey has. After all, the teacher is working with Neesey in extra tutoring sessions after school to bring her speaking and writing skills to the level that she expects them to be. Such an investment in her daughter, such concern for her future, is far more than Margarete has expressed. Again, she is only concerned about the resource value that Neesey has to offer. If she uses her up in that pursuit, then fine, but she does not expect Neesey to have any desires or aspirations beyond cooking, cleaning, and taking care of the baby.

This passage also reflects one of the few times in the novel in which Neesey is herself resentful about something, in this instance the baby that will take up the majority of her time once it arrives. Her teacher has opened different worlds of learning to Neesey, and she can see possibilities that she had not seen when she was in Virginia with Granma'am. However, the baby will potentially short-circuit all her plans. It is worth noting, though, that this objection is exceptional in the narrative. Mostly, Neesey just adjusts to circumstances and does what she is expected to do. In a situation in which she has little power, in a spatial dynamic in which she sleeps on a cot in a living/front room through which everyone passes, and in a stressful mother/daughter relationship, she is heir to an especially problematic homespace. Adults around her have their priorities elsewhere, and her wishes are valued only when they align with those other-focused directives.

A HOME ON A ... COT

It is in the mid-twentieth century that Neesey migrates from her grandmother's house in Patuskie, Virginia to a cot in her mother's apartment in Detroit. In her method of conveyance as well as in the things she carries, Neesey echoes many migrants from the rural South to urban enclaves in the North, especially as artist Jacob Lawrence depicts them in his "Migration Series."[24] Her grandmother enlists a trusted young churchman, Harold Grayson, to drive Neesey to her mother's home, with a stop in Washington, D. C. to share a meal with the young man's relatives. As was the case with many migrants historically, Neesey carries food that Granma'am has prepared for the trip, for, given the racial times, they did not want to risk unnecessary stops. Neesey notes that Granma'am packs "half the three chickens we fried last night, some biscuits she spoon-stirred this morning, a few apples and pears, two bananas. Three or four Mason jars with water, mint tea, and coffee. The hot coffee jars have pieces of wood spoon in the bottom to keep the glass from breaking."²⁵ Granma'am also sends them off with a pound cake. In addition, Neesey carries a precious folk concoction that Granma'am has prepared: "a small Ball jar of oil to help Margarete have the new baby."²⁶ Like those historical migrants, therefore, Neesey is carrying a part of the South in its food and folk traditions with her to the North. More important, she is carrying her southern self and all that means in terms of transporting a sense of home and a way of being in the world. As the South goes north *with* and *in* Neesey, she therefore takes the familiar into unfamiliar territory. She will spend years trying to merge the two.

Neesey's arrival at Margarete's house is an immersion into alienation even as Neesey tries to domesticate that alienation. Being assigned a cot as her sleeping quarters and the open space of the living/front room as her "bedroom," Neesey is awkwardly added on to the household instead of being thought of as an integral part of it. The front room where Neesey sleeps is also the entry point for the apartment. That means that, whenever family members come home from their various outings, they must violate Neesey's space to get to other rooms in the apartment. Neesey is therefore constantly being erased—visually and metaphorically—from her so-called family group. Any time the cot is put away, she is effectively "stored" as well. She is thus asked to fit into the small corners of her family's lives. At least John Grimes shares a bedroom with his brother, and even Pecola Breedlove has a bed. The living arrangement in which Neesey finds herself makes her a permanent squatter in her own homespace.

Constant spatial violation also has implications not only for Neesey's current privacy but for her potential growth into a healthy sexual being. While there is absolutely no hint of sexual impropriety once Neesey arrives in Detroit, it is something that has apparently crossed Granma'am's mind when Neesey recalls: "Granma'am and I had talked about Margarete's new husband, although he is not a very new husband anymore. Granma'am has told me he'll be glad that I have come to help, and that all I need to do is be nice to him and make sure I don't walk around the house half-naked."²⁷ Neesey certainly does not walk around the house half exposed, but she does have to use the facilities, take baths, get dressed, and carry out other toiletry business. Having to perform all those operations in an environment where privacy is barely given a thought must have some kind of effect upon Neesey, if it is no more than to push a relatively shy adolescent into more shyness. Also, she is close enough to Big Jim and Margarete's bedroom to hear, as Pecola and John Grimes do, the lovemaking that goes on there. How she might interpret such is left to reader imagination. While the brothers are seldom in the apartment for long stretches, they still must violate the space assigned to Neesey as they enter and exit, and the same is true of Big Jim and Margarete. Neesey, therefore, essentially lives in a miniature Grand Central Station, a space that can only truly be hers in the wee hours of the morning or the late, late hours of the night.

The cot also reflects the contradictions in Margarete's responses to Neesey. On the one hand, Margarete tells Neesey how valuable she is in the cleaning, cooking, and anticipated help with the baby. On the other hand, she expects Neesey to make all the adjustments (including returning from her grandmother's house) instead of Margarete's making any. Margarete is comfortable with Neesey on a cot; it is only when Big Jim forces Luke edward from the apartment that Neesey is finally assigned a bed. Neesey comments when Margarete and Big Jim are arguing about her sleeping on the cot:

> I heard him tell Margarete that we wasn't poor enough that I had to sleep on a cot in the front room. (Well, none of that was said before it was time to make space for his child.) And how long did she plan to let me just sleep on that cot? he wanted to know. Margarete told him I was all right. I couldn't even side with Big Jim cause he was being mean about my Luke edward, even though I did happen to be tired of that cot they bought.[28]

Noticeably, Margarete speaks *for* Neesey and effectively dismisses any discomfort Neesey may have experienced during the past several months sleeping on the cot. Also of note is the fact that neither Big Jim nor Margarete has altruistic motives about where Neesey should sleep. Big Jim just wants to get rid of Luke edward, and Margarete has not shown that she cares one way or the other.

With Luke edward's removal comes the opportunity for Neesey to sleep in one of the beds in the brothers' room, but Margarete even reneges on that assignment. Thus Neesey is expected to be "at home" in Detroit, but there is no true welcome into the home. Margarete does give a party once Neesey arrives, but it is obviously more for her and her friends than it is for Neesey. That one gesture, ostensibly well-intended though it might be, does not compensate for the overall lack of welcome (in the sense of *truly valuing* Neesey) that Neesey finds in the Detroit apartment. Neesey remains a present-absence in the apartment—she cooks and cleans, but she can be made to disappear simply by storing the cot away, since it is the most visible physical reminder of her being in the apartment. In the absence of a bed of her own (not to mention a bedroom), closet space (she lives out of her "grip"), and privacy, what Neesey experiences is not appreciably different from the lacks with which other literary characters contend in their homespaces. The lack of affection evokes Pecola's situation, and the sternness with which Neesey is forced to fry that chicken could compete with anything Gabriel dished out to John Grimes.

COMPETING FOR A LIFE

Though she is initially reluctant to attend school in Detroit, perhaps because she is fearful of her shortcomings in comparison to city students, Neesey eventually takes that step, relying upon Luke edward to walk her to school for a much longer period of time than he expects for a seventh grader. Once school becomes a part of Neesey's life, however, and once her teachers, especially Miss Pearson, invest extra time in helping Neesey progress, the prospect of the baby's arrival becomes more and more abhorrent to Neesey. For a long stretch of the novel, therefore, the competition between the baby and Neesey's education becomes an extended battle in which Neesey is determined to come out victorious. Again and again, Neesey's desire to learn takes second place to the baby: "I told Margarete I have to stay late at school to learn the rules a English, and she say I have to learn them by the new moon in March cause after that I have to be home, help with the baby."[29] When Miss Pearson starts to discuss college with Neesey, she reflects: "I was distracted early in the sentence: thinkin bout keepin in school and how Missus Pearson say I have to do the after-school work exactly from three to five-thirty, and how the baby comin soon and I will probably not have no spare time. Plus, Margarete done already told me I have to leave right when school end, come spring."[30] And: "Margarete had told me nine times if once that she needed me to help round the house and with the baby, and that I was gone need that know-how in my life for sure. And Margarete said I already know how to read and write and spell."[31] Thus Margarete sees functional, minimal, limited education as sufficient for Neesey. If Neesey remains totally devoted to school, that will reduce her use value from Margarete's perspective.

The competition between the baby and Neesey's education ensues throughout the latter months of the pregnancy as well as after the birth.

> Missus Pearson said that it was my not knowing the English language that cut me off from a bigger world. But it was Margarete's baby that kept me in the house, that cut me off from outdoors, even. Well, I figured if I could feed and wash the baby, douse her with powder and lay her down, clean and sweet, then I could look up all the words I didn't know and write them down in my school notebooks and try to reach to somewhere.
>
> I find other things to do besides cook, clean, buy meat, wash bottles, and diapers. I practiced how to write answers to questions. Every time I went to school, I took in extra I had done.[32]

In her desperate desire to continue some form of learning, Neesey uses every spare second available to her. Even when Margarete is in labor, Neesey does her math homework.[33] After the baby arrives, she recounts:

Lonely Place, Unwelcoming Space   87

> At home in our apartment, I wrote and wrote. At our kitchen table, or hunched over the coffee table, sometimes while I rocked Clara's bassinette swing. I looked up words in the dictionary, wrote their spellings and definitions ten times. Like formula, dismissed, perturbed, precipitation, barometer, proprietor. Used my dictionary for spelling and for meaning. I might put the baby to sleep, and then spread all my things out on the single bed I slept in in the room with the sleeping child. Or I might put the baby down and go back into the kitchen where I could smell that the kidney beans and neckbones were still cooking, about done, needing salt, or just about to burn.[34]

Neesey reads in between watching pots, does homework while the baby naps, and generally tries desperately to make the very best of an almost impossible situation. She carts the bulky baby stroller from the upstairs apartment to the street level when she takes baby Clara out for walks. She becomes, in effect, the baby's mother, even though she is only thirteen years old. She perhaps sees herself as standing in a gap that Margarete has created, for she notes, "Margarete does not seem interested in the baby," though Big Jim is consistently attentive once he arrives home from work every day. Many years later, when she returns from Hampton and is with Margarete and her baby sister Clara, Neesey observes: "I become the mother."[35] Immediately following the birth, however, Neesey almost drowns in the oceans of work connected with Clara.[36] Lisa B. Day states convincingly that Margarete relinquishes "her maternal responsibilities to Deneese much like a slave mistress giving her child to a black mammy to nurture."[37] Neesey is thus literally awash in work.

> Seem like I spent all my time cooking and washing, and toting Clara. I didn't mind so much, but I was surprised by the hill of diapers always need attending—either washed, folded, taken off or put on the baby. Thank the Lord for Margarete's wringer washer. I used it every other day to wash the twenty or thirty diapers that Clara either wet on, poo-pooed in, or that I slung across my shoulder for her to drool or spit up on . . . . Got so I could wash diapers in the morning, feed Clara, and then go on to school.[38]

Strikingly, Neesey consistently attempts to make the best of the situation by asserting that she "doesn't mind" the mountains of work that Clara requires. It is practically a miracle that Neesey is able to keep up any level of studies as she cares for the baby. Though she has to give up most of the afterschool sessions with Miss Pearson, she maintains interest in and completes work for her regular classes. It is Miss Pearson who inspires in her a desire to go to college, a desire to transcend the circumstances in which her family would seem to be very content to have her remain. After all, her older brothers appear to have no interest in higher education. The oldest one gets married out of high school, and the other drifts into a relationship with a woman who births a child for him.

Miss Pearson's desire to help Neesey leads Miss Pearson to a brief severing of the relationship with Neesey when Neesey makes a choice that appears to be as much out of the black past as Neesey's taking care of someone else's child appears to be. Neesey takes a job over one Christmas holiday, ostensibly to sort and package pins and buttons for sale. However, her pre-sorting job requires that she clean the bathrooms of the store where she works. As the closest thing to an othermother that Neesey has, Miss Pearson is outraged by that development and tries to convince Neesey that it hearkens back to days of Jim Crow and general servitude for black people. It is also the scene that provides the title for the novel. Miss Pearson avows:

> 'They got you in there cleaning toilets, making you a good little negress, and your mother's response to it is that you should buy the Christmas turkey.' Her face is pinched like a rodent's nose. 'Well, this is certainly not what I intended for you, Denise. And I don't think it is what your grandmother intended either. Your mother is very shortsighted about your future; I have told you that before.' She burrows. 'You can be like her if you wish, but where you will find yourself when it's over will be very close to where you are right now. Now, when you lift your hands and face and nose from the toilets, you can come back to see me. Until then, you are excused.'[39]

Miss Pearson's attitude is a direct contrast to Margarete's; when Neesey asks what Margarete thinks of the toilet-cleaning work that she does, Margarete merely responds that people sometimes have to do work that they do not like. Certainly that is true, but Margarete does not express any of the moral outrage that Miss Pearson feels, which means that Margarete continues to measure Neesey by a yardstick of use value. Her invoking expediency conveys yet again how un-engaged Margarete is in imagining long-term aspirations for Neesey. She wants a Christmas turkey, and Neesey has promised to purchase it with some of the money she is scheduled to earn. Turkeys and babies thus take priority over development of the mind, and Margarete is willing to sacrifice the intangible for the tangible.

Miss Pearson's reference to a "good negress" also provides an out-of-the-family commentary on how Neesey is being treated within her own family. She does a lot more subservient work than merely clean the toilet at home. She does enough work to warrant having the best of everything reserved for her. However, given the light in which her family views her, no one would consider that and no one objects seriously to her being the servant. Even Luke edward, the brother-god whom she worships, does not offer to help Neesey with any chores even when he recognizes that she is more like a maid than a sister. Again, it is a matter of diminished value as a female offspring and commodity value in terms of the labor that her body can provide; there is no appreciation for her mind. Throughout the novel, no family member expresses approval of or applauds Neesey's aspiration to finish high school and perhaps go on to college. Neesey has to determine that she will "write" her way into a future that includes high school graduation and normal school, and indeed she ends the novel enrolled as a student at Hampton Institute. Anything she achieves, however, has been in spite of her family, not because of any nurturing support they might have offered.

The novel is set in the 1960s, which makes Margarete's attitude toward Neesey's desire for education rather surprising. Many people of African descent on United States soil were eagerly pursuing any education available to them in the 1960s. No longer were they content to be domestic workers and purveyors of unskilled labor. That was especially the case if they migrated to the North, as Margarete has done. For her to be so willing to allow Neesey to clean toilets as the preparatory work for her sorting pins and buttons might thus be abstractly surprising but is less so when viewed in the context of Margarete's viewing Neesey as a commodity—perhaps not an expendable one but a commodity nonetheless. At least Margarete does not take Neesey completely out of school to care for the child, though Neesey cannot help but be aware of the implicit disapproval that Margarete holds toward her desire to learn and improve her mind.

This nonsupportive dynamic means that the family situation, the home environment for Neesey, will always be one of intrusive discontentment. As noted, she sleeps on a cot in the front room of the apartment, which allows her little privacy. Although she cleans out other people's closets, she is not assigned any closet space of her own. Once David gets married and the conflict between Big Jim and Luke edward escalates, Neesey graduates to being allowed to sleep in one of the twin beds in the room that her brothers shared. That, however, does not bring any appreciable relief. Margarete usurps that space as the room and the bed in which she prefers to give birth, so that her own bedroom can remain clean and unspoiled for Big Jim. It is a telling commentary on Margarete's relationship to her husband and daughter, as well as to her forthcoming child. Giving birth to her daughter seems unpleasant, dirty, and spoiling, thus she violates the space recently assigned to Neesey to contain all the pollution so that her husband will not have to see or be tainted by the giving of birth. There is no consideration for Neesey and certainly no asking what she might prefer in the matter. Margarete simply tells her, ""I'ma have the baby in the bed in your room . . . . keep this room clean for Jim.""[40] To be tossed from pillar to post, as the folk saying goes, is bad enough, but to be repeatedly denied privacy and a space of her own within that tossing underscores the troubled relationship that Margarete has with Neesey.

Indeed, no one mentions that she is without privacy and closet space until, months after her arrival and just before the baby is due, Big Jim comments to Margarete that they are not so poor that Neesey has to sleep on a cot. Her comfort is not his primary concern; he just wants Luke edward out of the apartment in anticipation of the baby's birth, and Neesey's situation is just another point in the case he makes to put Luke edward out and to take over the brothers' bedroom for Neesey and the baby.

Luke edward's position provides another vantage point from which to view Neesey's subservience. Here is a young man whose mother adores him, who has allowed him to remain at home even after high school graduation, and who makes no demands upon him to become a regular working person and contributor to household expenses. He keeps disruptive hours—often arriving home from nights out when other family members are sitting down to breakfast—and there is apparently nothing that he does for the household. Yet, Margarete and Neesey adore the young man. Remarkably, Neesey comments at one point that Margarete and Luke edward are more like sister and brother than mother and son. They form a unit in which they lock other people out, including Big Jim and Neesey. As long as mother and son can share jokes and enjoy parties, nothing else seems to be required of him. Certainly Neesey does not require more. She offers that Luke edward is her "god," and she suffers with him when Granma'am punishes him for stealing from a local store on his last visit to Virginia.[41] Neesey is equally forgiving of him when, following their father's death, Luke edward spends a portion of the money on candy that he and Neesey have been sent to use to turn the electricity back on in the apartment. To Margarete's and Neesey's minds, therefore, Luke edward, just by virtue of being male, articulate, handsome, and fun, can do no wrong. That Neesey has bought into this way of thinking about her brother emphasizes the gender preferences that mark the narrative. There is no way that Margarete would expect her son to do a fraction of the work that Neesey does; nor does Neesey expect him to do so. This relationship thus reflects her serving mentality, for not only is she serving the entire family with her cooking and cleaning, but she is serving Luke edward, her "god." This voluntary diminishing of self underscores yet again the problematic characterization of Neesey and the relationships that exist in the space she must call home.

The apartment, which is Neesey's temple of sacrifice to Margarete, Luke edward, and the remainder of the family, is also Neesey's prison. Like many devotees who were not allowed in ancient times to leave various sites or holy places of worship, so too her family would have Neesey remain in place to serve them. Imprisoned physically because she is a dependent adolescent and imprisoned psychologically because the skills she initially has do not enable her to conceptualize herself in any other way, Neesey is locked for the longest time in a family situation and a homespace that is more detrimental to her than not. Even when she manages to escape a few years later and attend Hampton, it is clear upon a return visit home that Margarete still wields power over her and that Luke edward still commands her attention and imagination. Sent by her mother to warn Luke edward that his boss is looking for him for possibly having stolen money, Neesey still tries to see her slacker brother, who is living with his girlfriend and their child, as the unblemished youth he was many years before when they first visited their grandmother. The fact that Neesey is matriculating to Hampton pales in comparison to her falling back into the patterns that dominated her early life. The apartment space has determined her outlook on the world, and her familial relationships have ensured that, though she may absent herself physically from Detroit, she can never escape the hold of subservience that her family wields over her.[42]

NOTES

1. A. J. Verdelle, *The Good Negress* (Chapel Hill: Algonquin Books, 1995). To date, there has been little sustained critical commentary on the novel. Reviewers were enthusiastic about it, but even they barely extended beyond a paragraph or a couple of hundred words of mostly summary comments. Shelley E. Reid intersperses a few comments about *The Good Negress* in her survey of novels and characters that have followed the works of Toni Morrison and Alice Walker. See Reid, "Beyond Morrison and Walker: Looking Good and Looking Forward in Contemporary Black Women's Stories," *African American Review* 34, no. 2 (Summer 2000): 313–28.

2. Sondra Washington has identified what she refers to as "girl-women" in African American literature and has focused her scholarly research on portrayals of such characters. She has also created a website that showcases research, conferences, publications, and blogs about black girl-women. See www.blackgirlhoodproject.com. I should also point out that some African American male adolescents were also conscripted to take care of younger siblings. James Baldwin provides one such example. For his discussion of his caregiving for his younger siblings (he was the oldest of nine children), see *Notes of a Native Son* (New York: Bantam, 1968).

3. Verdelle, *Negress*, 8.
4. Verdelle, *Negress*, 28.
5. Verdelle, *Negress*, 285.
6. Verdelle, *Negress*, 44.
7. Verdelle, *Negress*, 251.
8. Verdelle, *Negress*, 21.

9. Margarete's plan to turn over her baby to Neesey has echoes of what happens in Delores Phillips's *The Darkest Child* (New York: Soho, 2004; 2018). In that novel, Rosie Quinn insists that one of her teenage daughters, Martha Jean, assume primary responsibility for the unwanted, too-dark child to whom Rosie gives birth. Though Martha Jean is mute, she effectively raises the child as her own. While Margarete does not denounce her maternity as aggressively as Rosie does, it is still an abdication

of responsibility. Eventually, Rosie executes the ultimate rejection when she tosses her months-old daughter from her back porch into a ravine, thereby killing the child.

10. Verdelle, *Negress*, 115.
11. Verdelle, *Negress*, 87–88.
12. Verdelle, *Negress*, 9–10.
13. Lisa B. Day goes so far as to assert "that in form and content the novel both depends on and undermines the literary tradition of the slave narrative." See "'I Reach to Where the Freedom Is': The Influence of the Slave Narrative Tradition on A. J. Verdelle's *The Good Negress*," *Critique* 41, no. 4 (Summer 2000): 411.
14. Verdelle, *Negress*, 14.
15. Verdelle, *Negress*, 88.
16. Day, "Reach," 417.
17. Verdelle, *Negress*, 26.
18. Verdelle, *Negress*, 20.
19. Verdelle, *Negress*, 39–40.
20. Verdelle, *Negress*, 166.
21. Verdelle, *Negress*, 166.
22. Verdelle, *Negress*, 167–68.
23. Day, "Reach," 418.
24. See Jacob Lawrence's images at https://lawrencemigration.phillipscollection.org/
25. Verdelle, *Negress*, 63.
26. Verdelle, *Negress*, 65.
27. Verdelle, *Negress*, 84.
28. Verdelle, *Negress*, 218.
29. Verdelle, *Negress*, 120.
30. Verdelle, *Negress*, 122.
31. Verdelle, *Negress*, 160.
32. Verdelle, *Negress*, 192.
33. Verdelle, *Negress*, 257.
34. Verdelle, *Negress*, 191.
35. Verdelle, *Negress*, 284.
36. Verdelle, *Negress*, 193. This echoes again the kind of work that Rosie Quinn forces her teen-aged daughters to perform in Phillips's *The Darkest Child*. Martha Jean, the daughter to whom Rosie "gives" her last child, is especially put upon.
37. Day, "Reach," 420.
38. Verdelle, *Negress*, 255.
39. Verdelle, *Negress*, 209–10.
40. Verdelle, *Negress*, 251.
41. Verdelle, *Negress*, 273, 286.
42. Verdelle presents one very vivid example of parent/adolescent interactions in a troubled homespace. Two other novels that focus on female characters are Alice Childress, *Rainbow Jordan* (New York: Coward, McCann & Geoghegan, Inc., 1981) and Delores Phillips, *The Darkest Child* (New York: Soho, 2004; 2018). Although her homespace is slightly less troubled, Sistah Souljah's Winter in *The Coldest Winter Ever* (New York: Washington Square P, 1999) is also conscripted to take care of

her younger siblings. By contrast, a male teenager in Randall Kenan's *A Visitation of Spirits* (New York: Grove, 1989) is thoroughly alienated from his relatives and homespace, to the point of committing suicide. The adolescent, drug-using male protagonist in Alice Childress's *A Hero Ain't Nothin' But a Sandwich* (New York: Puffin Books, 1973) tries to find parental figures and places beyond his home to assist in navigating his difficult life journey. For poetic depictions of troubled homespaces, see Gwendolyn Brooks, *Children Coming Home* in *In Montgomery* (Chicago: Third World P, 2003), 77–103.

Chapter 4

A Mother's Desire, A Son's Hell
Daniel Black's Perfect Peace *(2010)*

Margarete is guilty of denying any educational aspirations Neesey may have and, without conscience, turning her into the equivalent of an enslaved person. She only values Neesey's labor, and she definitely does not want her newborn daughter. By contrast, Emma Jean Peace in Daniel Black's *Perfect Peace* (2010) represents the horror that a mother creates when she desires a child too desperately.[1] In this case, after she has six sons and is so devastated that her seventh delivery results in a son instead of a daughter, Emma Jean decides to raise the boy as a girl, a scheme that she succeeds in carrying out for eight years. The narrative begins in the 1940s in seriously isolated Swamp Creek, Arkansas, a place that only the most dedicated travelers can find. Emma Jean's husband Gustavus (Gus) Peace and his brother built the house in which the Peaces reside. As a home site, therefore, the house is away from neighbors and is not saturated with familial educational aspirations or enlightened approaches to living. The Peaces are farmers, with husband Gus having completed only the third grade and with Emma Jean not having appreciably more education. The isolation of the home and its physical space are matched in problematic creation by the family dynamic that gets carried out in that space. Home in the novel is one in which mother and father have a disturbing, at times disrespectful, relationship and where the mother's decision in response to the birth of her seventh child brings about decades of ramifications. What happens in their home, however, is a direct consequence of the impact of external forces upon it. The novel is exemplary in showing how what the world thinks about individuals and what those individuals have been taught to think about themselves can shape relationships and determine how characters view themselves in their own space as well as in connection to each other. It also epitomizes how race (the origin of pigmentocracy, or colorphobia, or colorism) and religion can destroy any potential family harmony.

Prejudices about skin coloring dominate almost everything in the novel and make it impossible for any of the houses to truly become homes.

PAINTED WITH A BRUSH OF TAR

Set against the backdrop of an American society that devalues blackness and has spawned in its own black citizens a hatred for themselves, *Perfect Peace* joins Toni Morrison's *The Bluest Eye* (1970) in illustrating how beauty culture in America and the devaluing of blackness taint characters' mental perceptions of themselves, their interactions with others, and any hopes they may have for envisioning healthy futures for themselves.[2] The issue of skin color, specifically the pigmentocracy that devalues dark skin color, informs almost all the events in the novel. It is what makes Emma Jean's mother treat her worse than any stepchild, encourages Emma Jean's sisters to join their mother in derisive and emotionally destructive behavior towards Emma Jean, leads Emma Jean to "settle" for Gus as a husband, prevents Gus from believing that his wife has any semblance of beauty, leads Emma Jean to decide to raise her youngest son as a girl, and serves as the impetus to antisocial behavior and lack of human kindness and forgiveness in almost all the characters in the text.

At points in African American history (and some would argue even contemporarily), persons of lighter skin tones were valued more highly than those with darker skins. Whether in folklore, tales of admission to various historically black colleges and universities (the brown paper bag test), applying for jobs, or a host of other incidents, darker-skinned black people in American society were taught that they were of lesser value. As the folk saying goes, "If you're brown, stick around, if you're white, you're right, if you're black, stay back." Numerous are the tales of black men asserting that they do not want to be saddled with "skillet blonds," which would describe Emma Jean perfectly. The history of devaluing and dismissal based on skin color found its way into the literature from the history of its creation on American soil. What is the passing tradition if not a rejection of darker skin? Frances Ellen Watkins Harper's *Iola Leroy* (1892) and Charles W. Chesnutt's *The House Behind the Cedars* (1900) are prime examples of passing novels.[3] Characters who are unable to pass also reject black skin or realize that others do so when gazing at them. Emma Lou in Wallace Thurman's *The Blacker the Berry* (1929) undertakes desperate attempts to lighten her skin, as does Florence in Baldwin's *Go Tell It on the Mountain* (1953). Little Lincoln West in Gwendolyn Brooks's poem is subject to the gaze of white gawkers who find him to be the epitome of their conception of the black and ugly racial stereotype. Pecola Breedlove implicitly rejects blackness in *The Bluest Eye* and bows to exterior gazes when her desperate quest for acceptance leads her to the imagined blue eyes that result in her mental instability.[4] As reflections of historical practices, the literature makes clear the rejections that such heavily-hued persons suffered—and suffer—in African American communities. In every instance, it is because the larger American society places more value on lighter skin, which in turn leads to their own black communities following suit, that each of these characters suffers as he or she does. Emma Jean is no exception; everything she does, everything she is has been shaped by her buying into a system of beauty that in turn has informed her home existence. For Emma Jean, the home of her childhood becomes a violent, unhealthy, and unsafe place for her simply because she is born the wrong color. Everything she does in life after that point is linked to that sad and destructive history of pigmentocracy.

Dark-skinned Emma Jean suffers through the trauma of her mother Mae Helen's considering her of significantly lesser value because of the darkness of her skin. This leads directly to Emma Jean's desperate desire for a daughter whom she can dress in girlie clothes and upon whom she can lavish the affection that was so missing in her relationship with her own mother. Born the third daughter of Mae Helen, who essentially prostitutes herself to get light-skinned children who will offset her own dark skin, Emma Jean Hurt is doomed to abuse and lack of affection from Mae Helen. In a brief flashback, readers meet Mae Helen, who has chosen her lovers solely for their skin color in order to ensure that she gives birth to light-skinned offspring. There is no desire for marriage and little for sustained relationships; she needs the men only as sperm donors. Her first foray into that venture yields two daughters, Emma Jean's older sisters, who are fathered by a man who does indeed pass on his lighter skin shade to Pearlie and Gracie. Emma Jean's father, even lighter than the sisters' father, sleeps with Mae Helen only to have Emma Jean "emerge" "with Mae Helen's navy blue complexion."[5] It is a comment on the internalization of self-hatred that Mae Helen has inherited and by which she lives that she despises Emma Jean. When Claude Lovejoy, Emma Jean's father, observes that Emma Jean looks "'jes' like'" Mae Helen, her response is "'Fuck you, nigga. Get the hell outta my house.'"[6] Claude is unable to convince Mae Helen to allow him to be a part of Emma Jean's life and unable, later—and after she has in turn been indoctrinated by Mae Helen—to convince Emma Jean to get to know her dark-skinned relatives.

Having dark skin in this fictional world is comparable to having leprosy. It will not wash away, and it pollutes everything around it. Those who have it struggle mightily to escape its clutches, and they hate themselves as well as those like themselves. The social pressures of this world are extraordinary, and weaker-willed persons, or at least persons of less authority and power, just get squashed by them. This is no more vividly revealed than on Emma

Jean's eighth birthday, when she asks her mother if there will be some marker of the occasion, perhaps some cake and ice cream. The vitriol that Mae Helen heaps upon Emma Jean is painful even to read:

> 'A party? Shiiiiiit! Ain't nobody wastin' no time on no goddamn party. We got work to do 'round here, girl.' She stood and stared at Emma Jean. 'I mean, who you think you is for real? You ain't nobody special. That's what I shoulda named you—Nobody.' . . .
>
> 'Ain't gon' be no goddamn birthday party 'round hyeah today, you black heffa!' Mae Helen screamed into Emma Jean's watery eyes. 'You must think you some rich white girl or somethin'. Well, you ain't! You's a po', ugly, black-ass nigga. That's what you is!' . . . .
>
> 'You think de world s'pose to stop and dance'—she mocked a jig—'jes' 'cause it's yo' birthday?' . . . 'You's a selfish li'l bitch, you know that?'[7]

Initially turning innocent childhood desire into calculated disruption, Mae Helen then adds injury to insult: "Mae Helen retrieved a cast-iron skillet from a nail on the wall . . . As though by reflex, she slammed the skillet against Emma Jean's forehead, then placed it on the stove," before ordering the dizzy, staggering Emma Jean to sweep the floor, then gather eggs for breakfast (she faints in the chicken coop).[8] The violent attack leaves Emma Jean with a "C-shaped mark" that onlookers will perceive as making her even more unattractive as she grows older.[9] Emma Jean receives such treatment while her sisters, who are a "golden hue," are allowed to remain in bed because "'pretty folks need plenty o' sleep.'"[10]

Thus Emma Jean is in an impossible situation, one in which her mother, having thoroughly absorbed the color preferences of her own community as well as those of the larger society, takes every opportunity to remind her how black and "ugly" she is. Of Emma Jean's hair, Mae Helen asserts: "'This is yo' daddy's nappy hair. My hair is nappy, but not like this. You need a mule and a plow for this briar patch.'"[11] In this home environment, Emma Jean is treated worse than in the many scenarios of maltreated stepchildren. At least stepchildren could hope for the possibility of rescue; Emma Jean is stuck with a violent, vengeful mother whose own self-hatred of her skin color leads her in turn to treat Emma Jean worse than any perverse stranger might. And the impetus to such treatment is always the white world that Mae Helen mentions in passing. Even as she asserts that Emma Jean must think she is some "rich white girl" to want a birthday party, Mae Helen's very existence is defined by the world of that rich white girl. Since Mae Helen obviously is not white, cannot date a white man (though she could have a child by one), and cannot bleach herself into that existence, she settles for the next best thing: she absorbs the skin value of that rich white girl and punishes Emma Jean's father and Emma Jean for not allowing her to approximate even more the traits of that world. The use of the word "nigga" (here and throughout the novel) is also an indication of self-perception from the perspective of white outsiders, and it is used insultingly again and again in the text. To Mae Helen, Emma Jean is an abomination, a throwback, a constant reminder that she, herself, has not met some abstract standard of skin color and beauty. Notably, skin color matters more than beauty; if Emma Jean were ugly but yellow, that would still satisfy Mae Helen. The fact that Emma Jean is labeled ugly *and* is decidedly dark-skinned is more than the self-hating Mae Helen can tolerate.

Distribution of resources that Mae Helen has also reflects a color bias. On one occasion, when she purchases beautiful yellow dresses for Easter for Pearlie and Gracie, she does not buy one for Emma Jean. That in itself is rejecting enough. Mae Helen carries it further, however, by refusing to allow Emma Jean to sit with the family on that fateful Easter Sunday. Emma Jean is relegated to a pew behind her mother and sisters, an occurrence that not only underscores a horrific family dynamic but the great division between professing Christians and the un-Christian, un-loving behavior that defines this family and so many characters in the novel. This spatial segregation in a public arena evokes the spatial and social separation that attends Emma Jean in Mae Helen's household, for she is always made to feel second-rate. Of note is the fact that Emma Jean's sister Gracie recounts this portion of the family history:

> 'Momma was wrong. She didn't have no business treating you that way. I remember you asking where your dress was and she told you to shut up and wear my old one. Of course it was too big and she never could get that huge chocolate ice cream stain off the front. Everybody told me and Pearlie how pretty we were, how pretty our hair was, how pretty our new shoes shined, and that was enough for Momma. We sat next to her on the front pew and she told you to sit behind us. She hadn't even done your hair.'[12]

It is perhaps difficult to imagine the intensity of this rejection based solely on skin color, especially when the rejection comes from the person who has given birth to the one being rejected. Equally worthy of note is that Gracie does not recount the incident because she, as one of the favored, felt any great sense of guilt at that point in time. She has come to Emma Jean to try to get her to visit their dying mother, and this is the tactic she uses in agreeing with Emma Jean that their mother has not treated her youngest daughter well—all because she did not have a "golden hue."

Mae Helen's hatred of blackness also extends to her curtailing Emma Jean's aspirations to become a dancer. Emma Jean's future, Mae Helen surmises, can only be one of subservience and childbearing: "She'd said, 'Is you ever heard of a black nigga dancer, girl? Huh? Is you? . . . Well, then! Do somethin' you can do . . . . Girl, find a man who'll have you and have as many babies as you can. Good as you sweep and clean up, you oughta be somebody's wife. If they'll have you.'"[13] On the scale of value by which Mae Helen operates, it is clear that she believes that Emma Jean is in the begging position, and it is only through the largesse of a generous man who will not mind her blackness (which Mae Helen credits more to Emma Jean's father's relatives than to herself) or her ugliness that she can hope to find some sort of fulfillment in life. Mae Helen wants Emma Jean to understand the bigness of the "If" in her final phrase, to understand that her position in the world is not something over which she has control, especially in a community in which most folks share her mother's perceptions. Being fed such poison so repeatedly, it is no wonder that Emma Jean rejects her father's overtures to get to know his family. She, like Mae Helen, in a class and color-inspired prejudice, looks down on the folks who live in the part of the town, "de Bottoms," associated with her father's relatives, and that is less a matter of geography than a matter of skin color. Without a solid rock of acceptance of any kind, Emma Jean can only be set adrift in terms of identity.[14] Thus she is doomed to perceive herself, even when she professes otherwise, through the eyes of others. Sadly, she has no living mirrors that project back to her any sense of value in herself.

Emma Jean's sisters, Pearlie and Gracie, echo their mother's sentiments in being fully baptized into self-rejection and embracing of colorphobia. They are also adamant in a similar judging of Emma Jean's chances in life. When the three are discussing boys they think are cute, for example, and whether or not they would "choose" a particular one, Pearlie "sneers" about one that Emma Jean mentions: "'You *couldn't* choose him, even if you wanted to!'" (italics in original), with the obvious implication that Emma Jean is too black and ugly for that young man to have the remotest interest in her.[15] The conversation continues as Emma Jean asks, "'Do y'all think I'm pretty?' Pearlie hollered. 'Of course not. But you nice, and that counts for somethin.'"[16] The sisters are silent when Emma Jean asks them if their mother, dark like her, is pretty, after which Pearlie offers what to her mind is the definitive explanation: "'Your looks come from your daddy,' Pearlie explained, 'and *your* daddy's people are real black jes' like you. He jes' happens to be yella,'" in response to which Emma Jean asks "'But cain't chu be dark *and* pretty'?,'" which leads the sisters to "frown" and reply "in unison, "'No'" (italics in original).[17] They put a coda to the conversation by expressing the same color and class sentiments that Mae Helen does by asserting that the Lovejoys, Emma Jean's father's people, "'live down in de Bottoms. It's a lotta dem Lovejoys runnin' 'round. They breed like rats, Momma said,'" which adds a sexual stereotyping dimension to their color and class phobias.[18] Absent living mirrors in her own home, and disallowing herself the opportunity to interact with them in the Bottoms, Emma Jean cannot hear when her father tells her that she is "'Black and beautiful jes' like'" his mother, so Emma Jean grows up apart from her family, herself, and the possibility of any truly healthy identity formation and movement into the future.[19] Her mind, her body, and everything that connects the two are thoroughly polluted as she enters adulthood.

While Gracie and Pearlie have been on the "right" side of color and have been more in agreement with their mother's disposition, Emma Jean has always caught the brunt of Mae Helen's disapproval as well as Mae Helen's verbal and physical abuse, which includes many beatings in addition to the skillet-braining. What will haunt Emma Jean throughout her life, however, is that fact that, despite the horrible things her mother has done to her, and despite the violence she has heaped upon her, Emma Jean still loves Mae Helen: "She loved her mother and that's what she hated most . . . . She hated how much she feared her mother, and she hated even more that she couldn't stop loving her."[20] Without any possibility of reciprocation from Mae Helen, Emma Jean is again doomed to an incomplete, unfulfilled emotional life and a hollow gap in the center of her being as far as parental connection is concerned. Given her home situation, in fact, it is a wonder that Emma Jean grows up with the modicum of common sense that she does have, though certainly some of the decisions she makes are highly questionable. In this world where Mae Helen judges the entire worth of her offspring on the superficial characteristic of skin color, there is little hope that a positive mother/daughter relationship could evolve or any healthy identity formation could result, and certainly there is no possibility for a healthy home.

With this negative home environment and Mae Helen's emotionally destructive parenting, therefore, it is no wonder that Emma Jean grows into an adult who passes down the same colorphobia poisons that have defined her existence. Though victimized by color discrimination, Emma Jean nonetheless inherits—and accepts—the aversion to dark skin that defines her mother and sisters. She is very much like a laboratory rat in an experiment, though the experiment and its results are one and the same. There is no opportunity for a do-over. Where she is at the end of living with her mother in terms of judging and responding to people on the basis of the color of their skin is mostly where she will be at the end of her life. She might not voice the same kind of ugliness that Mae Helen spews forth, but, in her interactions with her husband, sons, and neighbors, she is far from innocent in exhibiting color-based prejudices.

AN UNSAVORY BUT FUNCTIONAL MARITAL RELATIONSHIP

The extent to which Emma Jean has absorbed her mother's teaching is apparent initially in her attempt to find a marriage partner. Gus comes to her attention in the cotton fields, when his seemingly scrawny size belies the amount of cotton he can pick. Having picked three hundred pounds of cotton in a day, Gus catches Emma Jean's attention because "she knew Gus had to be a work mule, and more than anything, she liked working men."[21] Nonetheless, she finds Gus physically repulsive.

> However, his sharp African features disgusted her. With lips three times the size of her own, and big open nostrils that flared with each breath he took, Gus was rejected by most women, and Emma Jean most of all. Who would ever marry such an ugly, purple-black brute, she wondered. His smile and frown were barely distinguishable, and the first time Emma Jean saw his crusty, flat, fourteen-inch feet, she actually vomited.[22]

Locked into judging people by the superficial traits that her family has instilled in her, Emma Jean is just as judgmental of Gus as her family has been of her. As noted of Mae Helen earlier, she points out to Emma Jean that her choices are limited and that she should be responsive to any man who shows interest in her: "'You betta try to git dat man, girl!,' Mae Helen admonished after witnessing Emma Jean's repulsion. 'What other choices you got?'"[23] Eighteen when she meets Gus, Emma Jean swears that she will "never lay" with him, but, "a year later, after having been ignored by every other man in Swamp Creek, she cried her way to the altar and married the man she loathed."[24] He promises to keep working, and she promises to try to give him a son. There is no love lost on either side and no pretense that there is any romance or perhaps even liking in this union. It is a functional consequence of being in the environment they are in and adhering to the larger communal expectations that those of a certain age should get married.

With no love freely given and with only a perfunctory response to each other, Gus and Emma Jean embark upon a marriage that will yield sons but no true lovemaking and no true affection. They will live in a house and grow a family there, but there is little true valuing of familial relationships. They are committed to each other, but that commitment, again, is primarily a function of expectations of the time. His brother, Chester Jr., had helped Gus build a house because he *expected* that Gus would get married at some point. Gus is committed to working because he *expects* that he will have a family to support at some point. Gus and Emma Jean go to church together on Sunday because they are *expected* to do so; it is, after all, what families do, so Gus believes. There is no part of the implicit contract, no part of the bargain, which suggests a husband must compliment his wife on any consistent basis or bolster her self-image/ego. On their wedding night, for example, when Emma Jean asks Gus, "'Do you think I'm pretty?,'" "Gus stared at her sleepily and said, 'I ain't never really thought about it.' Emma Jean almost slapped him, but decided that, as long as he worked, she wouldn't trouble him about such frivolous matters."[25] Healthy self-esteem is obviously not a frivolous matter, but Emma Jean, just as her sisters will do later, has settled for the form of marriage if not the substance of it. And, with the bearing of children, some of the substance does arrive.

In the house that Gus and Chester Jr. have built, therefore, the idea of a true home is besmirched before Gus and Emma Jean even enter the dwelling together. Their interactions are defined by heavily prescribed gender roles (husband works, wife cooks and cleans) that reflect those of the era and the society in which they are created. Discussions about gender roles are numerous in the novel, and they range from children reciting what they have heard and witnessed with their parents, to church folks suggesting that such roles are Biblically based, to Gus's own experience in his father's house.[26] Between Gus and Emma Jean, therefore, there are only male and female roles to be played. There is no true intimacy, no expansive conversation, and nothing to deviate from the routine of farming and producing children into which they settle. And produce children they do. Six sons come in rapid succession: James Earl, Authorly, Woody, King Solomon, Blind Bartimaeus, and Mister. After the birth of Perfect, his seventh child, Gus sleeps on the floor to avoid further sexual contact with Emma Jean. In this community, with its emphasis upon church going and proper behavior, sex is viewed as the necessary pathway to procreation. Enjoyment might occur during that process, but it gets toned down in favor of what is more respectable, in this case, not showing open desire for one's wife—and refusing to admit directly that one even has desire. Black marks Gus's suppression of desire: "Gus, who usually slept like a hibernating bear—and snored like one, too!—was awakened by the sound of Perfect's lips smacking on Emma Jean's nipple, and, for a brief moment, he wished the lips were his own. However, as he recalled the connection between sucking Emma Jean's breasts and her subsequent pregnancies, his erection subsided and he returned to sleep."[27]

The circumstances surrounding the birth of the couple's seventh child have become the site of contention in the marriage and have led to sexual abstinence on Gus's part as well as to his sleeping on the floor. For Gus, the decision is perhaps more a matter of economics than it is the loss of pleasure. As a black man in the deep South who has sworn that he will not earn any of the financial support for his family by working for whites, Gus needs help from his sons with his farm, but he also realizes that the demands of feeding nine people on the iffy whims of nature are challenging at best. The Peaces are surviving financially, but just barely. Another mouth to feed, therefore, is something for which Gus is not willing to allow. If a father sleeps on the floor and a mother sleeps in the bed, the estrangement that that physical arrangement suggests must surely have ramifications in the interactions of that couple, and the sons in the family must undoubtedly sense some of that tension, especially since there are only two bedrooms in the house. Nonetheless, Gus and Emma Jean move forward with their lives in the union to which both are committed but in which neither finds long-term, sustained pleasure, not to mention happiness.

In settling for Gus, Emma Jean, as noted, brings with her the prejudices that she has acquired from her own family. Those prejudices continue to make clear that outside forces—not just from white society but from the white-polluted black families in the community—inform familial and domestic interactions. Emma Jean is as free in her references to her family as "niggas" as her mother has been in relation to her and as the larger white community is in relationship to all blacks. Derogatory references adorn her speech as she refers to her husband and sons as "greedy niggas."[28] Mae Helen's impact is constant, for, when she visits, she in turn refers to Emma Jean and Gus's sons as "'nappy-headed niggas'" who eat "'like hogs.'"[29] When Emma Jean chastises that Mae Helen talks "'about Gus like a dog'" and treats the boys "'like they ain't nothin'!,'" Mae Helen's retort is, "'I speak to dem ugly children all the time!'"[30] Finally fed up, Emma Jean tells Mae Helen to "'kiss her ass'" and puts her out.[31] Her physical removal, however, does nothing to erase the impact that Mae Helen continues to have upon Emma Jean and, notwithstanding Emma Jean's objections to her mother, the passing on to her own family much of the poison that Mae Helen instilled in her. Standards of beauty and acceptance continue to saturate Emma Jean's emotional life. Those prejudices mingle with Emma Jean's desire for a daughter to produce a strange concoction in this family.

A DEFENSIBLE DESIRE OR A PERVERTED DELUSION?

Having suffered through her mother's dislike and emotional and physical abuse, Emma Jean Peace envisions having a daughter whom she can use as a corrective in establishing a relationship that could possibly erase the bad memories of her interactions with her own mother. However, Emma Jean sees her dreams of an adorable and adoring daughter fade as she gives birth to son after son. She is so desperate that, although she loves her sons, she expresses frustration after each successive male arrival. When son number six arrives, and she sees its penis, "she looked heavenward and mumbled, 'Damn you.'

Then she screeched, 'Gus! Come get this!' He knew it was another boy. 'You name him whatever you like. It don't make me no difference.'"[32] On the other hand, "Gus thanked a merciful God he'd never have to raise a girl."[33] Emma Jean's disappointment and Gus's relief coalesce around the birth of the next child. Certain that her seventh pregnancy will yield the daughter for whom she has waited for more than twelve years, Emma Jean simply rejects the midwife's declaration that she has given birth to yet another son. Instead, she blackmails the midwife—who has a shadowy past surrounding her having taken her sister's child upon a delivery that killed the mother and informing her brother-in-law, whom she despises, that the child had died—into keeping silent about the gender of the child. Excited by her own audacity, Emma Jean decides to raise her seventh son as a girl. She does so as much out of her own desire as her belief that God is making mockery of her: "*God must think this is funny*, she thought. *Why does He love to watch people suffer? What kind of God is He anyway? Aren't people supposed to get* something *they want before they die, especially if they've never had anything?*" (italics in original).[34] Because "she couldn't foresee a future without the daughter she'd imagined," Emma Jean proceeds with her scheme to turn a boy into a girl.[35]

The scheme works surprisingly well for eight years, during which Emma Jean controls the situation by employing a couple of strategies. She makes sure that none of the males in her household ever changes Perfect's diapers or in any other way encounters her nakedness. She refuses to allow Perfect to play rough and tumble with her brothers, though Perfect would like to do that more than anything else. Everything is fine for those eight years and would possibly have remained so for longer if Perfect had not asked Emma Jean when she would start bleeding (menstruating), since one of her slightly more mature friends had informed Perfect that bleeding is something that all girls do. At this point, Emma Jean realizes that continuing the scheme is untenable, and she voluntarily reveals the child's true gender. Prior to that revelation, however, the lie has enabled Emma Jean to achieve what she has desired most of all—a loving, reciprocal relationship with a daughter. The consequences of Emma Jean's audacity, on the other hand, include further deterioration of her relationship with her husband Gus, violent eruptions from Gus, homophobia from the family as well as the community, a confused offspring who is fated to a lifetime of trying to sort through his identity, and a turn of events that leads to Emma Jean's mental deterioration and subsequent death.

Before things unravel, Emma Jean has benefited tremendously from the deception. Having a daughter is the fulfillment of her every dream. It enables her to smooth over the disappointments she has felt as a child with her own mother, it ensures a special bond with one of her offspring, and it allows her to parade her revised motherhood status before the community, a community that plays a key role in the sequence of events that occurs in the remainder of the novel. By making Perfect into a girl, Emma Jean rewrites the script of the most negatively memorable interactions she has had with Mae Helen. Initially, Emma Jean is able to dress her "daughter" Perfect in ways that Mae Helen never did with her. She thereby smooths over the hurtful memory of that fateful Easter Sunday when Mae Helen did not purchase a dress for her and did not allow her to sit with the family in church. Emma Jean forces her sons out of one of the bedrooms (the house has only two), has it repainted, and gives it exclusively to Perfect. This echoes the occasion on which Emma Jean's father arrives and invites her to get to know her people. Mae Helen is disappointed that Emma Jean has not gone and claims to Pearlie and Gracie: "'Ump, ump, ump. Y'all almost had a bed to y'allself,'" a statement that will remain imbedded in Emma Jean's mind and imagination for the rest of her life.[36] That a mother would dismiss or be willing to part ways with her daughter so easily can only traumatize Emma Jean even more. She never forgets what her mother's suggestion of her disappearance would have meant for the privacy of her sisters, so she provides Perfect the kind of privacy that she never had in Mae Helen's household. Emma Jean also takes from family belongings as well as from the family coffers to ensure that Perfect has pretty dresses and ribbons, again echoing that Easter Sunday incident. When she introduces the six-week-old Perfect to her church community, for example, she dresses her in an "exquisite white lace dress . . . fashioned from the one good tablecloth the family owned" and adorns her hair with yellow ribbons (yellow seems to be the constant reminder of the mistreatment in clothing that Mae Helen has heaped upon an innocent Emma Jean).[37]

Even more specifically in terms of rewriting the script of her own childhood, Emma Jean takes much-needed money from household expenses and purchases a doll for Perfect as her Christmas present when Perfect is four years old; this echoes the occasion on which Mae Helen bought a doll and said that Pearlie, Gracie, and Emma Jean should share it, though Emma Jean quickly concluded that there was no room for her in that so-called sharing. The doll is thus emblematic of the lack of parental affection that Emma Jean has experienced. More striking, however, is the fact that it brings sharply into focus the outside forces and standards of evaluation that have guided Emma Jean, her family, and their community, for the doll is conspicuous in its whiteness.

> 'Ohhhhhhhh,' [Perfect] cried as shreds of newspaper fell to the floor. 'Oh, Momma! Look! My very own baby doll!'
> 'That's right, honey, your very own baby doll. Now make sure you take care 'o her. Me and yo' daddy spent good money for that.'
> *I didn't spend nothin'*, Gus thought.

'Oh, I'll take care of her, Momma! I promise! She's so pretty!' Perfect studied the doll's yellow hair and aqua blue eyes, cast against an off-white face. She wore a frilly pink dress that flared at the waist, and snow-white shoes. The doll's legs were thick like table legs . . . .

' . . . And remember what I said: take good care of her. Most little Negro girls in Swamp Creek ain't never had no baby doll, and they sho ain't had no new one.'

'I love you, Momma!' Perfect embraced Emma Jean's waist tightly. 'You the best momma in the whole wide world!'

Emma Jean kissed Perfect's head. 'You welcome, sweetie. Ain't nothin' too good for my baby girl. Now run on and play and let me get breakfast ready.'[38] (italics in original)

Emma Jean has sacrificed much just to hear Perfect declare that she is "the best momma in the whole wide world." Making some of the same mistakes that Mae Helen did, Emma Jean is blind in her ignoring of her husband and sons in favor of Perfect. Gus clearly has not approved the purchase; Emma Jean has simply taken the money, bought the doll, and claimed that it was a joint mother-father effort. Perfect gets the doll while the sons get shirts and overalls. Indeed, Mister, the son immediately older than Perfect, gets slapped when he comments: "' . . . she got somethin' to play with and I didn't get nothin' but a old—'" (87), thus Mister, in this moment, is relegated to the same position of enviousness and jealousy that Emma Jean experienced when Mae Helen neglected her in favor of Pearlie and Gracie.[39]

External values attached to the doll get highlighted yet again when Perfect names the doll "Olivia": "'That's the woman's name on the radio show. She sounds really pretty. And white. Just like you.'"[40] With Emma Jean's help with the spelling, Gus then engages in a ritual in which he carves "Olivia" into the wall above the bed where Perfect sleeps, thus the doll will "'see it every morning when she wakes up!'"[41] So, too, will Perfect, and she will in turn be reminded constantly of the standards of beauty that are preferable in the world in which she lives. Although she imitates her mother in taking care of the doll's hair and complaining about its unruliness, that is simply a daughter imitating a mother, for "Perfect rubbed the doll's hair with envy. She wished her hair was like that: soft, silky, easy to brush."[42] And so continues the cycle of Maya Angelous, Pecola Breedloves, Pauline Breedloves, Emma Jean Peaces, and countless other historical and fictional characters who desired whiteness in their lives, frequently through references to hair and its manageability. On the other hand, Mister, in his jealousy, echoes the young Claudia MacTeer in *The Bluest Eye* when he wants "to yank the doll from Perfect's lap and rip it apart, one limb at a time."[43]

In a sequence that revises specifically the eighth birthday scene that she experiences with Mae Helen, Emma Jean plans an elaborate eighth birthday party for Perfect. It is the epitome of her re-writing the script of her life with Mae Helen. Three days before the party, Emma Jean goes through the neighborhood announcing the event in the manner of a town crier, "heralding Perfect's eighth birthday party like Gabriel proclaiming the birth of Christ."[44] In anticipation of the party, Emma Jean takes money from Gus's overalls and buys yellow ribbons to decorate the living room, then, together, she and Perfect bake a "three-layer lemon cake" with "chocolate icing" in another one of the bonding moments that her scheme has been designed to bring about.[45] When her efforts are rewarded with "the who's who of Swamp Creek's black elite" in attendance at Perfect's party, one of whom brings the gift of a scarf that "only white girls usually wore," everything seems to have reached the pinnacle of Emma Jean's desires.[46] "Emma Jean stepped back, folded her arms, and smiled with pride. This was the party she had envisioned forty years earlier. The yellow ribbons, chocolate-frosted cake, neighborhood friends, homemade ice cream . . . she had dreamed it all. Why couldn't Mae Helen have done this?" (ellipses in original).[47] She also regrets that Mae Helen did not "tuck" her "'in at night and read [her] bedtime stories. Like white folks do with their kids.'"[48]

The occasion is indeed the pinnacle of Emma Jean's imagined success, for that day begins the unraveling of her scheme. During the cake baking, Perfect has asked about menstruation, and, during the party, Emma Jean's two sisters arrive to inform her that their mother has died. Emma Jean, angry that her sisters would even think of suggesting that she attend her mother's funeral, throws a fit and disrupts the perfect party. Unable to get the question about menstruation out of her head, and knowing that it will not go away, Emma Jean takes control of the situation by ending the scheme herself, on her own terms, instead of having someone else do it for her. Thus, the day after the party is the point at which Emma Jean begins her confrontation with truth. She abruptly takes Perfect into the woods behind their house, cuts her hair, forces her to put on boy's underwear and overalls, and returns to the house to announce to her family that the child they knew as a girl is really a boy. Only Blind Bartimaeus had unknowingly discovered Perfect's secret when Perfect revealed that she had a "thing" like the bull who was having sex with a cow (Emma Jean has allowed Perfect to be in Bartimaeus's company more than the others precisely because he is blind). Shocked into silence, Bartimaeus had kept the secret and instructed Perfect never to let anyone touch her down there again or to see her without clothing. He had not, however, fully explained to Perfect what his discovery meant, so Perfect went on being a "girl."

To say that the sequence of events is traumatizing for Perfect would be a vast understatement. It is equally traumatizing for the males of the Peace household. Emma Jean's revelation, as noted, has intended as well as unintended consequences. Those consequences obviously start with Perfect, but they continue with Gus. A shaky marriage from the beginning must now undergo its severest test, and Gus is unforgiving in the face of Emma Jean's announcement:

> 'I lied. I told y'all the child was a girl, but it wasn't.'
> Now Bartimaeus understood.
> Gus inched forward in slow motion, studying Emma Jean's face.
> 'I needed a girl!' she proclaimed. 'Cain't you understand that? Every mother wants a girl. It's a woman's dream.'
> 'What?' Gus whispered in fury. 'You did what?' He was approaching like a starving lioness before the kill . . .
> Gus slapped Emma Jean so hard the boys gasped and held their breaths.[49]

Traumatized Perfect slips into the background as the shock of the revelation strikes the family. He is humiliated and traumatized even more when Gus insists that Emma Jean "prove" that Perfect is indeed male. Embarrassed by having to strip naked before his father and brothers, Perfect hears Gus exclaim, "'No! Oh God, no!'" when he sees the "miniature penis," which prompts him to attack Emma Jean.[50]

> Gus lunged at her before Authorly could restrain him. He smacked Emma Jean's face three or four times, then pinned her neck to the floor with his thick, rough hands. 'What did you do this for! You ain't got no right to do nobody like this! What the hell is wrong with you!' Emma Jean couldn't breathe. 'You didn't have to do this!" He might have strangled her to death had Authorly not jumped on Gus's back and, with Woody's assistance, wrestled Gus's hands away from her throat.[51]

Then, "too angry and confused to purge, he simply escaped to the barn and shouted every curse word he knew instead of murdering the mother of his children." [52] Thus the usually meek Gus turns to violence in direct response to what Emma Jean has done. This change in his behavior will mark a transformed Gus for the remainder of the narrative. Not only is he unable to forgive Emma Jean—though he does emphasize that they will remain together as a family—but he is unable, initially, to love the son he renames "Paul." Implicit in his reaction to what he learns about Perfect is an ingrained homophobia that reflects the larger community's attitude toward "sissies." It leads immediately to Gus's failure as a father and to his inability to respond in any healthy way to his youngest son. Initially, not thinking at all about Perfect, Gus is more disturbed for himself than he is considerate of Perfect's trauma as he reflects: "A boy? Perfect was a boy? All these years he had been kissing a boy."[53] With the focus on himself instead of upon the boy who has been traumatized, Gus will therefore join with his other sons in working exceptionally hard over the years to get "the girl" out of Paul. And he is nowhere near ready to love the transformed child, for "he stood there, like a ghost, unable to love the son he had adored as a daughter" and "Actually, he felt guilty that he couldn't love an innocent—and effeminate—son, so much so that he would kick the shit out of him."[54] Violent disruptions define Gus whenever he believes that Paul has reverted to his girlie ways. For example, when Gus learns that the newly created Paul has reverted to his old habits of playing with his friends Eva Mae and Caroline, his reaction is swift and physical:

> Gus's left hand struck Paul's neck so hard he crumpled to the ground. 'You don't play wit' no girls, boy! Boys play wit' boys!' . . .
> I ain't gon' have no goddamn sissy in my house!' Gus kicked Paul repeatedly. 'You gon' be a man if you gon' live here!' . . .
> Blood oozed from Paul's nose by the time the family appeared. Woody grabbed one of Gus's arms and Authorly took the other. 'Stop it, Gus! Stop it!' Emma Jean shouted.
> 'What'd he do, Daddy?' Authorly asked.
> Gus continued kicking him. 'You gon' be a boy! You gon' be a boy! You gon' be a boy!'[55]

Gus's reaction is not appreciably unlike the hatred that Mae Helen heaps upon Emma Jean—just for being who she was at the time. Gus, like everyone else in the text, is so saturated with the values of the surrounding society that he is superimposing that society's expectations upon his own home—to the detriment of a very sensitive and hurting young person who has only recently learned that he must live his life and reconceptualize his sense of self and identity in a totally different manner than the one he has been taught.

Gus's homophobia causes Gus to be equally unforgiving on the one occasion when Paul, as a teenager, goes to the barn and cross dresses in a dress and shoes belonging to Emma Jean—just because he misses what he has been told can no longer be a part of his existence. Gus's reaction is just as vehement as it was earlier, though on this occasion he does not go beyond slapping Paul.

> 'You ain't no punk, boy! I done taught you better! Boys don't wear no woman's clothes!' With each word, Gus ripped the dress until it lay in shreds across the barn floor. Paul covered his naked chest with his arms and prayed Gus wouldn't kill him.
> 'Is you just determined to be a sissy the rest o' you' life? Huh!' . . . 'You ain't no faggot, boy! You ain't!'
> Paul nodded.

'I done taught you how to be a man, me and your brothers, so ain't no excuse for this shit.' . . . 'Now clean up this crap and get in the house. And I don't wanna hear nothin' more about it.' Gus hobbled away heavily.[56]

Almost as disappointed in Paul's behavior as he has been with Emma Jean's, Gus nonetheless adheres to a standard of judgment that forces his family to comply with unwritten rules that outsiders have created. Such practices only intensify the unhealthy homespace and homelife.

What is especially striking about Gus's homophobia is that he himself had been suspected of being too effeminate when he was younger. After his mother died, he was inconsolable and cried all the time. Of his father, he remembers: "Those had been the only times Chester Sr. had beaten him—when he cried like a girl—and he promised his father, after the last lashing, that he wouldn't be a sissy. Now he promised himself he wouldn't raise one, either."[57] After his first beating of Paul, to which, hours later, he offers a mumbled "sorry," he tries after Paul's episode with a life-threatening fever years later to explain his intentions, which are based again in his own home life.

'My daddy taught me that ain't nothin' worse than a sissified man, and I didn't want you to be one. I still don't. I guess I been too embarrassed to talk to you directly. Folks' whisperin' made me nervous. You know how I am.' . . .

'I guess this ain't been easy for you, either, huh? I know the kids pro'bly tease you at school and stuff.' He paused. 'And I'm sorry for beatin' you the way I did that day. When I saw you comin' down the road, you was twistin' like a girl, and I got so mad I couldn't see straight. But I didn't mean to kick you. I even told God I didn't and God told me to tell you, but I never did. I was too 'shamed, I guess . . . . After Momma died, I couldn't seem to stop cryin'. Daddy and Chester poked fun at me and said I was gon' be a sissy when I grew up. I told them I wasn't. They said I was weak and didn't have no backbone 'cause ain't no boy s'pose to cry all the time. But I couldn't help it.'[58]

It is a testament to familial and communal pressures that Gus, despite his backstory, treats Paul the way he does initially. His finally talking to Paul and articulating what has happened to him might assuage his own conscience, and it might even make Paul feel better for a moment, but it does not negate the fact that Gus has allowed external and familial forces to shape his family life in a most detrimental way and to have a tremendous negative impact upon his home. Once he began his rituals of going to the Jordan and crying during the spring rains, his neighbors at least learned to tolerate his howling spells. And they, like Shadrack's neighbors in Morrison's *Sula*, learned to set aside a place for him in the community. "As much as they had criticized him, they needed ole Gus Peace now to confirm that the world wasn't coming to an end."[59]

Again, Gus's homophobia is drawn from and shared by Gus's community as well as the members of Gus's family, which means that a circle of disapproval recreates and strengthens itself repeatedly as the consequences of Emma Jean's actions are revealed at home as well as outside the home. Authorly, who is the second oldest of Emma Jean's sons but the one to whom the others look up, shares with Gus his distaste for "sissies" and assumes as his personal assignment Paul's transformation from girl to boy. He is impatient with Paul in all of his interactions with him, which perhaps reflects as much an anger with Emma Jean and the entire situation as it reflects a frustration with Paul's slowness in learning his new lessons. Those lessons include Paul's lowering the register of his voice from the "raspy soprano" that emerges when his brothers try to train him otherwise. "'Stop that!,'" Authorly shouts when Paul speaks his name, "'You gotta do it right! You can't go 'round this community soundin' like no sissy!'"[60] Authorly shoves Paul to the floor and forces him to repeat his name again and again. "'I don't want no sissy for a brother,'" he offers in explanation to his brothers, whom he considers to be "babying" Paul instead of insisting, as Authorly does, that Paul make more rapid progress on his path to de-girlification.[61] When Paul screeches like a girl when he sees a snake, his brother Mister chops the head off the snake, and Authorly takes over.

> Authorly lifted the headless creature and presented it to Paul. 'Hold this.'
> Paul froze.
> 'I said hold this! Ain't no country boy scared o' no snake. Here! Take it!'
> Even Gus thought Authorly was a bit too much, but he didn't stop hm.
> Paul stared at the snake dangling from Authorly's monstrous hand.
> 'Ima slap you if you don't take this snake, boy!'
> Woody and Sol expected Gus to say something. When he didn't, they stepped toward Authorly simultaneously.
> Paul wanted to obey, but fear paralyzed him.
> Authorly's left hand came so fast that Paul never saw it, but he felt the sting.
> 'I said hold this, boy!'[62]

Eventually, Paul obeys, but instead of being allowed to pinch the snake with his "thumb and index finger," Authorly forces him to grasp the snake "with his entire palm."[63] This brutal lesson comes shortly after Emma Jean's revelation, when Paul is still only eight years old. From learning how to hold his penis and urinate standing up instead of squatting to wielding the farm tools that his brothers and father handle with ease, Paul undergoes an unforgiving initiation that has as its primary impetus the refusal to allow a "sissy" to grow up in the Peace household. Although a couple of the brothers are not sympathetic to the pace at which Paul's lessons are crammed down his throat, they are all in agreement about the necessity of Paul's learning the lessons. It is not simply a matter of Paul's place within the family but also Paul's place within a community that Authorly believes will be equally unforgiving of a male child who has effeminate ways.

Authorly's fears are realized when the family returns to church for the first time after Perfect becomes Paul and reiterate, yet again, the impact of external forces upon homespace. Few of the neighbors actually have to vocalize the aversion to homosexuality, for the Peace family members have internalized the societal directive thoroughly. Nonetheless, these so-called Christians are as ugly and judgmental in their reactions to Paul as Gus and Authorly have been. "'I told y'all that heffa was crazy!'," offers Miss Mamie, a prominent member of the community. "'Didn't I tell you! Lawd have mercy! Ain't no tellin' what that woman done done to dat chile. How you make a li'l girl into a boy? Huh? Somebody tell me dat.'"[64] In response to Miss Mamie's grandson's declaring, "'That ain't no boy! And if it is, he gon' be a faggot the rest o' his life!,'" Authorly "slams" his fist against the critic's head. Miss Mamie and her grandson are representative of the general communal attitude toward Paul—judgmental, name-calling, and insensitive.[65]

Adults who profess to be Christian seem to take pleasure in gossipy responses to Paul, as an exchange at the local store to which Gus has sent Paul and Mister for supplies makes clear.

> From a distance, a group of old men, sitting on a worn church pew in front of the store, looked up as the boys approached.
>
> 'That's him right there,' Stump murmured. . . . He don't look like no boy to me. You ever seen a boy twist like that?'
>
> Charles Simmons, chairman of the trustee board at St. Matthew, shook his head sadly. He'd had a son *like that*, he remembered. Thirty years ago. Before he sent him away forever. 'That child ain't gon' never be right. You mark my word.' . . .
>
> 'That boy is sweet as sugar! Shit! I don't know what Gus gon' do with him,' Stump said.
>
> Paul was standing just inside the screen door, listening.
>
> 'I don't know, either, but I'm glad it ain't me. I couldn't have nothin' like that in my house.' Charles spit tobacco into the road. 'Gus need to send that child off somewhere.'
>
> 'What good would that do?'
>
> 'A whole lot! Least folk 'round here wouldn't have to look at him every day.'
>
> 'Well, maybe Gus is tougher than we thought. But I'm like you—I couldn't take it.' His face grimaced as if he'd suddenly smelled something dead. 'I can take a whole lot o' things, but I can't stand no punk. And that boy gon' be a punk the rest o' his life. That's for sure. Ain't nothin' else he *can* be.'[66] (italics in original)

And the men proceed to make jokes about Paul, who is devastated by the talk and even more devastated when one of the men asks if he is indeed a boy "*'for real?'*" (italics in original).⁶⁷ Paul is treated like a blood-thirsty two-headed monster or a devouring four-legged beast that is intent upon destroying his community. The intensity of dislike and disapproval, especially when one of the speakers is hiding behind his mistreatment of his own son, sets the pattern for neighbor reaction throughout the text. And it underscores the non-loving, non-Christian responses of these folks who are wrapped up in religious rituals and practices and who hold church offices from which they are expected, ironically, to be models of moral behavior for others.

Aside from his friends Eva Mae and Caroline, a sympathetic teacher named Miss Erma, and of course Emma Jean, Paul is adrift in a harsh world in which the consequences of Emma Jean's action redound upon his head again and again. Unable to perform—at least consistently—to the masculine imperative of his family and his community, Paul suffers repeatedly. His suffering obviously begins shortly after Emma Jean's revelation, when he sits and cries and is essentially relegated to visible invisibility while others discuss his fate. His aloneness and his new identity saturate his reflections.

> Everyone agreed that he was a boy now, and there was nothing he could do about it. In the past, Emma Jean had made the lump irrelevant, but now it seemed to be the center of things, hanging freely and shifting slightly whenever he moved. It obviously meant more than Emma Jean had said. Gus and the brothers' reaction to it, lying at the base of Paul's flat stomach, suggested that, in fact, it meant everything. They had stood and gazed, waiting to see if Paul had what other men have, and when they discovered he did, they immediately began constructing for him a new, masculine Self. It was as if the penis were the male identifier, the main thing, the *only* thing that made a boy *a boy*, and Paul now knew why Emma Jean had gone to great lengths to trivialize it.⁶⁸ (italics in original)

Reconciling what that penis means in his life, actions, relationships, behavior, education, and profession occupies Paul for the remainder of the text.

Thus the major consequence of Emma Jean's scheme is a permanent crisis in identity for Perfect-turned-Paul. Having been treasured, pampered, and valued as Perfect, Paul now finds that he is just another hard-leg male, who is to work like a mule in the fields, abstain from outward expressions of affection, and develop a nonchalant attitude about many things in the world. Detachment from emotional expression and not having anyone tell him how special and pretty/handsome he is become the major lacks in Paul's life as he tries desperately to fit into his newly created identity. That new creation means he and Emma Jean can never share the girly moments of intimacy in which he basked for eight years. It means initially a rejection of the relationship with Eva and then redefining that relationship. It means hostility from practically all the males he encounters, including the four who beat him mercilessly and rape him when he is fifteen. It means learning to perform as a male even as he is trying to determine what that really entails. Most important, it means a confusion and a mixture of erotic feelings. His friend Eva Mae has led him to discover the pleasures of the flesh during the days when they played house, but Paul is uncertain as to whether the "tingling" feeling his mother has told him he would experience when he fell in love is one that should be directed toward men or women. At times flailing in a world that he did not create with emotions that he must sift through, Paul finds himself attracted to the same young man, Johnny Ray Youngblood, who eventually works with Mister and the NAACP in registering folks to vote. It is a teenage crush that Paul sustains for years, only to discover that Johnny Ray is really in love with Paul's brother Mister. Thus one of the greatest ironies of the text is that the most virile, masculine-looking, and muscular of the Peace sons, namely Mister, is the one who embraces his homosexuality and eventually leaves to join Johnny Ray in a new life in Atlanta.

For Paul, the difficulty of treading his way through the uncertainty of an identity is not fully resolved by text's end. Certainly he is attracted to Johnny Ray, but he is also attracted to a young woman named Christiana and invites her to the fateful dance that brings several things to fruition in the text. Though Paul likes Christiana, it is clear that he will not move forward in a relationship and possible marriage with her. His confusion in identity, a consequence that Emma Jean obviously did not anticipate in her turning a boy into a girl, is realized more stereotypically in bisexual activities than homosexual activities, which means that he decides to become a designer, a male and female profession, and has no stated romantic involvement by the end of the text.[69] What he has achieved, finally, is uniform acceptance from his brothers and his father. Having begun with an inability to love the newly designated Paul, Gus moves to accepting and loving his son after he watches over him through that life-threatening fever. Sol, the singing son who has gone off to Howard University and earned a degree after Emma Jean took him out of school so that Paul could enroll, recognizes immediately upon his return to visit the family four years later that Paul is attracted to men. He asks Paul if there is someone he has been "looking at" and then follows up with "'What's *his* name?'" (my emphasis).[70] The other brothers meet Paul in New York and celebrate with him on the occasion of his first fashion show.

Since this latter scene occurs outside the space of Swamp Creek, it would perhaps be difficult to argue that a uniform "yes, we will embrace our possibly gay brother" attitude has emerged. It is perhaps safer to argue that familiarity in this case has lessened contempt. At least the brothers see, especially Woody the preacher, who has vehemently preached against homosexuality, that Paul has been able to make a life and a living for himself by doing something that he loves, that is, designing clothes.[71] As Sol has told him on that return visit to Swamp Creek, he needs to pursue his passion against all naysayers, and that is what Paul has done. Achievement thus overshadows rejection, and family togetherness overshadows family dissolution. The home environment for Paul might have been hellacious for years, but the entire family has perhaps matured into another space of operation. After all, in New York together, the brothers are able to witness all kinds of people and all kinds of behavior. They can see that, if their baby brother has made it in this kind of environment, then perhaps he can make it anywhere.

Paul survives and thrives. Emma Jean does not. The greatest consequence of her transforming a boy into a girl is the dissolution of her own mental health and her ultimate death. The midwife, Henrietta, responds to Emma Jean's scheme with a crucial question: "'You can't be serious! What kinda mother would do this to a child?'"[72] It is a question that Gus echoes later when he comments to Emma Jean "'This ain't gon' neva make no sense to me, woman. Neva. I cain't believe no mother would do this to her own child. I jes' cain't believe it.'"[73] Emma Jean can and does—at least for eight years. At that mark, when things unravel and she becomes less dominant in her own household, she begins to lose her way. Burned severely in a cooking accident, she deteriorates even further, which leads Gus to believe that this is just the beginning of Emma Jean's punishment, a sentiment with which Henrietta agrees.[74] The ultimate punishment begins when she enters into a bargain with Henrietta in order to get Paul a suit for that fateful dance. The vengeful Henrietta, who has sworn that she would make Emma Jean pay for blackmailing her if it is the last thing she does, has given up midwifing and turned to sewing when Emma Jean botches the suit she is trying to make for Paul to wear to the dance. Henrietta is her only hope for salvaging the suit. A gleeful Henrietta agrees to do so under a condition that will enable her to start her own clothing store: "'You don't get it, do you? I don't want no one-time payment. I want you to work for me. For free. For the rest of yo' life.'"[75] Only a truly desperate person would agree to such a bargain, and Emma Jean initially rejects it. Still unable to salvage the suit herself, she returns to Henrietta and begins her hell on earth, which is her voluntary enslavement to Henrietta. Her hell is cutting cloth for Henrietta, who, as the devil, oversees the process with unbridled glee and occasional taunting. Her hell is also being alone with Silence, the thoughts—mostly torturing ones from her mother—that eventually lead to her mental deterioration. Having refused to share with Gus and her family what she is doing when she leaves home early in the morning and returns in the evenings too tired to prepare dinner for her family, Emma Jean finds that her bargain, like Emma Jean's turning a boy into a girl, eventually is brought to light when Henrietta must seek out Gus to take the mentally debilitated and hallucinating Emma Jean from her shop when Emma Jean talks for extended periods to an invisible personage she has created.

Finally, the ultimate consequence of her boy-turned-into-girl scheme is that Emma Jean, haunted by her mother and their unresolved relationship, guilty about her treatment of Paul and her termination of Sol's education, resolves to quiet the voice that plagues her by killing herself. She does so in the Jordan River where her husband has cried out his misery each year during spring rains. It would be easy to assert that Emma Jean deserves her fate, that she is an evil woman for what she has done to her family and especially what she has done to Paul.[76] It would be equally easy to assert that the direct consequences of Emma Jean's scheme have shattered any possibility for a healthy homespace for the Peaces, though they continue to go through the motions of being a family and doing the things that families are expected to do, such as going to church together. It would also be easy to maintain that Emma Jean is just a crazy woman who, without the aid of a psychiatrist or some other mental health professional, could not work out the lingering issues that defined her relationship with her own mother. It might be easy just to agree with the community that Emma Jean deserves the fate that she has brought upon herself.

However, I wade into the waters of this confusion and defend Emma Jean for her desire to have a daughter. I stand with her against the church that would condemn her, the Peace family that does not remotely try to understand what she has done or why (another gender division?), the community that is unsympathetic to her, and the mother and sisters who shaped her into what she became. I argue that Daniel Black has not been able to disconnect readers from sympathy for Emma Jean in part because he stacks up her portrayal against that of the characters who surround her. Her mother is, by almost any standard of measurement, despicable. Emma Jean may be guilty, but the so-called church folks who surround her are equally guilty—of failing to be the Christians they profess to be, of overwhelming insensitivity, of the ugliness of their treatment of each other, of their general lack of concern about anything but their own entertainment. They especially find Emma Jean and her family situation entertaining. I am sympathetic to Emma Jean against this lot because she is no worse than they are. I am sympathetic because she voluntarily enslaves herself, sentences herself to hell on earth, for the love of her son and in a futile attempt to right some of her wrongs. I am sympathetic to Emma Jean because she finally decides to kill herself, and that in and of itself is a measure of the extent to which she is remorseful about what she has done. Mostly, though, Emma Jean is a sympathetic character because of the backstory that Black provides for her. If she had just emerged as a woman who, one day, out of the blue, decided that she wanted to turn a boy into a girl, that would perhaps be different. The desire she has, however, combined with a sense that fate is operating against her, makes her more tolerable than not. In the community in which she lives and in the family of which she is a part, Emma Jean is an engaging character who stands out in bas relief against so many who are despicable. She is forgivable also because Paul survives and is pursuing a lucrative profession; whatever damage may have been done to him recedes in the face of his success. While this does not exonerate Emma Jean, its inclusion goes a long way to mitigate final judgment of her, which means that she ultimately fares, in reader response, much better than the majority of the characters Black creates in the narrative.

THE WHOLE AWFUL LOT OF THEM

Daniel Black's fictional world in *Perfect Peace* is populated with characters who are uniformly gossipy, judgmental, hypocritical, homophobic, and generally not the type of folks that sane individuals would want to encounter on a regular basis. These folks are the vicious arbiters of behavior, the self-righteous intruders into the home environments of characters such as the Peaces, and the ultimate assurers that outside values and outside judgments will prevail in the minds of everyone in Swamp Creek. Like Mae Helen Hurt, these characters routinely refer to each other as ugly, as "niggas," and they denigrate each other whenever an opportunity arises. For example, in response to Emma Jean's blackmailing her, Henrietta thinks: "Black, ugly, insignificant Emma Jean Peace. Who would've thought?"[77] Implicit in her comment is that blackness and ugliness are antithetical to trickery and intellect. Henrietta, like everyone in Swamp Creek, disrespects Emma Jean to her face as well as behind her back. She visits Emma Jean to gloat after she suffers the burning injury, and she is quick to claim that all the punishment heaped upon Emma Jean is God's will. Miss Mamie, an elder in the church that the Peace family attends, is equally two-faced toward Emma Jean and equally unsympathetic. When she visits after the burning incident, she cannot resist the urge to comment on Emma Jean's scheme and to add: "'I didn't mean to upset you, especially not in yo' condition [Emma Jean has suffered third degree burns]. You done got enough punishment from God without me sayin' a word!' Mamie smacked her lips. 'And He might not be through with you yet.'"[78] She is the epitome of hypocrisy as she ostensibly comforts Paul after his overhearing of the conversation at the store even as she castigates Emma Jean for what she has done and speculates, as others do, on Paul's behavior and future. The unrepentantly self-righteous Mamie is similarly unkind to worshippers at the annual church picnic when she calls them to enjoy the food that has been prepared: "'Come and get it, I said!,'" and then she "mumbles," "'You greedy-ass niggas.'"[79] When Woody, the Peace preacher son, decides to marry a dark-skinned woman whom Emma Jean describes as having "'bone ugliness,'" Mamie is just as insulting by insisting that "'seem like to me that girl just *wants* to be ugly!'" (italics in original).[80] Worthy of note is the striking fact that Mamie carries the banner for her "Christian" community, that she is not alone in her less than charitable comments about others. Other women at church "yelp" "without shame" when Emma Jean brings Perfect to church for the first time, and they heap insult upon Emma Jean as well as upon her child: "'Do she think that peach dress go with that tired, ugly hat?,'" then "'And what mother in her right mind would *ever* put that many bright yellow ribbons on a black baby?'" (italics in original).[81]

These so-called Christians thrive on the misfortunes of other characters, and, to them, Emma Jean and her family provide spectacle entertainment for their blighted, pathetic little farming lives. They exercise freely the destructive power of words, and they show absolutely no remorse in doing so. Their portrayals invite speculation about Black's ultimate intent in limning his characters in this way. An obvious interpretive path leads toward Black's larger indictment of fundamentalist religious practices and those who carry them out. Church attendance is central to Swamp Creek, for that ritual provides as much of a social outlet as a spiritual one to the citizens of the community. Yet, as the folk saying goes, there is "form and fashion and outside show to the world," but there is no true religion, no true Christianity. Even when Emma Jean, in reaction to their learning that Perfect is indeed a boy, admonishes them to "'mind yo' own business and act like the Christians y'all claim to be!,'" no one steps forward to assume that behavior or that mantle.[82] The characters are in the habit of practicing religion, and habit may rule their lives, but, as with Gabriel Grimes, there is an exceptionally wide gap between form and substance in what they do. Indeed, while so many characters are quick to judge what is appropriate, right, or wrong in their community, none of them exhibits a true standard of morality. If what they practice is supposed to pass for Christianity, then they are all assuredly on their way to hell. That Black sets his tale among such unlikable and despicable characters suggests a different approach to what they all pounce on, that is, homosexuality. If these horrible characters with all their faults are the ones who object to homosexuality, then homosexuality must be the epitome of what is good and right, for it is highly preferable to those who object to it.

One of the few sympathetic characters beyond the Peace family is Sugar Baby, the wise fool who recognizes immediately when Emma Jean brings Perfect to church that something is wrong with the baby. "'That baby ain't right!' Sugar Baby screamed. 'That baby ain't right!'"; he keeps repeating the phrase—more stridently each time, and he is on the scene at crucial other moments in the novel.[83] When Emma Jean brings Paul to church for the first time and just before she reveals that Perfect is indeed a boy, Sugar Baby "laughed and shouted, 'He all right now! He all right now!'"[84] When Paul is beaten and raped, it is Sugar Baby who snatches up the wounded young man and delivers him to the porch of his home. It is Sugar Baby who intercedes when Gus takes his shotgun and goes out hunting for the criminals who have beaten and raped Paul. Sugar Baby takes him into the woods, to the hovel that he inhabits, and just shares time and space with Gus until Gus calms down. It is also Sugar Baby who assures Paul that he has a calling, a reason for being on earth and that he will not be able to depart until that mission is fulfilled. Sugar Baby, then, is the "crazy" antidote to the "sane" neighbors who torment and beat Paul and torture him emotionally.

Another contrast to the insanity that surrounds Paul is Eva Mae, his childhood friend who grows up to be a high school friend and who eventually falls in love with Paul—though she realizes that that love will remain unrequited. It is Eva Mae who serves as Paul's guide into sexual awareness, even though she does it through the stereotypical gender roles that she has observed in her parents and others in the community. It is also Eva Mae who decides that the Redfield brothers who beat and rape Paul cannot get away with what they have done. Although Paul wants to forget what has happened, Eva Mae takes it upon herself to set fire to the Redfield house. Her intent had been to burn just the section in which the brothers are sleeping, but the fire quickly gets out of hand, and the entire family dies. No one knows—though Sugar Baby suspects—that Eva Mae had anything to do with the fire, and there is no in-text punishment for her action. Yet, it is difficult for sensitive readers to believe that Eva Mae is the criminal that such an action might suggest. Just as it is difficult to damn Emma Jean completely for what she has done, so too it is difficult to damn Eva Mae. Arguably, the Redfield brothers are mean and evil homophobes who deserve the punishment that Eva Mae heaps upon them. If they are such Christians, in such a Christian community, then why would they have participated in the un-Christian act of ganging up on a young man and beating and raping him so badly that it took weeks for him to recover—just because he is not like them? There is no indication that Paul has on any occasion approached or made a pass at any of the male Redfields. They have merely set themselves up as judge and jury of someone else's life, in the manner of the old men at the store. Just as they have decided that they can be arbiters of life and death, so too does Eva Mae. Since morality is such a slippery issue in the text, judging her more harshly than the lot of them is not an automatic response.[85]

PERFECT PEACE

Ostensibly, the title of the novel refers to Emma Jean's naming of her seventh son. Her "daughter" is perfect, she avows, and so she gives her that name. Almost everyone finds it strange that a child has been so named, and the minister of the church the Peaces attend is especially resistant to the naming. In his fundamentalist mind, only God is perfect, and it is blasphemous to offer that appellation to anything or anyone else. When it finally sinks in that Emma Jean has indeed named the child Perfect and is not the least bit remorseful that she has done so, the preacher takes it upon himself to offer the only corrective available to him, the one through prayer. So, as he prays for the child, he concludes: "'None of us is perfect, oh Lord. No, not one . . . . Give us the humility, precious Savior, to know that all have sinned and fallen short of your glory. No one,' he shouted, 'can be called perfect in your sight, oh Lord. No one!,'" in response to which Emma Jean "rolls" her eyes at the minister and declares, "'*My* little girl *is* Perfect!'" (italics in original).[86] Perfection to Emma Jean is less the superiority of physical features than it is the fulfillment of a dream. And her dream wish has, in her mind, given her the perfect answer to her great desire for a daughter and all the mother-daughter things that she has envisioned doing.

Perfect peace is not only applicable to the child, however. Characters use it on other occasions to mark emotional states. Emma Jean asserts at one point that she has "perfect peace" in her relationship with her mother.[87] That is an obvious lie, for there never will be peace between the two of them. The tumultuous and unresolved relationship that Emma Jean has with her mother defines her entire life and constantly highlights the inadequacy of the space and the relationship that she identified as home. It is the voice of her mother, after all, that defines the Silence that haunts Emma Jean at Henrietta's shop, and she, like Pecola Breedlove in *The Bluest Eye*, is ultimately reluctant to have that at times taunting voice leave her. Perfection is therefore absent in this case just as it is absent in the naming of Emma Jean's seventh son. Nonetheless, characters keep evoking the idea. It also enters the picture when Gus imagines what his seventh son might grow up to be. He concludes that "perfect people only existed in his mind," and he has "no room in his heart for a son who, only yesterday, had been his daughter."[88] Of course Gus will modify his position later, but, in contemplating the idea of perfection, he echoes an implicit theme in the text.

The idea of perfect peace might also enter the conversation in connection with the entire community of Swamp Creek and what it *lacks*. And the one thing it lacks most conspicuously is any sense of peace, let alone perfect peace. This is a community that seems to thrive on division, insult, and a refusal to be truly neighborly. Characters almost applaud when bad things happen to folks they know. They have no respect for anyone, including, it seems, themselves. They are cruel and unforgiving (as in the case of the church officer who sent his son away because he was gay or in what Henrietta does to Emma Jean), and they thrive on the kind of gossip that Zora Neale Hurston used to describe small-minded characters who are jealous of Janie Crawford. Their home lives are judgmental (as in Gus's father and brother teasing him for crying after his mother's death) and violating (as in Caroline's father raping her repeatedly). Throughout the text, there is very little that can be said in a healthy or positive way about the community of individuals among whom the Peaces live. Of course we might argue that they are perfectly horrible in their lack of neighborliness or that they are the perfect example of how a community should *not* exist. The only perfection that could remotely apply to them is one of negativity, and that negativity has little counterbalancing weight.

Perhaps "perfect peace" is only truly applicable in one instance in the text, and that is when Emma Jean kills herself. Having endured her mother's taunting voice in her mental deterioration, and having failed utterly in her desire to have a daughter, Emma Jean finally finds peace in the cold waters of the Jordan River, the river to which Gus and Bartimaeus have gone each spring to wail out their frustrations under the cleansing power of a cooling rain. The father and son, who have undertaken this crying ritual for years without having to endure labels of being "sissified" for showing their emotions, have found in the power of rainwater a renewal that has lasted them throughout the year. In the stream into which those rains have flowed, Emma Jean finds an escape from her mother's voice, an escape from the guilt she has reaped as a result of her treatment of Paul and Sol, and the quiet termination of a life that has been filled, especially in its final decade, with more anguish than most people experience in a lifetime. Emma Jean goes to a much deserved, quiet rest, one in which she ostensibly finds the peace that could never be available to her again in her family or her community. In her authoring of Perfect's life of femaleness and sweet mother-daughter interactions, she also authored the plan for her own demise. That plan comes to fruition with her full acceptance and embracing of it, and it is that embracing and that welcome that make the title of the novel more applicable to Emma Jean than to any other character. On the banks of the Jordan—conveniently named for its Christian implications—"Emma Jean didn't hesitate. Unable to foresee herself in the future, she marched boldly to the edge of a jutting rock and, with the help of God's heavy hands, plunged headfirst into the chilly Jordan . . . . She'd gotten precisely what she'd come for. She was cleansed now, and no one—including Mae Helen—could tarnish her again. The hope for perfect peace had finally been realized, and now she'd have it forever."[89] She is beyond pain, beyond frustration, beyond guilt, beyond disapproval, beyond torturing herself mentally for her past action. Emma Jean has found a home, and she walks into that home as if bright yellow ribbons and chocolate-frosted cake, attended by a chorus of welcoming voices, make her feel as if she is the absolute best and most perfect being in that after-world.

NOTES

1. Daniel Black, *Perfect Peace* (New York: St. Martin's, 2010).

2. Toni Morrison, *The Bluest Eye* (1970; New York: Plume, 1994). While it is intriguing to consider *Perfect Peace* in connection to Toni Morrison's *Sula* (1973), especially given the same provocative last name—Peace—for the families in each novel, the issue of skin color in *The Bluest Eye* is more immediately relevant for comparison. Suffice it to say that there is little Peace in *Sula* or in *Perfect Peace*, and both of those conditions have to do with the relationship of mothers to their children. While Emma Jean Peace robs Perfect/Paul of a stable identity, Eva Peace simply kills her son Plum when he does not live up to her expectations. Eva's is another homespace, therefore, in which more troubling and tragic occurrences take place than nurturing and supportive ones. Pigmentocracy is also an issue in Morrison's *God Help the Child* (2015), in which the strikingly black Bride has her relationship with her mother interrupted and where she learns to use her skin tone in fashionable ways. As a child, Bride, like Pecola and Gwendolyn Brooks's Mabbie in "the ballad of chocolate Mabbie," learns quickly that the color of one's skin can make one an outcast, a lesson that is also absolutely vital to Emma Jean's growth and development—or lack thereof. See Brooks, *Selected Poems* (New York: HarperPerennial, 1963, 2006), 7.

3. Frances Ellen Watkins Harper, *Iola Leroy* (1892; Boston: Beacon, 1987); Charles W. Chesnutt, *The House Behind the Cedars* (1900; Athens: U of Georgia P, 1988).

4. See Wallace Thurman, *The Blacker the Berry: A Novel of Negro Life* (Maccauley Company, 1929); Gwendolyn Brooks, *Selected Poems* (1963; HarperPerennial, 2006); and Toni Morrison, *The Bluest Eye*.

5. Black, *Perfect*, 23.

6. Black *Perfect*, 23.

7. Black, *Perfect.*, 20.

8. Black, *Perfect*, 20–21.

9. Black, *Perfect*, 24.

10. Black, *Perfect*, 23.

11. Black, *Perfect*, 23.

12. Black, *Perfect*, 48.

13. Black, *Perfect*, 56. Mae Helen's comment echoes Big Jim's in *The Good Negress* when he asserts that, because of her cooking and cleaning skills, Neesey would make some man a good wife.

14. Black, *Perfect*, 55.

15. Black, *Perfect*, 55.

16. Black, *Perfect*, 55.
17. Black, *Perfect*, 55.
18. Black, *Perfect*, 55.
19. Black, *Perfect*, 56.
20. Black, *Perfect*, 54.
21. Black, *Perfect*, 75.
22. Black, *Perfect*, 75.
23. Black, *Perfect*, 76.
24. Black, *Perfect*, 76.
25. Black, *Perfect*, 76.
26. For these experiences, see Black, *Perfect*, 38, 44–46, 61, 73–74, 95ff, 139, 140, 160, 213.
27. Black, *Perfect*, 83.
28. Black, *Perfect*, 115.
29. Black, *Perfect*, 52.
30. Black, *Perfect*, 53.
31. Black, *Perfect*, 54.
32. Black, *Perfect*, 12.
33. Black, *Perfect*, 12. Emma Jean's response echoes that of the jaded Mem Copeland in Alice Walker's *The Third Life of Grange Copeland* (1970), who, when she looks out of her sharecropper shack after just having given birth and sees nothing but brown fields, names her son "Brownfield."
34. Black, *Perfect*, 13.
35. Black, *Perfect*, 13.
36. Black, *Perfect*, 58.
37. Black, *Perfect*, 66.
38. Black, *Perfect*, 87, 88.
39. Black, *Perfect*, 87.
40. Black, *Perfect*, 88.
41. Black, *Perfect*, 89.
42. Black, *Perfect*, 90.
43. Black, *Perfect*, 93.
44. Black, *Perfect*, 114.
45. Black, *Perfect*, 120.
46. Black, *Perfect*, 117, 118.
47. Black, *Perfect*, 120.
48. Black, *Perfect*, 146.
49. Black, *Perfect*, 131, 132.
50. Black, *Perfect*, 133.
51. Black, *Perfect*, 133.
52. Black, *Perfect*, 134.
53. Black, *Perfect*, 133.
54. Black, *Perfect*, 179, 180.
55. Black, *Perfect*, 174, 175.
56. Black, *Perfect*, 209–10.

57. Black, *Perfect*, 140.
58. Black, *Perfect*, 212–13. Uzzie T. Cannon argues that Gus exhibits traits of the "two-spirited" nature that defines certain persons in Native American cultures, in that he showcases both masculine and feminine traits; the same would be true for Bartimaeus. See "Tears, Fears, and Queers: Transgendering Black Masculinity in Daniel Black's *Perfect Peace*," *CEA Critic* 78:1 (March 2016): 45–58.
59. Black, *Perfect*, 139.
60. Black, *Perfect*, 147.
61. Black, *Perfect*, 148.
62. Black, *Perfect*, 150–51.
63. Black, *Perfect*, 151.
64. Black, *Perfect*, 155.
65. Black, *Perfect*, 158.
66. Black, *Perfect*, 181, 182.
67. Black, *Perfect*, 184.
68. Black, *Perfect*, 143–44.
69. In one of the greatest, if perhaps not *the* greatest, ironies of the text, Paul and Eva Mae seek out Henrietta after Emma Jean's death for her to teach Paul the sewing business. That Black allowed this development in the text might be viewed as an insult to Emma Jean's memory and an implicit approval of the woman who has played a major role in Emma Jean's demise. On the other hand, a less prejudicial reading might allow for Henrietta's taking on of Paul as a student as a way to expiate her own sins. Fortunately, Paul's working with Henrietta is *not* dramatized in the text, so readers can only surmise her motives as well as the daily interactions between Paul and Henrietta.
70. Black, *Perfect*, 335.
71. Like Horace Cross in Randall Kenan's *A Visitation of Spirits* (1989), Paul seeks out a preacher relative to ask questions about why God creates human beings the way they are, about why some people are different from others. Woody is initially just as un-understanding as is Jimmy Greene in Kenan's novel. Echoing Jimmy, he tells Paul: "'You just need to pray, boy. God'll answer all yo' questions . . . . You cain't be saved yet, boy. Not while you still a sissy. You gotta get delivered from that first . . . You do gotta believe, but you cain't be no sissy. You gotta get rid of that before He can do anything with you. He hates sissies'" (229, 230). Mister is a bit more understanding when Paul confides in him, and we later learn that Mister himself is gay.
72. Black, *Perfect*, 15.
73. Black, *Perfect*, 142.
74. Black *Perfect*, 166, 169.
75. Black, *Perfect*, 270.
76. In his review of the novel in 2009, Nathaniel Norment Jr. asserts that "Emma Jean's desperate need to have a daughter causes her to commit an evil/cruel act of deceit." He goes further to label her act "the ultimate betrayal to a boy's manhood, to her husband, to her sons, and to the will of God." See the review of *Perfect Peace* in the *CLA Journal* 53:1 (September 2009): 114. Uzzie T. Cannon refers to Emma Jean's

decision to raise Paul as a girl as "perceivably abominable" (45) and "psychotic" (52). Norment's and Cannon's comments reflect positions against which I argue.

77. Black, *Perfect*, 32.
78. Black, *Perfect*, 169.
79. Black, *Perfect*, 260.
80. Black, *Perfect*, 298.
81. Black, *Perfect*, 67.
82. Black, *Perfect*, 159.
83. Black, *Perfect*, 69, 70, 71.
84. Black, *Perfect*, 155.
85. Eva Mae's burning of the Redfields evokes Nel and Sula's accidental drowning of Chicken Little in Toni Morrison's *Sula* (New York: Knopf, 1973). While Eva Mae's act is deliberate and Nel and Sula's is accidental, none confesses to what has occurred, which lands them in the same arena of questionable morality that guides both texts. The witnesses to both deaths are the village fools, Shadrack and Sugar Baby, neither of whom is positioned to counter any alternative narrative any of the girls could provide—even if they were inclined to do so.
86. Black, *Perfect*, 68–69.
87. Black, *Perfect*, 48.
88. Black, *Perfect*, 138.
89. Black, *Perfect*, 333.

Chapter 5

A Mother's Domination, A Family's Submission

Dorothy West's The Living Is Easy (1940)

The ugliness that defines the Peace home in rural Arkansas in the mid-twentieth century is matched by the ugliness that defines a northern, urban African American home in the second decade of the twentieth century. The color politics that shape Mae Helen's and Emma Jean's interactions with their families also inform the interactions of the characters in Dorothy West's *The Living Is Easy* (1948).[1] While the Peace family is pretty much "dirt poor," as the saying goes, the Judsons of Boston are more financially secure; indeed, the husband owns a lucrative business across the street from Boston's famed Faneuil Hall. That success, however, does not satisfy his wife, who wants to migrate into the upper ranges of middle classness. Thus the class issues that may have been implicit in *Perfect Peace* but could not be acted upon because characters did not have the economic or social means to carry out their exclusionary practices are given more rein to operate in West's novel. Cleo Jericho Judson, around whom the action of the novel revolves, is a striver in the very traditional sense of that word, that is, she desires a champagne lifestyle on beer money, and she will do everything within her power to accomplish her objective of renting a house in the "right" section of Boston (as close to Brookline as possible and away from the South End, which is dominated by blacks newly arrived from the South), training her daughter Judy in what she deems to be proper etiquette, disrespecting her husband Bartholomew (Bart) Judson by marking his blackness as the whipping post against which she uses her lighter skin to wield control of everything but especially finances, and forcing her sisters to acquiesce to her domination of their lives.

Thus, several factors ensure that the homespace over which Cleo presides will not be a healthy one. Initially, she allows everything she believes about living and interacting with her family to be shaped by external forces, specifically the black Boston upper middle class to which she aspires and which is defined by history, manners, legacy, and a pronounced pigmentocracy. That class's values, their ways of being in the world, their overall position in the society dominate Cleo's imagination and *all* of her actions. From adopting this set of values and beliefs, Cleo moves to lying about how she acquires the house that she hopes will impress that upper middle class. Those external values and beliefs also lead her constantly to insult and berate her husband Bart, whom she views through the lens of use value. Comparable to Margarete's reaction to Neesey in *The Good Negress*, Cleo sees Bart only for the labor he can provide, and that labor produces the finances that underwrite her planned upward mobility. Use value also dominates her interactions with her three sisters, whom she brings from South Carolina to Boston solely to satisfy her own starved need for someone to adore her. Perhaps most detrimental to her home, she allows the external values of colorism to distance her emotionally from her daughter Judy. She does not reject Judy in the outward, vocal ways that Mae Helen rejects Emma Jean, but the impact is just as negative in destroying the potential for any healthy homespace that Judy could experience.

Writing in 2007, Meredith Goldsmith commented that "West's *The Living Is Easy* continues to receive scant critical attention in studies of both the African American novel and Harlem Renaissance women's writing, despite the praise the novel garnered when it was published." Echoing some of the political and critical responses to Margaret Walker's *Jubilee* in 1966, Goldsmith continues:

> West's fiction seemed almost self-consciously out of step with the vernacular and proletarian aesthetics of its literary moment; for example, while Ann Petry's best-seller *The Street* portrays the struggles of single mother Lutie Johnson against the forces of racism, sexism, and poverty of wartime Harlem, West depicts the social ambitions of black bourgeois heroine Cleo Judson to enter the cloistered elite of black Boston.[2]

With Richard Wright having published *Native Son* in 1940 and having firmly established the Protest Tradition in African American literature, West's *The Living Is Easy* did indeed seem out of step. The novel does not engage politics beyond the ineffectual efforts of the black upper middle class to retain their positions and status, and the only protest apparent is Cleo's personal affront at what offends her or hinders her attempt to claim membership in the upper level of black Boston society. While varying content and character may have accounted for initial neglect of the novel, they are insufficient to account for decades of less than sustained treatment. Perhaps that has more to do with character type. Cleo Judson, like Rosie Quinn in Delores Phillips's *The Darkest Child* (2004), is written against the grain of expectation for what black female characters should, ought, or can be.³ It is difficult to read about black mothers who do not like their children, and, in Rosie's case, who actually kills two of them. Received critical traditions in African American literary studies perhaps have difficulty accounting for or treating such characters. Perhaps that trend will change as younger scholars such as Delia Steverson and Sondra Washington take on these complex and enigmatic female characters.⁴

Unlike Emma Jean Peace, whose insatiable desire for a daughter leads her to make a desperate, spur-of-the moment decision about turning her seventh son into a "girl," Cleo has no such remotely noble or individualized intentions. All of her motives are materialistic and superficial. There is not a hint of altruism here, nothing beyond bald, uncontained, egotistical and selfish pursuit of a singular objective. Cleo is painted as a shallow, money-grubbing, calculating, and mostly despicable liar who uses everything at her disposal, but especially her good looks, to manipulate Bart, intimidate Judy, and force her sisters Charity, Lily, and Serena to abandon their husbands and join her in her effort to invade the upper middle class in Boston. She wants to be a part of the black elite in this city, and she deploys whatever options are available to her to try to attain that status. In the process, she stunts her daughter's emotional and psychological growth, browbeats her husband, and adheres to an evaluation of skin privilege—or lack thereof—that is just as devastating as the colorphobia to which the characters are heir in *Perfect Peace*. Cleo allows nothing to stand in the way of her trying to move up the social and class ladder. She sacrifices her own marriage as well as those of her sisters in an externally imposed system of values that is just as destructive as the color-defined one in *Perfect Peace*. I would venture to say, however, that, whereas a modicum of sympathy could be spent on Emma Jean, it is nearly impossible to bestow the same largesse upon Cleo, though, by the colorphobic standards of her creation, some might excuse her simply because of her beauty.⁵

ACQUIESCING TO BEING "MISTER NIGGER"

How does a character shape the world in which she lives and control all the others in it to conform to her sense of reality? Cleo uses her physical features as well as a couple of strategies to achieve her purposes. She combines being light-skinned and beautiful by the standards of the day with being an unconscionable liar and a verbally abusive mother, wife, and sister to bring a toxicity into her homespace that is more detrimental to the emotional health of its inhabitants than any wife-beating husband might be. A fierce independence, a decided straying from any teachings her parents provided, and an uncontained willfulness thus define a woman who recognizes no limitations, no restrictions on her behaviors, and no boundaries that she feels compelled to respect. Her ongoing and aggressive negative behaviors therefore make it impossible for her to build an emotionally healthy home life with Bart.

The husband/wife relationship in this home is accordingly informed by lack of intimacy, manipulation, and constant insult. Cleo's parents had sent the beautiful Cleo to the North in an effort to save her from possible sexual violation in the South. Bart discovered her working for a white woman in Springfield, Massachusetts and recognized immediately that the young white man in the home in which Cleo worked had designs on her—even if he had not yet physically acted upon them. Bart proposes to Cleo to effect a rescue, and she marries the twenty-three-year older, dark-skinned man "without thinking about it" and certainly without any thought of love.[6] Thus begins a relationship in which Cleo holds herself away from Bart sexually, fights against any and every urge to show tenderness or feeling for him, and insults him at every turn. West notes:

> When Cleo was twenty, their sex battle began. It was not a savage fight. She did not struggle against his superior strength. She found a weapon that would cut him down quickly and cleanly. She was ice. Neither her mouth nor her body moved to meet his. The open eyes were wide with mocking at the busyness below. There was no moment when everything in her was wrenched and she was one with the man who could submerge her in himself.[7]

The battle is especially poignant because "there was no real abhorrence of sex in her. Her need of love was as urgent as her aliveness indicated. But her *perversity* would not permit her to weaken" (my emphasis).[8] Given these interpersonal dynamics, it is impossible for this ever to be a happy home. Unfortunately for Bart, he is desperately in love with Cleo and perhaps heir to the color dynamics of the time in which darker-skinned blacks often aligned themselves with lighter-skinned blacks at whatever personal cost was necessary. The personal costs to Bart come in a suppression of self, a loss of dignity, and a general lack of respect from the woman he has rescued. Throughout their marriage, Cleo and Bart never share the intimacy that might be expected from a voluntary union. And not only does Cleo deny Bart sexual and affectionate intimacy, but she also denies him spatial intimacy when her sisters arrive. Prior to their arrival, Bart had at least been able to share the same bed with Cleo. Once her sisters arrive, he is relegated to "the small back room on the second floor," a space that he will eventually share with the young son of one of Cleo's sisters.[9] Cleo has been distinctly uninspired in preparing Bart's bedroom space: "Bart's bedroom on the second floor, habitually kept closed from public view because of its ugly meager furnishings that Cleo had bought with haste and disinterest at the shabbiest of second-hand stores" is only transformed for the infamous Christmas party, when it is "turned into a scented bower for the ladies, with something borrowed from each room upstairs."[10]

Despite her disrespect for Bart, Cleo still expects him to take care of all the expenses of the house, to believe whatever she says, and to trust her to manage household expenses. Given this leeway, she manipulates Bart at every turn. When she manages to secure a ten-room house to rent in Roxbury (across the street from Brookline), she tells Bart that the rent is fifty dollars for the first month and forty-five dollars thereafter when the landlord, who is prejudiced against the Irish and wants to get away from their encroachment, actually rents it to her for twenty-five dollars a month. Cleo is thoroughly satisfied with the house as she looks around and beyond the "gracious room" she has entered: "The lacquered floors were of fine hardwood, the marble above the great hearth was massive and beautiful. The magnificent sliding doors leading into the dining room were rich mahogany, the wallpaper was exquisitely patterned. From the center of the high ceiling the gas chandelier spun its crystal tears."[11] Lying about the amount is but the first of many deceptions about the rent, for Cleo changes the amount (from forty to sixty dollars) with her audience and tells whatever lies will suit the moment; she even erases and substitutes the amount on the rent receipt in order to continue her lies about what she has paid. Documenting Cleo's lies in the text would take a chapter in itself, for they are the staple of her existence. In the world that she has created and within the perverted system of values to which she adheres, lying is equivalent to and comes as naturally as breathing, and Bart is more often than not the audience for and recipient of those lies. Even when he is aware that Cleo is lying, he refuses to scratch the surface of her artifice for fear of the consequences, ones that usually involve ugly verbal abuse.

Cleo has no conscience. Even as she manipulates Bart financially, she also steals from her daughter Judy's piggy bank. She believes that Bart is a bottomless well of financial resources, and she believes such resources should be spent instead of saved. As "The Black Banana King" of Boston, who owns "Bartholomew Judson, Foreign and Domestic Choice Fruits and Vegetables, Bananas a Specialty," which is located in one of the most profitable business districts in Boston, there is no doubt that Bart initially has resources.[12] However, he also has major expenses, even as he is fixated upon planning and saving for Judy's future. As far as Cleo is concerned, Bart is simply lying about the money he has, and she believes that he can supply all of her needs and many of her whims. The only future she is concerned about is the one in which she sees herself on par with Althea and Simeon Binney, who represent the very best of Boston's traditional black upper middle class. In order to get the things that will enable her to interact socially and on par with that group, Cleo wages constant financial war against Bart in the same way that she wages sexual war against him. To her mind, her needs/wants/desires are all that matter. Resources should be allotted and expended solely to achieve her objectives. While those objectives might be in the service of getting improved social status for her husband and daughter, they simultaneously entail trampling on any and all desires of that husband and daughter. In other words, Cleo makes decisions and acts for everyone around her. She gives no thought to what they might want or to how they may feel about decisions she makes; it is her world, and she is lady and master of it.[13]

To retain that mastery, she cultivates browbeating tactics that make the enthralled Bart seem like a self-deprecating denizen in a nightmare from which he has no ability and seemingly no desire to awake. The color and class dynamics that inform all of Cleo's waking hours also inform her relationship with Bart. Her light skin and beauty feed his fascination with both to ensure that he is a lapdog for life to whatever Cleo wants. While many black women of the early twentieth century might have addressed their husbands as "Mr. So and So," those appellations were ones of respect for marriage and perhaps respect for differences in ages. The age difference might apply to Cleo when she calls Bart "Mr. Judson," but no such justification applies to Cleo when she refers to Bart as "Mister Nigger."[14] It is purely with the intent to insult and control, and Bart clearly has no retort and no defense against these attacks. Cleo first refers to him as "Mister Nigger" when Bart mistakenly follows the false clue she has given and thinks that she is pregnant.

> 'Mister Nigger,' said Cleo coldly, 'who told you I was going to have a little shaver?'
> 'You address me by name. You told me yourself sitting right in my store.'
> 'I beg to differ, Mister Nigger. You told me.'
> 'Cleo, don't you start that again. Why in the name of God did you take money from me to go to the doctor if you knew it was a fool's errand?
> 'I never refuse money when it's offered me,' she said imperturbably.[15]

While it might seem that Bart is arguing, he most assuredly is not, as he finally concludes that "'man gets so he'd rather let things slide than see you get so excited.'"[16] That is the constant counter strategy that Bart employs with Cleo. He would rather let insults slide than get into arguments with Cleo, for, with her volatile nature, there is no telling when she might dissolve their marriage, though, arguably, she likes what she perceives as easy living far too much to risk its total dissolution. If she can insult Bart—as she does constantly—and still keep him attached to her, then she will have obtained her objective of refusing him intimacy, tenderness, courtesy, or consideration, and yet maintaining the source of funding that she needs to pursue her upper middle class dreams. Cleo references Bart as "Mister Nigger" again when her sister Serena is considering getting a job to help out after the siblings have descended upon the Judson home. She uses the phrase "venomously" in an attempt to shame Bart for not quietly assuming the additional financial burden of six people (all three of the sisters come, and each has a child).[17] She also refers to Bart when she tells her sister Charity that she spoils that "nigger" when Charity is only trying to respect a man who has accepted so much additional financial responsibility.[18] Yet again she refers to Bart as "Mister Nigger" when she is trying to cajole him into paying for a lawyer for Robert, Serena's husband.[19]

With Bart, the "nigger" references might be related directly to skin color and previous condition or point of origin. Like the characters in *Perfect Peace*, Cleo has developed a derogatory racial politics that allows her to denigrate everyone around her by calling them "niggers," and Bart receives the brunt of that denigration. Readers who search for reasons why Bart acquiesces to Cleo's domination might need to look no further than the fact that he is a man intent upon supporting his family and doing whatever he can to ensure that they have a present and a future. That explanation, however, pales in comparison to the venom that Cleo heaps upon him every day. Thus the question still remains: Why does he not simply walk away? Perhaps, again, color politics ensure that he does not. The novel is set between 1914 and 1919, which are not only the years that encompass World War I but also reflective of the time in African American history when those of lighter complexions, epitomized in W. E. B. Du Bois's Talented Tenth, still dominated the black masses, as the Boston society backdrop against which the novel is set illustrates clearly. Somewhere in that mixture of color, class, reputation, and desirability is Bart Judson's weakness for Cleo. After all, she is an excellent trophy wife for a man of his skin color and business statue. He is therefore willing to sacrifice some self-esteem (if not all) to be a doormat for Cleo, to keep that image going. Readers need but consider his excited reaction to Cleo and Judy when they enter his store and his two white helpers see them to get a glimpse of what family means to Bart: "He jerked around, then his whole face splintered into smiles. He opened the office door and rushed forward, holding out his arms to Judy."[20] It is truly his sad fate that family does not mean the same to Cleo.

Cleo's battles with and denigration of Bart are also gender informed. Cleo is apparently jealous of what she perceives as the privileges and freedoms that men enjoy. "Men were her enemies," she contemplates, "because they were male."[21] Because Bart can do the things that she cannot, therefore, is perhaps yet another reason for Cleo's mistreatment and apparent jealousy of him, especially in terms of his business skills and earning ability. "Her despotic nature found Mr. Judson a rival."[22] Having turned Bart into a "rival" and willing to wage war in the gender arena, Cleo adds yet another layer of conflict to her relationship to her husband and makes it impossible for them to ever make a healthy home together.[23] The text notes that "it had never occurred to her in the ten years of her marriage that she might be his helpmate. She thought that was the same thing as being a man's slave."[24] And later: "He was not a companion. He was a good provider. Had he tried to be a companion, Cleo would have said that he talked her to death. As it was, she said he bored her to death."[25] Destining herself to struggle in a competition in which she cannot possibly come out the winner, Cleo nonetheless girds on her armor and will not surrender. It is only fate that rescues Bart from her clutches.

After years of trying to get Cleo to be more frugal, and after four years of supporting her six relatives and having paid for an expensive lawyer for the husband of one of the sisters, Bart has no resources on which to fall back when the vicissitudes of war and business converge and result in the sale of the block on which he has his business. Diminishing contracts over the years and the impact of World War I upon routes of delivery of fruit, combined with the sale, leave him virtually destitute. He buys as many groceries as he can, passes along as much cash to Cleo as he can (around $300), and leaves Boston for New York to start over again. The scene in which he presents the food and money to Cleo sees little change in her, though she does offer the money back to him in a misguided belief that he can undo his fate. Beyond that, there is little remorse, little genuine affection for Bart. The only real thing that Cleo feels is that there will no longer be anyone to love her "best."[26] There is no sorrow for Bart's plight, no apparent regret that she has contributed in part to his financial reversal, no sustained awareness of anything or anyone beyond herself. Even her attempts to comfort Bart are awkward and insincere. Most worthy of note is that she is still lying as much at the end of the novel as she was at the beginning. She hands Bart money that she has received from Lily's husband Victor and declares that he gave it to her "for being so good to [Lily] and [her daughter] Vicky" when Victor really brought the two hundred dollars to pay for a divorce after Cleo turned Lily against him, one hundred of which Cleo pocketed (stole) and eighty dollars of which Lily took to pay back rent.[27] Thus, even as her marriage dissolves officially (for Bart realizes he will not be in touch unless he has cash to put in an envelope), Cleo is still the self-centered liar that she has been throughout the text. Only a few years from sixty, Bart may be hardy, but it is doubtful that he will be able to start over again, so perhaps this is effectively the beginning of the end of everything for the Judsons.

Given Cleo's personality and means of interacting with everyone, there is simply no way that a foundation for a good marriage and a healthy home can be constructed in *The Living Is Easy*. Cleo's jealousy, striving, lying, and perversity make such an outcome impossible. At times it seems as if Cleo works against her own good fortune in the pursuit of some standard of acceptance and social status that remains as elusive to her at the end of the novel as it was at the beginning. Cleo fails miserably as a wife because she sees her husband as the enemy, a man against whom she must use her wits to put forth her own agenda. Her inability to believe that she could work in unison with that husband and that they could achieve much together is an idea that she rejects out of hand. To her mind, she is the only person who is right in the relationship, with the right attitude toward where the Judsons should live, the right attitude about where Judy should go to school, and making the right decisions about what is good for her sisters—despite what they and their husbands might want. In many ways, Cleo is a beautiful, vampiristic monster who sucks the life blood out of those around her, who drains them so thoroughly that they do not have the energy or the inclination to resist her wiles and her guile, for which she has been in practice since she was an adolescent and teenager. In this portrayal, West depicts a married woman who will never consent to be a wife—sexually, socially, financially, spiritually, or any other way—and a mother who is saddled with a child toward whom it is impossible for her to ever show genuine affection—and certainly not love.

WHERE DID THIS CHILD COME FROM?

West writes Cleo's daughter Judy as a child—initially five years old—being shaped by a thin, light-skinned, beautiful mother who is constantly impatient with the darker, thick-legged, and slightly stout child. Cleo's system of values in relation to color has been derived in part from her background in the South and her free association with a young white girl as well as from her interactions as an adult with privileged black folks whom she judges to be the "better" classes and whom she seeks to emulate. There is no mother pounding preferences into her head, as Mae Helen did with Emma Jean, but there is tremendous leeway extended to Cleo because of her light skin advantage. She also learns from the adoration of men that she is a prize for whom almost any of them would be willing to make sacrifices. Bart Judson proves himself to be more than willing, and he therefore commits himself willfully to the hell that Cleo puts him through. As demonstrated, Cleo is a strong-willed and strong black female character who has the ability to turn the world upside down for just about everyone around her. A bothersome presence in and appendage to Cleo's world, dark-skinned Judy can never receive the undivided love that a child might expect from a birth parent. Certainly Bart loves Judy and interacts with her as frequently as Cleo allows, but she often forces him to wash his hands or take baths in preparation for his playing with Judy and the other children, a directive she gives him before the famed Christmas party that she hosts: "Her last command had been that Bart must take a bath and put on a fresh nightshirt. Since his last bath he had probably picked up enough germs to kill the hardiest child. And God knew they had a fertile field in which to stay alive."[28] That Bart acquiesces—and even lies on top of the bed and covers with a quilt instead of "dirtying up" Cleo's sheets—is but yet another indication of the blind, lifed love that defines his relationship to Cleo, who, despite her seeming concern for Judy, has serious gaps in her commitment to the role of mother.

To the light-skinned Cleo, dark-skinned Judy is a puzzle on the one hand and her biggest challenge on the other. Unlike Cleo in temperament and honesty, Judy learns early to tiptoe in the space that belongs to her mother. Yet she serves as the impetus to Cleo's wanting a bigger house and the privileges that come from moving up in elite black Boston society. By teaching Judy to adopt Boston manners, so to speak, and by training her to be "a little Boston lady," Cleo expects to reap the reward of entry into the society that will distinguish her from the hordes of black people arriving from the South.[29] The mother-daughter relationship, however, is just as tainted as that between Margarete and Neesey or between Pauline and Pecola. For Cleo, Judy is mostly a bothersome burden that she cannot return to the place from which it came. It is clear from her interactions with Judy, her thoughts about her, and Judy's responses to her aloof but demanding mother that this can never be a healthy relationship and that the home Cleo pursues will always be valued more in the abstract that in any tangible reality, for the reality of Judy's dark-skinned, Negroid features and Judy's general awkwardness will never allow Cleo to be satisfied completely with Judy.

It is immediately clear upon entering the text that this mother-daughter relationship lacks any of the tenderness that might be expected of a mother interacting with her five-year-old child. Cleo is incapable of showing affection, let alone love for her daughter. Within the first couple of pages of the novel, readers learn that Cleo "hisses" at Judy "fiercely" as they are walking to the streetcar, that she has "a lollipop for Judy in case she got tiresome," and that she has "a change purse with silver, half of which Cleo, clandestinely and without conscience, had shaken out of Judy's pig bank."[30] Later, she will speak to Judy "coldly" and with "charming insincerity."[31] With the money that she has finagled out of Bart to rent the house also in her purse, Cleo is presented as a woman whose schemes matter more to her than her relationship with her daughter or her husband. Judy must tag along because there is nothing else Cleo can do with her at this point. The impatience Cleo exhibits, along with the personality traits that West showcases in her, sever any hint of tenderness from her in her role as mother. It quickly becomes apparent that part of Cleo's dissatisfaction with her daughter comes not only from her "stoutness" and slowness but also from her color and Negroid features.

On the streetcar, Cleo is conscious of white observers noting the contrast between her light skin and Judy's dark skin, as well as Judy's Negroid nose. Cleo is thus impatient when Judy presses her nose against a window and flattens it even more. "Judy's nose was pressed against the glass. Cleo nudged her and whispered, 'Judy,' what do I tell you about making your nose flat?,'" which makes Judy realize that the people on the streetcar who are stealing surreptitious glances and raising their eyebrows are probably wondering "where Cleo got her"[32]:

> She was dark. She had Papa's cocoa-brown skin, his soft dark eyes, and his generous nose in miniature. Cleo worked hard on her nose. She had tried clothespins, but Judy had not known what to do about breathing. Now Cleo was teaching her to keep the bridge pinched, but Judy pinched too hard, and the rush of dark blood made her nose look larger than ever.[33]

Features and manners get tied together as, in response to Judy's "grinning" at a little dog that she sees from the streetcar, Cleo "hissed in her ear: 'Don't show your gums when you smile, and stop squirming. You've seen dogs before. Sit like a little Boston lady. Straighten your spine.'"[34] Thus destined to her mother's disapproval and corrective practices, there is little hope that Judy can ever live up to the abstract standard that Cleo envisions for her. It would be difficult for Judy ever to feel comfortable with her mother or content that she has remotely achieved Cleo's expectations for behavior or her transforming her blackness into something more acceptable. While she might momentarily appreciate something about Judy, as she does once when glancing down at her skin, Cleo is mostly unapproving and dissatisfied with her offspring.[35] Therefore, throughout the text, Cleo exhibits impatience more than acceptance with Judy, and she judges her constantly by externally exposed standards. "Cleo wished that poor little Judy had lovely curls like that [Simeon's]. Braids were fine if they fell to your waist. But two braids bobbing on a colored child's shoulder looked like pickaninny hair, no matter how you dressed it up with expensive ribbons."[36] Unvoiced yet unflattering thoughts about her child speak to Cleo's unwavering lacks as a mother to Judy.

As she learns more about her mother and observes her operating in the world, Judy suffers in silence but quietly begins to carve out a definition of self that is different from what Cleo may want. When Cleo refers to other blacks as "niggers," for example, Judy is "shocked" because she has been taught that that is a bad word.[37] She begins to see that Cleo preaches one thing and acts another, so she learns to tiptoe around her mother and her actions. She internalizes her feelings and suffers in "injured silence" in a situation in which she knows that she cannot possibly win.[38] In later years, after the sisters and their children have arrived in the Judson household, Judy grows to understand Cleo's whims more and more, and she navigates around them as best she can. She sees clearly the impact that Cleo has and determines that, comparable to John Grimes's advice to his baby sister, "she was going to leave home and get married and never come back. She thought it would be an act of folly to return. Cleo would try to turn her against her husband. Cleo would try to take away her children."[39] Thus her views are different from Cleo's nieces and nephew: "Her cousins thought Cleo could stand up to anything," a nine-year-old Judy thinks, but she "felt secret pity for her where the others felt secret awe. Cleo made a big noise to scare people into letting her be boss. Judy was beginning to see that Cleo was the boss of nothing but the young, the weak, the frightened. She ruled a pygmy kingdom."[40] Nonetheless, Cleo *does* rule, and Judy must be as wary of her moods as are her cousins. The fact that a child is put in such a situation is further testament to the unhealthy home environment that Cleo creates and to the psychological damage that accrues to all within that environment. As an additional indication of estrangement between mother and daughter, Judy refers to Cleo with the formal "Mother" instead of "Mom" or "Mama" or "Mommy."[41] While Judy remains critical to and the motivating factor behind Cleo's desire to move up in Boston society, Cleo does not really approve of Judy in her current physical manifestation, a conclusion that the young Judy must be made aware of again and again. Judy is thus a necessary appendage—crucial to upward mobility but a drawback in terms of personality and physical features. Indeed, Cleo reflects at one point that "sometimes Judy bored her," and she cannot understand why their landlady in the first house in which they lived could possibly find Judy interesting enough to engage in conversation.[42]

In terms of dysfunctionality and overall negativity, therefore, Cleo creates an environment in which Judy, and, later, the cousins are forced to recognize her as the goddess of creativity, punishment, and survival, or as the queen of her self-created kingdom. Though her creativity lies mostly in the realm of lying, it is still a useful force in her arsenal of deception. She easily assumes the role of disciplinarian in connection with her nieces and nephew, which means that their own mothers get pushed to the side. Most important, she undermines each sister's homespace and charts the course of survival for the Jericho sisters as being only through her. How she treats Judy and what she thinks about her is certainly unmotherly, but what she does to her sisters is unconscionable and immoral. She turns her newly acquired ten-room house into a castle, then a prison from which it will take the sisters almost four years before they even attempt to free themselves. One manages to escape the physical premises while the other two end up with dead-end jobs that will ensure their continued dependency upon Cleo and Bart.

MY SISTERS, MY (UNSTABLE AND TEMPORARY) KINGDOM

A hunger in Cleo that is perhaps more gnawing than her desire to move up in Boston society is her desire to have her three sisters with her during that process. With the renting of the new house, she intends to bring all of them under the same roof, and she sees her task as "to lead Mr. Judson by degrees and duplicity" in the matter of getting her sisters to Boston.[43] In her manipulative lying, Cleo has no respect for the wishes of her sisters, no respect for their husbands, and no respect for the lives they have created in South Carolina and New York. All she knows is that she has a lack and that she imagines her sisters will fill that lack. Everything else is secondary. She begins her scheme by hinting to Lily, her sister in New York, that her marriage to Bart is in trouble, then she writes to Charity and Serena and hints to them that Lily is in trouble. She has already succeeded in turning Lily against Miss Fannie, the woman their father married once their mother died.[44] That is the reason Lily, who hates to travel, had left home and ended up in New York and married Victor, the Pullman porter who befriended her along the way, directed her to a rooming house once she decided that she would not travel another mile, and ended up marrying her.

The sins that accrue from Cleo's unscrupulous manipulation of her relatives boggle the mind, for she is unrelenting in her scheming. She maintains at the beginning of the project to get her sisters to Boston, when she deliberately writes a letter and misleads Lily into thinking that she is having marital difficulty and needs sisterly support, that she must continue her campaign quickly with Charity and Serena:

> She smiled with satisfaction. Lily would think she was leaving Mr. Judson. Since Lily, along with poor misguided Serena and Charity, was such a firm believer in the bonds of matrimony, she would brave the iron monster to shepherd her sister back into the marriage fold.
>
> This speculation produced a natural sequel in Cleo's wily mind. She released a quiet chuckle, then touched the tip of her pencil with her tongue and began to scribble furiously on a second sheet of paper. Things got done if you did them without thinking. If you thought, your scruples stopped you. It was always better to do today what your conscience might not let you do tomorrow.[45]

What Cleo's wiliness and repressed conscience allow her to do is lie to Lily to get her to Boston, then lie to Charity and Serena by suggesting that Lily is the one having marital problems and needs their support when she arrives in Boston. Thus, all the sisters depart for Boston in response to what they believe to be various family crises that need their immediate attention. In her ever judgmental and interfering role, the monstrous Cleo decides that her sisters are "misguided" and need to be motivated to put their husbands and marriages on hold as they head from South Carolina and New York to Boston. "All of her sisters," Cleo thinks, "were as blind as bats when it came to their husbands. They loved them. What could they find in them to love? Not a man among them was a decent provider"—in contrast to Bart obviously, though she does not offer the comment in any way to heap praise upon Bart.[46] Cleo therefore positions herself as the center of her sisters' lives just as she will shortly become the center of their children's lives.

The kingdom that Cleo seeks to create with her sisters transplanted to Boston is thus built from the beginning upon a shaky foundation, and that shaky foundation will lead to physical and mental deterioration within the homespace that Cleo constructs. Cleo easily convinces her sisters upon arrival that there has been mutual misunderstanding all around, that all is well in her marriage, and that Lily is perfectly fine. The stage is thus set for the ultimate undermining of the marriages, for Cleo initiates shopping sprees and sightseeing ventures that dazzle her less-advantaged and less-traveled siblings, which delay their departures. Their trips down memory lane, with Cleo at the center of reminiscing, also keep them enthralled with the house and the city in which Cleo resides. For this rich and rather pleasant time, therefore, Cleo succeeds in recreating the home life that she has romanticized from her youth in South Carolina. Her efforts to maintain it indefinitely lead to the second phase of her plan, that is, her intent to keep her sisters with her permanently. She begins to achieve that by attempting to turn each of her sisters away from her husband. Such a move is loaded with irony, for Cleo, financially secure in her troubled marriage to Bart, never contemplates severing the relationship with her own husband. What she does is perhaps worse, for even as she enjoys the company of her sisters, she puts Bart out of her bed, relegates him to a closet of a bedroom, and sends Serena's son Tim to sleep with him as she invites Judy into her bed; Charity sleeps with her daughter Penny, and Lily sleeps with her daughter Victoria. This spatial configuration of the sleeping arrangements in the house mirrors Cleo's sense of the world, that is, one in which men are absent or relegated to insignificant spaces and insignificant roles. Fittingly and even more ironically, she thus assumes the role of head of the household—usually identified as male—and "husband" to her three sisters as well as "husband" to her husband in her ability to direct and orchestrate his every action in the space of the ten-room house. Her kingdom very quickly devolves into a psychological as well as a physical prison for the majority of its inhabitants.

To ensure that the shaky kingdom thrives for as long as it can, Cleo determines that she will keep her sisters in Boston. She uses a combination of strategies to achieve her objective, all of which are shady, unscrupulous, and unconscionable. First, Cleo pours gasoline on the strained relationships between the sisters and their husbands when the sisters become so enamored of Boston that they extend their original plans for visiting. Cleo's old practice of insulting and denigrating men is crucial to this strategy. Second, Cleo works to entrap them even further when she becomes ill in response to their new plans for departure. Having been the center of their attention most of the time when they were children, Cleo calls upon those reserves and evokes a sense of guilt in all her sisters, none of whom will then be so heartless as to desert an ill Cleo. Third, their delayed departures make them completely dependent financially upon Cleo—using resources that Bart has provided, of course. It is a dependency that Cleo relishes—at least initially—for the queen can only be queen if she has subjects, and Cleo can only keep her romanticized dream of recreating her southern family on northern soil if the sisters remain willingly. In a period that is consonant with the movement north of many who participated in the Great Migration, the sisters may follow the physical path of that migration, but its results are far from the images that James Van Der Zee pictures in such photographs as "Couple in Raccoon Coats."

Cleo is heartless in her response to the dissolution of her second sister's marriage. Charity's husband Ben has been clear on her departure that his faithfulness would depend upon her quick return. While that honesty is noteworthy, it also speaks to the fact that Charity has probably married a man whom she might have been better suited to have avoided. In replying to her repeated questions about whether he will remain true to her while she is in Boston, Ben simply asks: "'How long you figure to be away?'"[47] He is clearer in seeing through Cleo than Charity can ever be, and he is skeptical about her motives: "'That Cleo and her letters! That Miss Big Dog!' The words were spat. 'Wouldn't surprise me if it ain't her back of the bust-up of Lily and her man. I'm giving you warning. You stay out of her clutches. I wouldn't put it past her to turn a baby against its mother's milk.'"[48] Ben's insightful observation has no impact upon Charity, so she goes to Boston, stays longer than she expects, and finds her marriage dissolved when Ben writes to tell her that he has another woman and that he is sending her and Penny's clothes to Boston. Despite the fact that Charity and Ben had a good marriage, Cleo dismisses it and denigrates Ben: "Cleo sat down on the edge of the bed. Her face was cold. 'Charity, I'm going to talk harsh to help you over the hurt. That dog did you so dirty it makes you think you lost the moon and the stars. All you lost was a nigger who didn't have a dime when you married him and's got no more now. I've been wanting to say this for years. You were always too good for him.'"[49] Charity still avows love for Ben and wonders if he would leave the other woman if she returned, to which Cleo's response is "'Go back for her to cut you in ribbons? Go back to hear Ben say what it came near killing you to read? How could I live with my conscience if I sent my own sister into a cage of lions?'"[50] Thus Cleo, who holds the purse strings, puts the period to the end of Charity's marriage by not providing resources for her to return to South Carolina. The outcome might indeed have been as Cleo predicted, but Cleo does not give Charity a choice. She makes the decision that keeps Charity in Boston and without financial resources beyond those that Cleo supplies. Cleo makes Charity a "man-size breakfast" as a pacifier to grief and refuses to leave the table until Charity eats it all.[51] After eating, crying, and sleeping, Charity concludes: "What happened to her happened to other women. They went on living in their twilight. If you kept your stomach full, looked like nothing seemed so bad as when your stomach was empty"; thus begins an eating disorder that will lead to Charity's being confined to the house for four years and to her "laming" "herself with gluttony."[52] Indeed, Meredith Goldsmith refers to Charity as "the first compulsive overeater in African-American fiction."[53] Nonetheless, as Goldsmith also notes, Charity uses the stereotype of the overweight, "she must be a good cook" black woman to get out of Cleo's house when she accepts a job that she aligns with the visual image of her body: "In a reversal of power, Charity's acquiescence to this stereotype offers her a measure of freedom from the increasingly claustrophobic household."[54] Charity might not be completely free of this unhealthy homespace, but she does make a decision independent of Cleo.

Playing a more direct role in the dissolution of Lily's marriage, Cleo continues without conscience. When Victor writes a letter from New York, Cleo lies to the gullible Lily about its contents. Cleo's influence over Lily has already turned Lily against their father's new wife. Cleo is even more effective in turning Lily against Victor. Cleo "got Lily so stirred up that she was afraid to open Victor's next letter. As if it were a hot coal, she handed it to Cleo to open for her."[55] Cleo thus interprets as dangerous and intimidating a letter in which Victor simply entreats Lily to return: "'He's not messed up with any woman. But he's fixing to mess you up as soon as he sees you. I won't tell you what he said word for word. No sense in scaring you. But I wouldn't trust him not to beat your brains out. That's why I was sorry when you married him. You never know when a low-class man is going to get ugly. My advice to you is to sit tight until his temper cools off.'"[56] Totally in control of Lily's psychological and emotional response to Victor, Cleo unsettles Lily so much that when Victor comes to Boston, Lily literally attacks him, tearing at his face with her fingernails, and ending the attack by calling him a "black nigger."[57] Colorphobia is also at work here as the brown Victor is "savagely conscious of Lily's white skin and the golden skin of her sister."[58] He departs and will not return until four years later when Cleo will refer to him as "Mister Nigger" and will steal part of the money he has given her for Lily to get a divorce.[59]

Ugliness on Cleo's part reigns in the novel, but her interference in and responses to the marriages of her sisters take her to new lows. She is undeniably evil, but they are undeniably stupid. Charity knows that she loves Ben, yet she makes no effort to try to save her marriage. Lily knows how helpful Victor was to her when she was on the train from South Carolina and how he came to her rescue in New York, yet she refuses to read the letters from him, believes everything Cleo wants her to believe about him, and is more than willing to allow her daughter to grow up without a loving father. Both are like laboratory animals in an experiment of influence, and Cleo wields the potion of influence potently, effectively, and without an iota of remorse. In both marriages, the husbands were supportive and loving; it is only because of Cleo's intervention that things take a turn for the worse.

It is only Serena, the youngest sister, who stands by her husband against Cleo, but his life after Serena leaves for Boston becomes so unhinged that he suffers mental deterioration. A fragile young man who is victimized by his outsider status as mixed race, so light that he could pass for white, Robert viewed Serena as the stable force in his life. When she departs and leaves him living with her father, he moves to another town to try to find work. Passing for white and working as a police officer, he kills another officer who is attacking a black man during a riot. Having learned of his fate through a visitor to her home, Cleo at least persuades Bart to hire an attorney for Robert, and that attorney succeeds in getting him freed. Nonetheless, Cleo is tactless when she informs Serena that Robert has "committed murder": "Cleo said, 'I wanted you to know what kind of man you married. I wanted you to see I was right to want to separate you.'"[60] Transported to Boston, Robert is confined to a mental facility, the expenses for which Serena provides when she leaves Cleo's house and becomes a live-in maid. Though Cleo does not denigrate Robert as much as she does Ben and Victor, she is still unrepentant and, from her perspective, "right," in her meddling, and it is still the sequence of events that she has set into motion that leads to the situation in which Robert finds himself.

Cleo's carefully constructed kingdom of cards has clearly diminished in stature by the fourth year the sisters are in Boston. Her sisters' desire to separate themselves from Cleo is obvious when she gives the infamous Christmas party that she believes will cement her position among the black elite in Boston society: "part of her mind was quite certain that this was the hour which gave her whole life meaning."[61] This sentiment echoes a moment earlier in the narrative when Cleo, visiting one of the black elites, had thought: "She would give her soul to sit behind this exquisite tea-table and pass these fragile cups to the admiring ladies of her acquaintance."[62] And, indeed, her soul is about the price she pays for all the events leading up to this fateful Christmas gathering. Though the caterer outdoes himself in producing a feast for royals, no one in Cleo's household will join her in the downstairs celebration. Everyone, including Bart, provides excuses and disappears to the upper portion of the house for the evening. Cleo, undeterred, lies her way through questions about the whereabouts of her sisters.

> 'My sister Charity lost her husband in early September. She's now away on a visit to Father. I wanted him to spend Christmas with us, but the long trip here and back would give him too short a holiday before he returned to his teaching duties. My sister Lily is away, too. Her husband travels for a firm that sells improvements for stubborn hair.' . . . 'He telephoned Lily last night to meet him in New York this morning . . . . As for my youngest sister—who sends her apologies, Tim's quite feverish from too much Christmas excitement—her husband, who is very fair, is working as white in a very prejudiced part of the South. It means indefinite separation.' . . . She smiled brightly at her own ability to taste untruths on her tongue and make no betraying grimace.[63]

Meanwhile, everyone in her family is upstairs being as quiet as proverbial church mice. In her explanations, Cleo has promoted her father from farmer to teacher, the non-traveling Lily is now a jetsetter, and Serena is nursing a sick child. Her textual audience is no less mesmerized by Cleo and her lies than the reading audience, for Cleo takes prevarication to an art form. No art form, however, can supplant reality permanently.

The constant drain on Bart's finances over the four-year period has been astronomical, with rent, food and clothing for the household, and utilities being ongoing major expenses. And of course there are the expenses connected with Bart's business. With only Bart as the primary breadwinner, and with Cleo constantly scheming and taking money intended for one purpose to use for another, there is no way that the kingdom can stand. The last sequence in the novel has Cleo desperately trying to figure out how to pay eighty dollars in back rent by 4 p.m. on the day that a dispossess notice is to take effect, Charity is desperately trying to mix ingredients to make cheap food appetizing to the children when they come home from school, Cleo fails in her attempt to rent out rooms in the house, the children want Easter outfits so they will not be embarrassed before the bragging Irish students at their school, Lily has only eight dollars to contribute to household expenses instead of her usual twelve, and Bart is awaiting his fate in the sale of the block on which his business is located. Yet, despite the hammer of doom hanging over her head, Queen Cleo continues to lie, scheme, and lie some more. She tells a visiting Thea that the phone has been disconnected because someone down the street with the same name has not paid their bill, and that that family of Judsons has been confused with hers. She tells Lily that Victor left a hundred dollars for a divorce when he really left two hundred, and she allocates its expenditure with the passing observation that, "Lily didn't want a divorce. It was Victor who wanted one. Let him get one the best way he could."[64] And she tells Bart that Serena has not contributed anything to household expenses when she finally has to seek the rent money from him because she has spent the previously allotted amount.

It would be fair to say that Cleo is the *lying-est* black character in African American literature. Her inadequate status as a mother might find some competition in the likes of Margarete Palms or Emma Jean Peace, but no character, *absolutely no character*, surpasses Cleo for being a despicable liar. Her ability to execute the lies raises comparable questions to Emma Jean. How can a single individual control the lives of at least a dozen people through the sheer force of her dominant personality and lying art? What does that set of circumstances suggest about the characters around the liar and their general intelligence? Bart knows Cleo lies, but he does not know the extent to which she does. His deliberate and willful blindness enables Cleo to get away with a host of untruths. And not only is he aware of her lies, but he is equally aware of her duplicity. When she comes seeking money for a lawyer for Robert, Bart remonstrates: "'God knows I'm sorry for Serena. God knows I wish there was some other way to save Robert. But you're the one that took that girl away from her husband. You're the one kept her away. You got what you wanted. Now ask God's forgiveness for the sin on your soul.'"[65] Bart has issued no such assessment and offered no such directive for the majority of the time the sisters have been living with the Judsons. He has stood by silently through the lies and the deception. His fear of losing Cleo ultimately backfires into the very thing he has accepted her lies to prevent: the dissolution of his marriage.

Cleo's sisters are certainly not painted as being as intelligent as Cleo, but they are not completely devoid of abilities to think and reason. Yet they seem to cast all their common sense aside in giving over their lives, indeed their very imaginations, to their older sister. And that giving is not handled tenderly. Contemplating Cleo's verbal abuse of the husbands makes that clear. Also, Cleo grows to heap verbal abuse directly upon the sisters, especially Charity. After eating herself into an inability to socialize, Charity is confined to Cleo's house and the cooking duties that accrue to being an indigent relative. Cleo at one point refers to her as an "ignorant darky" and insults Charity with the size she has grown into over the years: "'You haven't put the first foot outside the front door in four years. You've lived for this kitchen. Pretty soon nothing will fit you but a tent. No wonder you're worried about keeping a roof over your head. I'd worry, too, if I thought they'd have to cut a bigger door to get me out.'"[66] Cleo has thus grown to disapprove of what she herself has created; she feels sorry about the horrible comment almost instantly, but she has not cultivated a habit of apologizing for anything. When a neighbor wants to hire Charity to cook, Cleo refers to Charity's size as a way to discourage her, though she relents. Later, she will tell Serena yet another lie—that she had to force Charity out of the house to accept the job.[67]

As Cleo herself recognizes, she is a grand and glorious performer. Although she maintains that she prefers to tell her lies one on one, she nonetheless performs well when she has more than one person in her audience, as she does on the occasion when she lies to her guests about the whereabouts of her sisters during the Christmas party. The performing aspect of her character can perhaps be traced in part back to an early desire of Cleo's. While in Springfield, Cleo thinks that she is "going on the stage," though she is careful to indicate that she "wasn't going to sing an old love-song with any greasy-haired coon. She wasn't going to dance any cakewalk with him either, and let his sweaty hand ruin her fancy costumes."[68] The substance of the dream might get pushed to the side, but the reality does not. Cleo is constantly "on stage" and performing, and she is constantly aware of what her staging means to her as well as to those around her. She even admires herself for lying so boldly to her Christmas party guests. She combines her manipulation of audience with her need for audiences. This enters into her adult relationship with her sisters when she "longs" "for the eager audience they would have provided, the boisterous mirth she would have evoked when she flatfooted up an imaginary flight of stairs, agitating her bottom," and it is realized when the sisters show up and she regales them with countless tales.[69] A listening Judy wonders why Cleo captivates her sister audience so effectively: "Was it her voice? Did they like to listen to her talk just to hear the music sounds she made? Was it because she was so full of life that she made things move inside you, tears or laughter or anger, and when she went out of a room something like something alive left with her?"[70] Judy's implicit awareness of the vibrancy of Cleo's performances mirrors how the sisters react to Cleo, for they are unfailingly enthralled.

Whether performing for her sisters or for the innocent who are stupid enough to believe what she tells them, Cleo links theatricality and untruthfulness in a powerful blend that sustains her throughout the novel. The world is indeed her stage, and she consistently owns it. No one in the text can match her for theatrical manipulation—not that anyone would necessarily want to do so. And no one can match her finesse in delivering falsehoods. When she tells Bart that she is getting furniture for the house from a white woman who had initially offered it to Thea, she threads the narrative in such a complicated way that Bart dares not approach the woman to inquire about the deal (Cleo really got the furniture *for free* from one of the elite black women). She maintains that she needs two hundred dollars to pay for the furniture and will not agree to Bart's confronting the woman to seal the deal. Following several lies that go in complex directions after Cleo multiplies them to cover initial falsehoods, Cleo "heave[s] a long sigh of relief" when Bart leaves the matter to her instead of attempting to handle it himself, which leads her to conclude: "If you could tell a bold enough lie, you could get anyone to believe you."[71] Audience manipulation and performance combine to give Cleo the upper hand in almost all of her dealings. Without conscience or morality to guide her (though, ironically, she thanks God for setting the pieces in motion that enable her to pay the rent on the dispossess day), Cleo is a force set loose on those in her world, an amoral one against which those with whom she interacts are obviously no match for her performances.

There is simply no bottom to Cleo's duplicity, her guile, or her lies. Such portraiture raises questions about West's overall intent in limning Cleo the way she does. By making Cleo as despicable as she is, is West in some way getting revenge on a mother who allowed her own relatives to invade her home? By creating a character whom readers would judge and almost certainly reject, is West putting her own mother in the place to receive this "justice" for what she perceived to be her sin of homespace violation? If there is no such "justice in fiction" motive operative here, then what other explanation might come to mind? Perhaps West, strikingly before her time, is interested in pushing the limits of black female representation to encompass some of the things that tradition separates from depictions of black female characters. Tradition, for example, would very easily reject Cleo for not sacrificing for Judy in a more morally acceptable way, for being out of the church, for using her physical features to the detriment of those around her, and for having a personality that perhaps only a mother could love. West paints Cleo outside of just about everything readers have come to know as representative of African American literature and outside of what many would consider remotely acceptable behavior for a black female character. And yet, there she is, and with her presence, there is a rationale for her creation. The likeliest explanation seems to be a combination of the biographical and the fictional, as West went on a journey perhaps to understand for herself how such a character and the workings of such a mind could find a place in a literature that, prior to this depiction, had been pretty pristine in its representation of black female character.

Experiment, revenge, or something more, what is clear in *The Living Is Easy* is that, in what is rapidly becoming another tradition in African American literature, there are few secure, healthy, or happy homespaces. Cleo's relationship with Bart and Judy was one of deception and turmoil before the sisters arrived from South Carolina and New York, and it continues to be so even more after their arrival. The roominess of the house that could have been home to so many becomes a house of horrors. The memories that Cleo wants her sisters to bring into this space in the re-creation of their lives in South Carolina become heavier than chains as the women find themselves emotionally locked in a space that is more dungeon than castle. It is a space where things substitute for love, as the children are given countless gifts for Christmas but receive no expressions of love—or even acceptance—from Cleo. It is a space where one sister grows monstrously obese, another deserts, and the third flits from one inadequately paying job to another because she does not have the backbone to stand up to any of her employers. Characters do not grow in this space; they diminish—or they leave. The children are not growing into who they can be as individual, autonomous beings; they are growing into competition with the Irish, another despised group. There is thus no broader vision for human growth and development that exists in this space. Instead, it is a space where dreams go to become dormant—if not to die altogether, and that includes Cleo's dreams, which are perhaps better labeled schemes than dreams. No matter her attempts to join the elite, Cleo will remain an outsider without the name and generational currency that will enable her to be anything but an errand girl for the Altheas and Simeons of that world. Whenever she looks around her and sees a huge house that needs constant repairs, she can be conscious that this house will never be the home that she intended. Thea and Simeon might have financial reversals, but they are still Binneys, and the Binneys have been a part of Boston society for generations. Cleo might stretch her financial resources to the limit to entertain them, but she will never be one of them, no matter how many large houses she inhabits or how many parties she hosts. Whether she is willing to admit it or not, her dream is pretty much dead at the end of the novel. Her wistful contemplation of who will love her most and settling on her nephew Tim is a desperate attempt to salvage something from the losses she has endured. What she can never salvage, however, is the substance of a mother who could have been willing to make a home for her husband, her child, and the relatives whom she invites into that space.

NOTES

1. Dorothy West, *The Living Is Easy* (New York: The Feminist Press, 1982). While the novel may be read satirically, I have chosen instead to read it in the same mode as the other fictional works I cover, for, even if it is designed to sting, it nonetheless makes sufficient points about class, strivers, pigmentocracy, and black family life and homespace.

2. Meredith Goldsmith, "The Wages of Weight: Dorothy West's Corporeal Politics," *Mosaic* 40, no. 4 (December 2007), 35.

3. Delores Phillips, *The Darkest Child* (2004; New York, Soho, 2018). In "A Different Image of the Black Woman," *Callaloo*, vol. 16 (October 1982): 146–51, I discuss how unusual Cleo is as a black female character.

4. Delia Steverson is working with Delores Phillips's family to publish more of her work. Sondra Washington included commentary on Phillips's *The Darkest Child* in her dissertation and is currently at work revising that project for publication.

5. Dorothy West, who was one of the youngest members of the Harlem Renaissance, had arrived in Harlem from Boston when she was a teenager. West's mother, like Cleo Judson in the novel, brought her extended family to live with her, her husband, and her daughter, with the husband, like Bart Judson, being saddled with responsibility for the entire lot. Under five feet tall, dark-skinned and visibly Negroid, West perhaps based the character of Judy on her own family history, for, like Judy, she was the dark and, in her own estimation, homely spot in a family of light-skinned beauties. In her "Afterword" to the Feminist Press edition of the novel, Adelaide M. Cromwell, who knew Dorothy West personally, notes that "The West family home on Brookline Avenue at one time included thirteen persons, all relatives of Rachel West [Dorothy's mother], who was one of twenty-two children" (360).

6. West, *Easy*, 35.
7. West, *Easy*, 35.
8. West, *Easy*, 35–36.
9. West, *Easy*, 199.
10. West, *Easy*, 242–43.
11. West, *Easy*, 45.
12. West, *Easy*, 57.

13. For an extended discussion of class, race, and the spatial dynamics that define them, set against the historical Boston Brahmins, see Cherene Sherrard-Johnson. "'This plague of their own locusts': Space, Property, and Identity in Dorothy West's *The Living is Easy*," *African American Review* 38, no. 4 (2004): 609–24.

14. West, *Easy*, 150, 234, 276.
15. West, *Easy*, 150.
16. West, *Easy*, 151.
17. West, *Easy*, 234.
18. West, *Easy*, 213.
19. West, *Easy*, 276.
20. West, *Easy*, 72.
21. West, *Easy*, 38.
22. West, *Easy*, 70.

23. Pamela Peden Sanders offers a detailed discussion of gender in the novel in "The Feminism of Dorothy West's *The Living Is Easy*: A Critique of the Limitations of the Female Sphere through Performative Gender Roles," *African American Review* 36, no. 3 (2002): 435–446. In contrast to my reading, Sanders is much more optimistic about the ending of the novel, by which point, she argues, Cleo has merged the masculine and feminine traits of her personality and is poised to move forward into a healthier future.

24. West, *Easy*, 71.
25. West, *Easy*, 146.
26. West, *Easy*, 347.
27. West, *Easy*, 345.

28. West, *Easy*, 267.
29. West, *Easy*, 39.
30. West, *Easy*, 3, 4.
31. West, *Easy*, 89, 90.
32. West. *Easy*, 38.
33. West, *Easy*, 39.
34. West, *Easy*, 39.
35. West, *Easy*, 42.
36. West, *Easy*, 137.
37. West, *Easy*, 5.
38. West, *Easy*, 38.
39. West, *Easy*, 301.
40. West, *Easy*, 308.
41. West, *Easy*, 220.
42. West, *Easy*, 219.
43. West, *Easy*, 75.
44. West, *Easy*, 51–52.
45. West, *Easy*, 83.
46. West, *Easy*, 50.
47. West, *Easy*, 158, 160.
48. West, *Easy*, 158–59.
49. West, *Easy*, 177.
50. West, *Easy*, 178.
51. West, *Easy*, 178.
52. West, *Easy*, 179, 292.
53. Goldsmith, "Wages," 37.
54. Goldsmith, "Wages," 46.
55. West, *Easy*, 179.
56. West, *Easy*, 180.
57. West, *Easy*, 181, 182.
58. West, *Easy*, 182.
59. West, *Easy*, 336.
60. West, *Easy*, 304.
61. West, *Easy*, 245.
62. West, *Easy*, 115.
63. West, *Easy*, 246–47.
64. West, *Easy*, 338.
65. West, *Easy*, 276.
66. West, *Easy*, 309, 290.
67. West, *Easy*, 323.
68. West, *Easy*, 29.
69. West, *Easy*, 44.
70. West, *Easy*, 202.
71. West, *Easy*, 153.

Chapter 6

Wrapped in Imagination and Desire

Countee Cullen, "Heritage"; Ann Petry, "Mother Africa"; Lorraine Hansberry, **A Raisin in the Sun** *(1959); Alice Walker, "Everyday Use" (1973); Toni Morrison,* **Song of Solomon** *(1977); Phyllis Alesia Perry,* **Stigmata** *(1998); Yaa Gyasi,* **Homegoing** *(2016); James Weldon Johnson; Sterling A. Brown*

In her scheming to rent a house that is impressive enough for her to claw her way into interaction with those of the upper echelon of Boston's black elite, Cleo reflects a pattern of migration and attempted integration that is duplicated many times over in African American history as well as in the literature. The characters may migrate from the South or from the Caribbean in attempts to transform their previous existences into something that is more conducive to their conceptions of the possibilities of living. In this context, Cleo shares kinship with Silla Boyce in Paule Marshall's *Brown Girl, Brownstones* (1959).[1] Like Cleo, Silla wheels and deals, schemes and lies, only to get the brownstone she wants at the loss of her marriage, the death of her husband, and almost at the price of her relationship with her two daughters. In both instances, migration has served as a major factor in the women's desire to acquire houses and establish homes that are dramatically different from the ones they have known. Cleo wants to erase her southernness (even as she appreciates the culture and oral traditions that define it) while Silla, having come from Barbados to the United States, must find a way to lessen her ties to that countrified background. Both women end up with the huge houses but without the relationships that would truly define them as homes. Cleo tries desperately to rent rooms in the ten-room house that is slowly deteriorating by the end of the novel. Silla acquires ownership of a brownstone that she believes will mark her arrival in America and signal a shedding of some of her foreign, Bajan status as she moves toward acceptance into American society, or at least into greater acceptance among the other house-owning Bajans who reside in her New York neighborhood.

The possibilities that appeal to both women characters are aligned with northern United States territory and frequently with urban areas. What the North represented to those abandoning one kind of home and seeking another has been well documented, with Isabel Wilkerson's *The Warmth of Other Suns* being a classic in that documentation.[2] Beginning in the nineteenth century, however, with the founding of various colonization societies during slavery and with missionaries such as Alexander Crummell electing to complete work in Africa, a corollary—though far less dramatized—pattern involved the movement of peoples of African descent in the United States back to the Continent, to what they perceived as their ancestral home. Certainly the case of Liberia is well known. It would take the concerted efforts of a small group of intellectuals, however, to posit the appeal of Africa in the early twentieth century. This was especially the case with some of the intellectuals of the Harlem Renaissance, such as Alain Locke and Aaron Douglas, who embraced African culture and art as the distinct heritage of blacks in the United States. Visual imagery of African art and sculpture thus adorned such publications as Locke's *The New Negro* (1925).[3] Evocation of African scenes and figures was key to many of Douglas's paintings, images of which often graced various publications of the period, such as James Weldon Johnson's *God's Trombones* (1927).[4] Scholar J. Lee Greene notes that "in embracing the African past as part of the period's artistic movement in primitivism, African American artists in essence sought to effect or to recapture an Edenic ideal, which existed more in their imaginations than in reality. To them, Africa represented a simpler, idyllic life, void of racism and other dehumanizing conflicts."[5] While such embracings may have been heartfelt, they did not reflect the attitudes of the majority of black intellectuals during the period, and they certainly did not reflect the opinions of the average working class black person. Africa, even to people of African descent, was still largely a place of mystery and a source of stereotype. It would be well into the mid- and late twentieth century before there was widespread embracing of Africa as the natural heritage of black people in America and before there was measurable pride in associating with the Continent as homeland. During this time, then, another pattern develops in the literature: a return to Africa. Prior to such progressive response to the

Continent, Africa was a troubled space for defining African American identity. Awakening to Africa and problems with Africa can be traced from the Harlem Renaissance.

MYTHOLOGIZING HOME

When Langston Hughes threw his books into the Harlem River just before he departed for Africa in 1923, he thought he was on a voyage home.[6] He embarks upon his journey, therefore, with hopeful anticipation of becoming a "new me," of being welcomed home. That enthusiasm continues as Hughes makes an initial landing on African soil and remarks upon the place and the people. Upon arriving at Dakar, Senegal in 1923, Hughes rhapsodizes in this manner: "My Africa, Motherland of the Negro peoples! And me a Negro!," he wrote, "Africa! The real thing, to be touched and seen, not merely read about in a book."[7] That enthusiasm waned fast as he complained about clothing and his rejection by Nigerians, who labeled him a white man. Such a response might not have wounded him permanently, or totally transformed his idea of Africa, but it might have conveyed to him the fallacy inherent in assuming unquestioned embracing from Africans. The Nigerians let him know that he was not home, that he was just as alien to them as the whites whose genes had infected his skin color.

Hughes had not contemplated fully how Africans would respond to him. Certainly, as Hughes's biographer Arnold Rampersad points out, Hughes had some reservations[8]; still, he believed in his ability to re-enter what he perceived to be his lost motherland and be welcomed there, a situation that would certainly have been a motivating force for optimism. It was only after more encounters with Africans that, as Rampersad asserts, Hughes's excitement waned, and Hughes was forced to revise his views of Africa, especially when, because of his lighter skin color, the people he anticipated would welcome him as a brother labeled him a "white man."[9] Hughes, as many life writers after him would do, documented his experiences on African soil. Others resorted to fiction and poetry to imagine an Africa on which they never had an opportunity to set foot or before such opportunities presented themselves. Perhaps one of the best known such poetic renditions is Countee Cullen's in his long poem "Heritage," published in the 1920s.[10] The fact that Cullen even penned a poem about Africa is an indication, as with the Locke volume, the Douglas paintings, and the Hughes memoir, of the concern of intellectuals of the period with the Continent. What is striking about Cullen's poem, however, is that it is cut from whole cloth, so to speak, in that it is based more in fantasy than in fact.

Cullen derives his Africa from books and imagination. "What is Africa to me," he intones, and proceeds in droning fashion to answer that question.[11] The source of his "knowledge" about Africa combines with the sing-songy rhyme scheme of the poem and his play on "lying" to create something that never existed in reality. Cullen's Africa is one that has strong men and women, "wild barbaric birds," "young forest lovers," beautiful animals and vegetation, "Jungle boys and girls in love," and an overall lush natural environment.[12] Cullen's images and conception of Africa, however, come from "A book one thumbs/ Listlessly, till slumber comes."[13] Having no real encounter with the Continent, the speaker resorts to reading, which is the next best thing for information to supply his imagination. His Africa is one of picture books and creative inspiration, bolstered by a chorus of stereotypical drumbeats that the repetitively-stressed lines reiterate. Africa is being beaten into his head even as he puts forth the pictures that the book and his imagination evoke. From the perspective of image and rhythm, Africa is inescapable to the speaker, and he tries his best to control the impact the Continent has upon him emotionally, physically, and spiritually. His Africa is one that draws upon him, pulls upon him, beats into his very blood. Even as he questions what Africa means to him, he collapses lying in bed with lying about his relationship to the Continent. As he is in the process of exploring what Africa might mean to him, he is also in the process of trying to deny its hold upon him and therefore lying to himself about how strong that hold really is. His denial is couched as "unremembering," which introduces a tie between history that is learned through books and history/culture that is inherent in one's very being. Having moved beyond the realm of remembering, which is as fleeting, he avows, as last year's snow, his body and the beat of the rain replace what his mental faculties will not yield, for they focus on the qualities of Africa that are essentially written within his being, which means that the body remembers what the brain does not.

Caught between Old World images and New World reality, the speaker contrasts Africa to America in terms of physicality and religion. Despite his efforts to contain the call of Africa, he nonetheless hears it in his very body as well as in the rain. He can thus "find no peace/ Night or day, no slight release/ From the unremittent beat/ Made by cruel padded feet/ Walking through my body's street./ Up and down they go, and back, /Treading out a jungle track."[14] At war with himself for containment to thwart the call of a physical force against which he has little resistance, the speaker "twists," "squirms," and "writhes" in response to the magnetic pull that commands, "'Strip!/ Doff this new exuberance./ Come and dance the Lover's Dance!'"[15] His ultimate attempt to resist is to resort to asserting his Christianity, which he offers as a contrast to the "Quaint, outlandish heathen gods/ Black men fashion out of rods,/ Clay, and brittle bits of stone,/ In a likeness like their own,/ My conversion came high-priced;/ I belong to Jesus Christ,/ Preacher of humility;/ Heathen gods are naught to me."[16] This movement in the poem pits mythological conceptions of Africa as "heathen" against the "Christian" West into which the speaker has been born. There may be conflict, but there is also stereotype, and the stereotype, the myth that captures the speaker's imagination, is one in which "civilized" America is supposed to be superior to "heathen" Africa. The "lying" mythology about the Continent has fully saturated his consciousness, but it ultimately fails, for the speaker recognizes that he is not only lying *about* Africa, but he is lying *to* himself.

> Father, Son, and Holy Ghost,
> So I make an idle boast;
> Jesus of the twice-turned cheek,
> Lamb of God, although I speak
> With my mouth thus, in my heart
> Do I play a double part.
> Ever at Thy glowing altar
> Must my heart grow sick and falter,
> Wishing He I served were black,
> Thinking then it would not lack
> Precedent of pain to guide it,
> Let who would or might deride it;
> Surely then this flesh would know
> Yours had borne a kindred woe.[17]

Lack of identification with an "alien" god, drawn in Christianity as not having suffered in the same ways that people of African descent have, gives the speaker just enough hesitation about western religion to link him irrevocably with his imagined Africa and its many gods. As he fashions "dark gods," he knows that he is outside the expectations of and perhaps anathema to Christianity. In order to be Christian—or pretend to be—he must "*Quench* [his] *pride and cool* [his] *blood*" (italics in original) to prevent himself from "perishing" "*in the flood*" (italics in original) of memory and unqualified identification with Africa.[18]

No matter his attempts to control the flood, his final conclusion is that the call of Africa has a more lasting power than the Christian West. "*Not yet has my heart or head*," the speaker asserts at the end of the poem, "*in the least way realized/ They and I are civilized*" (italics in original).[19] That lack of realization echoes Claude McKay's "Outcast," in which he maintains that, by being born away from Africa and in the West, he was born out of place and time.[20] While Cullen takes a leisurely, repetitive route to arriving at that conclusion, McKay is much more direct, as he necessarily has to be in sonnet form. Cullen's pondering fits his just-before-sleep contemplation, and it reflects his inability to contain the very containment that has occupied him throughout the poem. The call of Africa is stronger than his Christianity, stronger than his body's desire to resist, stronger than his immersion in the West. Still, the fact that he presents that call in the context of civilization versus lack of civilization nonetheless mires the poem permanently in the realm of myth and stereotype.

Although Cullen never specifically posits Africa as home, the fact that he engages it at all suggests a recognition of kinship at some level—or at least a place of origin. He recognizes his kinship when he asserts that the "regal black/ Women" are ones "from whose loins [he] sprang."[21] His undeniable ties to Africa leave him conflicted, and that may be appropriate for the time period in which he penned "Heritage." Authors and life writers in the mid-twentieth century would experience no such ambiguity in embracing Africa. Just as the Kwanzaa holiday was created to note African American origins in and ties to Africa, so fictional and autobiographical works of the period made similar claims. Some, such as Don L. Lee's "But He Was Cool or: he even stopped for green lights," implicitly chastised people of African descent in America who believed that African speech and dress, mere superficial markers, were sufficient to show kinship to Africa.[22] Others, such as Marita Golden in *Migrations of the Heart: A Personal Odyssey* (1983), met and interacted with Africans in communities of foreigners in the United States, made the trek to Africa, and wrote about their adventures. Specifically, Golden married a Nigerian and spent three years on the Continent. She wrote about those years in her memoir, and, while in Africa, she interviewed other transplanted black Americans and published articles about their efforts to find home in Africa. Repeatedly, such migrants viewed Africa as home in part because they were among a black majority. Some felt they had more freedom than America could ever provide. Golden herself remarked:

> To set foot on the continent that we no longer called home but that, in a historical sense, had birthed us, had become a necessary pilgrimage. A way of discovering who, indeed, we were. In the sixties Africa was a symbol and source of pride and regeneration. Renouncing the horrors of our slave past in America, we psychologically leapt past cotton fields and auction blocks back to the empires of Timbuktu and Mali, village life, Swahili, noble kings and tribal tongues. Hungrily we read, exchanged and discussed the books that revealed Africa's resilient cultures, its plunder at the hands of white conquerors, and its betrayal by its own sons. So those of us who became women and men in the late sixties sojourned to Africa in the seventies because peace of mind and self-definition required nothing less.[23]

In her embracing of Africa generally and Nigeria specifically, Golden exhibits what I articulate as "African fever":

I use the phrase African fever specifically to refer to people of African descent who are born in the United States and who long fervently, urgently, for re-connection to Africa; that longing might be manifested socially and politically in clothing and actions in the United States or in actual travel to the continent. As with any fever, African fever reflects a burning that can be alleviated only with the palliative designed specifically for that condition. In the case of African fever, the burning is the sensation that people of African descent in the new world have been thrust from the breast of their rightful mother, that is, the continent of Africa. The burning is a desire to be re-united with that lost mother, for the belief is that it is only her breast milk, so to speak, that is, her nurturing, that will soothe the cast-aside child. The return to Africa is the palliative. Setting foot on the continent, persons with this condition believe, will eliminate the burning.[24]

Golden embraces Africa in a highly romanticized way. She praises market women and hints that they are superior to African American women, ignores the faulty infrastructure (poor roads, on-and-off electricity), and, for an extended period, tries to reconcile with her husband's and his family's ill-treatment of her. The idea that she has returned to her ancestral home is the most important thing to her. She observes early in her memoir:

In six weeks I had roamed from Accra to Takoradi, through Dahomey to Lagos. And as I explored this small portion of Africa, I passed through a jungle of startling, new, often wonderful emotions. A sense of community enveloped me during the journey. The tensions inbred by a society intent upon convincing me I did not exist had miraculously disappeared. No longer constrained to apologize for the accident of color, I'd felt free, for the first time in my life, to become whatever *else* there was inside me, and I knew there was much more than a black woman defined by white America.[25]

To Golden, Africa means a more expansive identity, one that is vastly broader than the black-white dichotomy that has defined her existence in America. Therefore, for the longest time, Golden ignores the warning signals that clash with her romanticized notions of home. Nonetheless, the contradictions are striking. Golden is a subjugated woman in an aggressively patriarchal society. She is a mother in a culture that gives primary ownership of children to men (when she finally decides to leave her husband and escape from Africa, she essentially has to kidnap her son and leave under cover of darkness in order to retain custody). And she is an abused woman. Although she asserts that her marriage is more the problem than Africa is, she fails to admit that the two are inseparably entangled. Without her intensely romanticized notions of Africa and her desperate need to claim it as an ancestral home, she never would have gotten into the situation in which she finds herself.

Golden's narrative is one of several book-length explorations of the return to Africa that began in the mid-twentieth century and continue into the twenty-first century. Richard Wright and Maya Angelou document their treks to Africa in the mid-twentieth century.[26] Alex Haley's famed return to the Continent in preparation for his writing of *Roots* (1976) might also be included in life writings about Africa.[27] In addition to traveling to the Gambia, Haley stripped to his underwear and spent a night in the hole of a ship to get a sense of what his focus character, Kunta Kinte, might have experienced during the Middle Passage. Well-known literary scholar Saidiya Hartman's *Lose Your Mother: A Journey Along the Atlantic Slave Route* (2007) and Africana studies specialist Molefi Kete Asante's *As I Run Toward Africa: A Memoir* (2011) are two of the more notable examples of returns to Africa from the twenty-first century.[28] Both the idea of losing a mother and running to a place of origin capture the idea of Africa as ancestral home that informs so much of the generic life writing in this tradition.

These life writers joined authors such as Ann Petry, Lorraine Hansberry, Alice Walker, and Toni Morrison in referencing Africa in their works. In a slightly less romanticized but no less distorted version of Africa, Petry portrays the transformative effect that thoughts of Africa have upon Emanuel "Man" Turner, her protagonist in "Mother Africa," which appears in her collection *Miss Muriel and Other Stories*.[29] A junk collector in Harlem, Man, also known as "Rags, Ole Rags, Junk, Ole Junk, Bottles, Ole Bottles" and "Mannie," had dropped out of social interactions and become a disheveled and funky trader in discarded items after his wife died in childbirth.[30] Twenty-five years later, he is gifted a statue from the white employer of his one remaining friend. Made of metal, the nude statue evokes unexplained emotions in Man, who anoints her "Mother Africa." Initially determined to sell the statue, Man instead becomes inexplicably attached to it. Not only does Mother Africa disrupt his interactions with his neighbors and others who buy his junk, as well as with one of his tenants, but it has a dramatic effect upon him. He protects the statue from neighbors who adorn it with clothing, plants a plot of grass so that it resembles statues in a nearby park, and moves his entire junk yard to a newly-built shed so that Mother Africa will not have to endure the bawdy comments and "horny" caresses of male visitors, the disapproval of his female customers, or the giggles of their children. Over several weeks, he views the statue, modifies his responses to it, and accepts it as an integral part of his life.

Man imbues the statue with an almost otherworldly aura after he cleans it. "When he was finished he stared up at her, entranced. The dark naked figure glowed. That was the word for it, he thought; glowed. He felt something stir within him, an emotion that he could not put a name to. It was like seeing something dark and beautiful beyond description for the first time and yet recognizing it, because in the deepest part of your mind you had always known that that kind of dark glowing beauty existed. Mother Africa, he thought. That's what she really is: Mother Africa."[31] Whatever Man bestows upon the statue exists only in the imaginative reaches of his mind. While he might not be as expansive in the traits he assigns to her as Cullen's narrator, he nonetheless claims some atavistic tie to her. That imaginative conception of Africa embodied in the statue as an emblem of it leads Man to change several things in his life. He displaces a tenant who attacks the statue (something he has never done before), takes three baths before he believes he has eliminated the accumulated funk of years, gets a haircut and a shave (which severely challenges the barber's skills), and changes the pants he has worn for years. Having assigned the statue an African connection, Man allows it to operate upon him as effectively as Kwanzaa may have upon various practitioners of that holiday. While it is unclear where all the changes could lead Man in terms of altering his life, those registered are sufficient to illustrate that he has some romanticized notion of what Africa can or could be. It is only when—yet again—he removes clothing that neighbors have put on the statue that he comes to his Langston Hughes-type comeuppance. Climbing a ladder to remove the headdress from the ten-foot statue, he exclaims: "'Jesus Christ!'" and comes crashing to the ground, where "He lay still, too shocked to move. It had never occurred to him that this alive-looking statue was of a white woman. There wasn't any question about it—tell by the hair, the straight sharp nose, the thin-lipped mouth. He'd been so busy looking at her breasts and her thighs, he hadn't paid any attention to the face."[32] Thus disillusioned, he races to sell the statue to Harlem Metalworks as the story ends.

The ending does not belie the fact that Man has a longing, an unfulfilled desire, that leads him to believe so fervently the statue represents/is Mother Africa. In his longing, he joins many life writers and literary characters who hope for something antithetical to their American existences in what they imagine Africa to be. Frequently, that imagining conceptualizes Africa as home. As Barbara Puschmann-Nalenz notes in her study of Petry's story, the statue "represents the origins of black Americans, a symbolic 'home,' the roots of the African American."[33] Keith Clark observes in *The Radical Fiction of Ann Petry* that "Mother Africa" "unsparingly scrutinizes black cultural beliefs and practices—specifically, the extolling of a quasi-African ontology and epistemology by blacks born on American soil and the knotty gender politics underlying this 'recuperation,' as well as blacks' eternal search for a homeland."[34] Clark further asserts that Petry "demythologizes" the idea of Africa as a lost Eden. The very fact of engaging it, however, places Petry among African American writers who recognize that blacks born on United States soil remain captive to and ever inventive of an Africa of their imaginations. So too with other literary characters.

One of Beneatha Younger's suitors in *A Raisin in the Sun* (1959) is Asagai, who is from Nigeria.[35] As the nationalistically progressive member of her family, Beneatha embraces Africa as the true source of her identity, and she makes a dramatic visual change during the course of the play when Asagai presents her with robes that he has gotten from his sister's wardrobe. Beneatha cuts her hair and dons the robes, perhaps only half-heartedly expecting that her family will understand or embrace what she has done. While her sister-in-law Ruth is finally embarrassed that Beneatha has moved so far away from what makes Ruth feel comfortable, her brother Walter Lee embraces the transformation. However, it is in a drunken ritualized performance that raises questions about the seriousness of his temporarily taking Africa seriously. In the context of home, Beneatha embraces Africa not only as the place of origin for persons of African descent on United States soil, but she also embraces it as a source of pride, invention, and cultural development that is superior to the West. While her embracing might be more fact-based than Cullen's speaker (in that she *does* have authentic African robes and authentic African music), it is nonetheless more in the realm of exploration and imagination than it is in the realm of reality, since Beneatha has not had a chance to set foot on the Continent. It is still where Beneatha looks to affirm her identity, as she tells Asagai when she first meets him (he teasingly recalls that she approached him by saying, "Mr. Asagai, I am looking for my *identity*"—italics in original).[36] By making such a move, she claims Africa as home in the way that Hughes and others did.

Asagai also labels Africa as the only true home for Beneatha. After Walter Lee has stupidly given away the family inheritance from his deceased father's insurance policy, Asagai arrives to find Beneatha in a state of despair for fear that she will not be able to attend medical school. Seeking to change her mood, he observes—and rightly so—that a family's future should not depend upon the death of its patriarch. Then, in what Beneatha initially takes to be a superficial romantic gesture, Asagai asks her to bring the skills that she will acquire in medical school "home" to the African Continent. "My dear, young creature of the New World—I do not mean across the city—I mean across the ocean; home—to Africa . . . Nigeria. Home."[37] Though she initially misunderstands, Beneatha finally ponders the invitation seriously, at least seriously enough to discuss it with Mama Lena. Going home to Africa is an option that is not pursued beyond conversation in the play, but the suggestion still aligns Beneatha with other fictional characters of the period who look to the Continent for original and ongoing identification.[38]

That is equally true for Dee/Wangero, a character in Alice Walker's "Everyday Use" (1973).[39] Although her actions are mostly misguided, Dee models her transformation from Negro to black American on her sense of Africa. Having had her consciousness raised while attending college,

Dee returns to her family's country home in clothing that she presumes to be African-identified and with the Muslim connections that she imagines authenticate that process. Accompanied by a young man who is similarly indoctrinated, Dee proceeds to lecture her mother and sister on how they do not understand their heritage (since the mother gives the quilts that represent her family history to her daughter Maggie instead of to Dee, who plans to hang them on her apartment walls as art objects). Proceeding ignorantly, Dee suggests to Maggie: "'You ought to try to make something of yourself, too, Maggie. It's really a new day for us. But from the way you and Mama still live you'd never know it.'"[40] Making something of themselves apparently means being more than sharecroppers/farmers; never once does Dee consider that her mother and Maggie might be content with their lives and their appreciation of family heirlooms. Not only does Dee's lecturing reflect a scandalous lack of understanding of history and culture, but Dee's general posturing and dress distort what Africa truly means. For Dee and her ilk, such as Don L. Lee's narrator, encounter with Africa is something that they can accomplish with minimal effort, such as changing hairstyles, learning a few phrases of Swahili, and donning what they take to be traditional African clothing. Despite the wrongheadedness, though, Dee's movement toward an ancestral heritage is in keeping with many of the characters portrayed during this period.

Alice Walker, like many of her contemporaries of the mid- to late twentieth century, not only wrote about Africa, but she also traveled to the Continent, travels that she documents in various of her writings. Africa also appears in more of her fictional works, including *The Color Purple* (1982), where Celie's sister Nettie ends up as a missionary in an African village, and *Possessing the Secret of Joy* (1992), in which Tashi, who was a young girl in *The Color Purple*, is prominent in a narrative that focuses on female genital mutilation.[41] Noteworthy in this context is Walker's research and documentation on female genital mutilation, which led her to collaborate with an Indian filmmaker, Pratibha Parmar, on *Warrior Marks: Female Genital Mutilation and the Sexual Blinding of Women* (1993).[42] It is perhaps fair to say that few contemporary African American writers have engaged the African Continent imaginatively or physically more than Walker.

In considering romanticized treatments of Africa, however, Toni Morrison's *Song of Solomon* (1977) stands out in providing a subtext of how an African American is almost worshipful of one of his ancestors as well as of the place that has given birth to him.[43] I am referring specifically to Milkman Dead and the legend of Solomon, about whom Pilate sings throughout the novel. As Susan Byrd tells the tale, Solomon was one of the Flying Africans who, once his life in America became unbearable during slavery, winded his way back to Africa.[44] The legend of Solomon's Leap has been around for generations, but, once Milkman becomes aware of what the song his aunt Pilate sings means, he is giddy with excitement. When he shares his heritage with Sweet, a woman he encounters on his trip to the South to learn more about his family and ostensibly to locate gold that he believes is stashed in a cave, his excitement is almost uncontainable:

> 'The son of a bitch could fly! You hear me, Sweet? That motherfucker could fly! Could fly! He didn't need no airplane. Didn't need no fuckin tee double you ay. He could fly his own self!'
> 'Who you talkin 'bout?' Sweet was lying on her side, her cheek cupped in her hand.
> 'Solomon, that's who.'
> 'Oh, him.' She laughed. 'You belong to that tribe of niggers?' She thought he was drunk.
> 'Yeah. That tribe. That flyin motherfuckin tribe. Oh, man! He didn't need no airplane. He just took off; got fed up. *All the way up!* No more cotton! No more bales! No more orders! No more shit! He flew, baby. Lifted his beautiful black ass up in the sky and flew on home. Can you dig it? Jesus God, that must have been something to see. And you know what else? He tried to take his baby boy with him. My grandfather. Wow! Woooee! . . .
> 'Where'd he go, Macon?"
> 'Back to Africa . . . .'
> 'Who'd he leave behind?'
> 'Everybody! He left everybody down on the ground and he sailed on off like a black eagle. 'O-o-o-o-o Solomon done fly, Solomon done gone /Solomon cut across the sky, Solomon gone home!' (italics in original)[45]

In his excitement, illustrated numerous times over with the exclamation points, Milkman loses the import of Sweet's very pertinent question: Who has Solomon left behind? Milkman is callously unaware of how seemingly individual decisions affect numerous lives when he replies "Everybody." His appreciation for the fact/belief that one of his ancestors could fly leads him to ignore or dismiss the suffering and loss that Solomon's family has experienced as a result of the decision he made to abandon them in order to save himself (unheroic, to say the least, which Milkman does not register at all). That family not only includes Jake, Milkman's grandfather, but twenty-one other people (Jake's wife and an additional twenty children). To Milkman, the important thing is that Solomon flew. And not only did he fly, but he flew home to Africa, which is the equation that other writers make as well—America is alien, not home; Africa is home. The mythic representation of the ability gained from being African and from "that tribe of niggers" is what impresses Milkman most, and the fact that Sweet is aware of the legend of the Flying Africans gives the belief even more currency in the folk tradition.

Thus Milkman's response to Solomon aligns him with other characters who bestow special and imagined qualities upon the Continent as an ancestral home. Milkman therefore romanticizes Africa and Africans almost as much as Langston Hughes and others do.[46]

In taking this position, I realize that some readers and scholars may interpret Milkman's progression in a much more positive light and may celebrate with him. I acknowledge unquestionably that Milkman grows in the text, that he learns about his African ancestry, and that his father's comment about Pilate's being evidence of their African background is something that he internalizes. None of that progression, however, changes the fact that Milkman celebrates individual relief over communal suffering. Jill Matus agrees when she comments about flight in the novel:

> Though Solomon's flight may offer inspiration as a version of the celebratory legend of the Flying African, the novel also emphasizes the grief and mourning of those who were abandoned . . . . Solomon miraculously flies off, becoming a symbol of transcendence and escape, but bequeathing also a legacy of bereavement, loss and forgetting, . . . Morrison therefore uses the myth of the flying African both to celebrate and to mourn . . . . In some ways, *Song of Solomon* can be characterized as a mythologising of desertion. [47]

By celebrating Solomon, Milkman denies the adage by which Pilate has lived: "You just can't fly on off and leave a body."[48] In addition, as Robert B. Stepto notes, "The myth Milkman discovers is a wonderful story insofar as it provides him with genealogy, family pride, and a masculine identity (however outsized) . . . . But a myth of departure is a story of people left behind."[49] Nor does it change the fact that Milkman is the direct cause of both Hagar's and Pilate's deaths. Even if we place him within the realm of legend that asserts that he flies at the end of the novel so that tales of Flying Africans can continue (Morrison's prefatory note that "The fathers may soar/ And the children may know their names"), there are no witnesses to his feat to carry on those tales. I could assert that absence of witnesses simply means that the tale of his flying would survive that much more strongly in the folk imagination and inform generations to come, but that argument pales in comparison to the unresolved situation with which Morrison ends her novel. Also, since Milkman is not a father, and since he abdicates the responsibility that Pilate has enjoined him to assume with Reba, the couplet seems less applicable to him. Finally, it appears as if Milkman, no matter what he has learned, is just as carefree in his celebration of Solomon (individual rather than community) as he has been throughout the thirty-three years of his life.

While Walker's Dee, Hansberry's Beneatha, and Morrison's Milkman imagine an Africa that is mostly benign and apparently emotionally supportive, the Africa that Elizabeth (Lizzie) Dubose and her great-great-grandmother imagine in Phyllis Alesia Perry's *Stigmata* (1998) is about as troubling and perhaps even more complex than Dana Franklin's labeling of a cruel plantation in Maryland as her home. Perry's Africa is initially one of loss, of separation of parents from children, and of the cruelty of enslavement.[50] It then becomes an idea that Ayo, Lizzie's great-great-grandmother, carries with her through the Middle Passage and through her existence on United States soil. That Africa is one of longing, of the desire to be with what Ayo refers to as the *"forever people"* (italics in original), those who, inexplicably, have the ability to be reincarnated across time and generations.[51] Still, another evolution takes place when Ayo herself comes to represent Africa to her granddaughter Grace and her great-great granddaughter Lizzie. Ayo is certainly an Africa of loss, but she is also an Africa that devolves into the suicide of the Middle Passage, the chains and whips of slavery, and the almost inexpressible cruelty that leads her to torment her descendants into recognition of their past. This Africa is merciless, unforgiving of memory lapses, and utterly intent upon descendants retaining ties to ancestors, no matter the cost to those descendants.

Given the circumstances under which Ayo is snatched from her mother, a master dyer, on African soil, it is no wonder that she feels the sting of separation so acutely. On an otherwise uneventful day, she had accompanied her mother to market, only to be distracted, separated, captured, middle passaged, and taken by *"ghost people"* (italics in original) to America, a *"ghost land"* (italics in original).[52] For Ayo, Africa is the vision of wholeness that leads to a hole in her soul after her separation from her mother. Throughout her life, therefore, she holds Africa in her imagination as the place where all was well, all was whole. She has indeed, as Saidiya Hartman asserts, literally and figuratively "lost her mother." That loss, combined with the atrocities she suffers during slavery, informs the remainder of her existence. Because she cannot return to Africa, that place looms exceptionally large in her mind. It becomes for her the site on which health and healing are possible, as evidenced when her mother, a representative of that place and soil, comes to her after an especially brutal beating during slavery and wills her back to health. Africa, to Ayo, is thus not simply a geography, a place, a home, but it is also something that transcends mortality. Out of the uniqueness of her situation, Ayo imagines Africa as the transcendent site of ultimate escape, the place that gives rise to people who can be born again and again. In a scenario that echoes the legends of the Flying Africans, Ayo posits that she and others like her are in a circle of reappearance in the world. That circle is powerfully enabling: *"We are forever. Here at the bottom of heaven we live in the circle. We back and gone and back again"* (italics in original).[53] According to Ayo, her granddaughter Grace cannot be born until Ayo has departed, for the circle always skips a generation: *"She cant get here cause Im in the way . . . But when Im gone she come to take my place"* (italics in original).[54] Lizzie tries to convince one of her psychiatrists of the truth of this phenomenon when she insists that she "likes circles," that "the world seems to move in cycles," and that she is "the circle" "standing before" her interrogator.[55] Lizzie remarks near the end of the text, after her mother Sarah has finally come to understand what is going on, that "the circle is complete and my daughter sits across from me with the gap finally closed."[56] Reincarnation thus becomes the antidote to slavery, the antidote to cruelty, the antidote to forgetting, and the repetitive pattern that ensures wholeness (complete circularity) in family ties.[57]

As the figure whose genes deposit Africa into Grace, her granddaughter, and Lizzie, her great-great-granddaughter, Ayo becomes for her descendants a painful puzzle that they must work out. Their task is not merely to understand Ayo's life and what has happened to her, but they are doomed, literally, to *experience* that life and those cruelties. Thus Lizzie Dubose, who inherits Grace's quilt and Ayo's diary (written by her daughter Joy) in the contemporary portion of the novel, bleeds from chains around her wrists (even in pristine, middle class, twentieth century Tuskegee, Alabama) and shackles on her ankles. She also suffers as Ayo did from inhuman beatings. It takes her fourteen years confined to mental institutions before she comes to accept fully that she is the reincarnated Ayo and Grace and that she has work to do in remembering her ancestors. That work consists in part of making a quilt to tell the story of Grace's abandonment of her family (she left when Ayo's painful beatings and bleedings led her to realize that her husband George, whether he wanted to or not, would probably have her confined to a mental institution). More important, that work consists of the reclaiming of Sarah, the five-year-old daughter whom Grace was forced to leave and who must now be led, gradually and gingerly, to believe that her daughter Lizzie is also her mother Grace. By the time Lizzie learns to control her responses to the episodes of intervention from Grace and Ayo, that is, when she learns to embrace the interlocking of her life with theirs, Africa has become as symbolic for her as it was for Ayo.

To Lizzie, Africa is a lost mother and a frightened and a bewildered daughter. Her images of Africa are of the tall, "full-brown woman" (Ayo's mother) and the young girl (herself, Ayo, and Grace) who lost that mother.[58] Her sense of the connections among all of the females centers in part upon a bit of blue cloth that Ayo was clutching from her master dyer mother when she was snatched into slavery. That blue cloth, which will be passed down among the women until Lizzie receives it in her inheritance from Grace in the late twentieth century, symbolizes loss and wandering, but it also symbolizes the possibility for reconnection, for reaffirmation of ancestral ties. When Lizzie sews the last tiny bit of the blue material into the quilt that she is making to tell Grace's story, it is the signal that Sarah now understands the circle that encases her ancestors as well as her descendants, that Lizzie has made peace with the demons that Ayo set in motion, and that there might be a less painful and more forgiving future possible for these women without the bloody consequences of forgetting to remember.

The blue cloth also locks Lizzie's perceptions of Africa squarely into the realm of imagination. Color symbolism suggests that blue is reflective of sky and sea, which is most appropriate in thinking of the Middle Passage, but it also represents imagination. For Lizzie, who, like Beneatha and Dee, has never set foot in Africa, she can only think, like Countee Cullen's persona, of what it must be like. Heir to Ayo's memories, she can see—often with the aid of a mirror in her bedroom—the African ancestors from whom she is descended. The shadowy realm that leads others to believe that she is insane is also the realm that gives her access to what has occurred before her. The intangible (images of Ayo and her mother) combines with the tangible (bleedings, whippings, and chains) to lead to an unholy mixture of what can be experienced and what can only be imagined. The cloth, the quilt, and the diary are all keys to the unwanted but necessary journey on which Lizzie is set. It is not too far-fetched to picture her as an ancient heroine who must undergo painful and transformative trials in order to save her people or her "kingdom."

As the most recent in a long line of female characters in the text, Lizzie underscores the point that, often, ancestry or concern with ancestry rests with the females of families. Although Grace also left twin sons who are nine years older than Sarah, she is less concerned about reclaiming them than she, as Grace-Lizzie, is concerned about reclaiming Sarah; after all, "little girls especially need their mothers," and the "Mother-daughter-mother" trio had "the tighter connection."[59] The text dismisses an equal application of maternal concern to the males by asserting that "the twins were at that age when they didn't want to be associated with their mother [they were fourteen]. But little Sarah had been [Grace-Lizzie's] shadow."[60] This not entirely convincing argument reiterates the fact that lineage in this text is in the realm of females. How they react to their ancestors and their history is the important thing. Though Lizzie's journey to acceptance is far more painful and bloody than the encounters of other literary and historical narrators with their African ties, it is perhaps fair to say that Lizzie nonetheless arrives at a more palatable and productive connection to her African past and African/American ancestors. She might not be in a blissful state at the end of her journey, but she is in a far healthier one than the condition in which she began.[61]

A REALISTIC APPROACH TO THE MOTHER LAND

A more mediated, recent fictional focus on Africa is Yaa Gyasi's *Homegoing* (2016). It originates and ends with characters in Africa. Though they return, they do so realistically instead of with the wide-eyed, mythologically informed expectations that previous characters and life writers have exhibited.[62] Gyasi, a young writer of African and American descent, depicts an epic, panoramic vision of the dispersal of African peoples from their native cultures to others on the African Continent as well as to the western hemisphere. For those who are snatched from what they know and sold into slavery as a result of interethnic conflicts on African soil, or those who just get caught up in the madness that others perpetuate around them and find themselves in the dungeons of Cape Coast Castle on their way to the Americas, the experiences of dislocation, relocation, loss, and alienation as a result of losing home are comparable in the anguish they cause. Gyasi showcases vividly how, for so many Africans and descendants of Africans, home is a concept as well as a place. For displaced Africans, an intangible concept of home must suffice when all vestiges of familiar physical space have disappeared and they find themselves in the strangeness of the New World. For descendants of those displaced Africans, home involves changes of location from village to village as well as from the smallness of villages to the busyness of the Cape Coast. Mostly absent in all these movements is a sense of human dignity, of the realization that human beings captured during African interethnic conflicts or as a result of raids between groups are indeed human beings. The ways in which Africans treat other Africans as chattel, "things," property to be sold sadly anticipate ideas on the inhumane treatment of people of African descent on United States soil. Throughout the narrative, however, Gyasi is less intent upon, less interested in, judging and indicting than she is in depicting, and what she depicts is a fictionalized history of African peoples and the Diaspora that is so graphically poignant that it evokes visceral responses from readers.

Homegoing begins in loss. It is the story of two sisters who, evoking Mama Day's search for her ancestor Sapphira in Gloria Naylor's *Mama Day* (1988), are aware of each other's existence but never manage the feat of actually meeting, though, early in the novel, they literally occupy spaces within a few feet of each other.[63] Effia, who is born to an Asante mother who is the servant of a Fante family, is the older of the sisters. When her mother sets a fire to escape her employer's/lover's household, Effia is left with her father. Her mother, Maame, returns to her village, marries a "Big Man," and gives birth to Esi. Many years later, when Big Man's village is raided, Maame refuses to run again; instead, she gives Esi a black stone by which to remember her and literally disappears from the text (that is the dominant pattern for characters throughout the novel). Meanwhile, "Effia the Beauty," as she becomes known, becomes the "wife" ("wench") of one of the white British slavers at Cape Coast Castle. Her cruel stepmother orchestrates the plan for her to marry the officer and leave village life. It is only when Effia's doting father dies many years later that Effia's stepmother gives Effia the matching stone to the one she has given Esi. The two are held together spiritually by these talismen; however, that connection is brief for Esi. She is captured by the Asante, sold to the British, and housed in the Cape Coast Castle where her sister Effia lives just above her in luxury. In those dungeons, Esi wallows in the fecal matter, urine, and dead bodies that define the existence of those destined for enslavement in the western world. She tries to save her precious stone by burying it in the polluted soil, but she is selected for transport to America before she has a chance to retrieve it.

With the two sisters positioned as they are, Gyasi traces them and their descendants over a period of more than two hundred years. Each chapter follows, alternately, a descendant of Effia and a descendant of Esi. The destination for Esi's descendants in America might be more stereotypically horrifying, but Effia's descendants on African soil fare only minimally better. Both sets of descendants, as are their mothers, are beset with displacement, disruption, loss of home, unfulfilled familial longings, and alienation from their new environments. Whether that alienation manifests itself as phenotype, cultural practice (religion, customs, manners), linguistic expectations, or the intangible psychological shocks of no longer inhabiting the familiar, the majority of Gyasi's characters suffer in some way. Yet, their family lines continue, and that continuation ultimately takes precedence over the suffering, though it is only in the purview of the reader to know the fate of many of these characters. In their immediate circumstances, suffering of one kind or another reigns, as they are sent, taken forcibly, or driven from their families and what they have known as home.

In this very non-romanticized view of Africa, *everyone* is to blame for the condition that saw millions of native Africans removed from their homespaces and dispersed to the other side of the world. In Gyasi's fictional rendition, there are no innocent natives or foreigners. As one of Esi's twenty-first century descendants posits, everyone is responsible for what happened on the African Continent that led to centuries of enslavement in that space as well as in the New World. Again, under Gyasi's pen, no one, absolutely no one, is innocent. There are obviously victims, but even victims such as Esi have themselves tasted of the egotistical fruit of dehumanizing their fellow human beings.

Disappearing people and disappeared homes are thus the nature of enslavement, and migration (most often forced) and homelessness undergird practically every chapter in the novel. As stated, Gyasi does not use her fictional tale rehearsing the Middle Passage, renditions that might echo Olaudah Equiano's *Narrative* (1789) in an early version or Toni Morrison's *Beloved* (1987) in a later one.[64] Nonetheless, what the women (men are there as well, but, because of Esi, the focus is on the women) experience who are disappeared into the dungeons at Cape Coast Castle is arguably its own form of middle passage. As they are stacked on top of each other and must lie in the collective filth from many misused, mistreated, malnourished, and dying bodies, they echo the spoon-fashioned stacking, deprivation, and violation of human beings that characterized the historical Middle Passage. For these women, the dungeons are the pre–middle passage Middle Passage, the liminal space between what they know from their family/cultural ties and the unknown territory they are about to enter, and those dungeons serve as effectively to sever their ties to everything they have known as the expanse of water that spans the Atlantic Ocean. These women are stripped of home and kin in the dungeons; the water passage simply puts the exclamation point on their inability to return to anything with which they are familiar.

Thus, instead of rendering the traditional Middle Passage, Gyasi treats the gap of the Atlantic Ocean as the additional space of loss of home, the point of no return that is a given. Its consequences, however, extend for generations. Each representation of one of Esi's descendants on American soil is a representation of loss and homelessness. For those representations, Gyasi seems to have compiled a list of the iconic places and practices that led historically to African American homelessness. These include, first of all, the buying and selling of human beings, the disruptions of family life that characterized the lives of the enslaved from the time they set foot in America (Esi's daughter Ness). There is the attempted escape and its consequences (Ness is recaptured, but her son Kojo ["Jo"] goes North with an African woman, Ma Aku, who has befriended Ness). Gyasi also pays homage to the Fugitive Slave Act of 1850, the legislation that led to many recently liberated and some never enslaved African Americans on northern territory being snatched from their homespaces and remanded to slavery (Kojo's wife Anna). The convict lease system of the late nineteenth and early twentieth centuries finds its way into the novel as well, as black men are forced to trade their freedom (H, Kojo's son) for work in the mines around Birmingham, Alabama that Douglas A. Blackmon documented so vividly in *Slavery By Another Name: The Re-Enslavement of Black Americans from the Civil War to World War II* (2008).[65] Nodding to the Great Migration, Gyasi depicts one of Esi's descendants in the early twentieth century who makes her way from Alabama to Harlem in hopes of a better future (Willie, H's daughter). It is this descendant's grandson, Marcus, who brings the book full circle; by voluntarily leaving Harlem and matriculating to Stanford to get his doctorate in Sociology, he meets Marjorie, the last descendant of Effia, who has migrated with her family from Ghana to Huntsville,

Alabama and is now herself a graduate student in California. For Marcus, the aspiring Sociologist, leaving home is a way of securing home, for he follows in the path of many African Americans who believed that education was/is the way out of impoverished or other socially disadvantaged circumstances.

Over hundreds of years and many generations, however, few of Effia's and Esi's descendants attain happiness or homespaces. As mentioned, they are adrift in any number of ways. While their displacements, relocations, and alienations replicate various African and African American histories, they also ultimately point toward the future, a future that has the power to restore some of the loss and perhaps even to alleviate some of the suffering. Once Marcus and Marjorie become friends, they make a trip to Ghana. There, they visit Cape Coast Castle, experience it viscerally—in spite of its being a tourist trap—and engage forces that are larger than themselves. The visit to the Castle has such an impact upon Marcus that he rushes out onto the beach beyond the Castle, although he is deathly afraid of water. Marjorie, who, because of what she knows about her grandmother, is deathly afraid of fire, follows him. On the beach is a blazing fire that Marcus invites her to approach, and she then invites him into the water to encourage him to lessen his fear of that great expanse. Significantly, the black stone that Marjorie has inherited from her grandmother is front and center in this moment in the novel. It contains the history to which neither of the young people is fully privy. Its presence, however, indicates that lines continue, histories go on, and families survive in spite of the horrors—self-imposed and otherwise—that might wipe out some or even a large portion of its members. It is thus fitting that Marjorie, nestling in the water that she so enjoyed with her grandmother and that she has invited Marcus to enter, lifts the stone from her neck, places it around Marcus's, and intones: "'Welcome Home.'"[66]

Home indeed. But . . . is it? It is worthy of note that Gyasi titles her novel *Homegoing* instead of "homecoming." The latter is a term that people of African descent (and obviously lots of other folks) use in ways that suggest a return to something familiar. Historically, African Americans have had homecomings at churches, and parishioners who may have left many years before return on an annual basis to celebrate the ties that bind those who departed to those who remain. Such events are communal celebrations and recognitions that kinship carries more weight than geographical location. So, hordes of the recently—or not so recently—migrated return to the site of departure (usually a North to South pattern). Public embracings set the tone for such occasions, for both those departed and those who remain are aware of histories that tie them together.[67] On the other hand, "homegoing" in such communities has come in recent years to substitute for the word "funeral." Such communities now have homegoing celebrations of those who have departed through death, which means that the emphasis is on the realm of movement from the natural to the extra-natural. However, there is still communal engagement with this particular use and practice of the word, for countless numbers of people participate in funeral rituals. In the context of Gyasi's novel, community desires and embracings are emphasized less than individual questings. Those individual journeys might be accomplished against a community backdrop, but it is the individual on whom Gyasi focuses. It is thus up to the individual to "go home," to make a conscious choice to do so, no matter how the folks at home may feel about that desire. Marcus and Marjorie are thus both inside and outside community, though we could begin to read their togetherness as the formation of a new community. Still, their situation is counter to what might historically in African American communities be considered a "homegoing."

Throughout the text, Gyasi has focused on leavings, on departures from spaces that characters called home. Now, in this moment of intense revelation and transcendence for Marcus and Marjorie, "home" takes on connotations far beyond the physical spaces from which various characters have been snatched. It is now global in context, historical in meaning, and colored by African American and African history. Here, home, the physical space of Africa, is posited as a restoration of loss. Marcus becomes, like so many characters pictured in African American literature, the lost brother who has returned to the bosom of Mother Africa.[68] That return is represented powerfully by its manifestation in the water, for not only is Marcus returning to Mother Africa in terms of land, but he is returning to the bosom of the earth, the water over which so many of his ancestors were taken to be enslaved in the New World. So, is this a cleansing? A reconciliation between Old World daughter and New World son? Is this a reinstatement of the romanticization with which twentieth and twenty-first century African Americans imbue Africa? How Gyasi positions her characters is significant. An African woman who has migrated to the United States and who is herself perceived as alien when she returns to Ghana assumes the role of spiritual guide to an African American male who has never set foot on the African Continent. While it is certainly understandable that she is in the best position to extend the mantle of welcome, it is no less true that, against the backdrop of what the text has depicted, Africa is perhaps anything but a relatable home. Even more unfortunate is the fact that there is no space comfortably identified as such anywhere in the text.[69]

By contrast, it would probably not be too far-fetched to assert that some historical African Americans who reached out to the Continent in emotional and physical embracing in the mid-twentieth century considered that move almost comparable to arriving at a state of bliss. They definitely viewed Africa as a haven from the troubles of the world that they had experienced in western society, and, dare we say, some of them may even have viewed Africa as a kind of heaven.[70] The Africa they carried in their minds was one of hope for restoration of a particular kind of status, the promise of peace and contentment after racist and social limitations in America, and the freedom of being in a majority culture for once in their lives. Just as African American folk tradition paints heaven as answering all the needs and providing all the comfort that is antithetical to life on earth, so Africa perhaps became that for many black Americans who sojourned there. Still, Africa is of and in this world. Beyond that, African American folk and religion tradition posits that the true home for black people is not of this world; it was forged by God in a heaven that it as vivid as the one James Weldon Johnson describes in "The Creation," the one depicted in the spirituals, and the one that leads gospel— and even some blues—singers to belt out their anticipation of removal from this physical world to a place of comfort in eternal life and the presence of Jesus. That space, so the tradition goes, is the home to which all should aspire.

THE ULTIMATE HOME

"Weep not, weep not," James Weldon Johnson intones in "Go Down Death—A Funeral Sermon, "She is not dead/ She's resting in the bosom of Jesus." The first stanza continues:

> Heart-broken husband—weep no more;
> Grief-stricken son—weep no more;
> Left-lonesome daughter—weep no more;
> She's only just gone home.[71]

Johnson's poem captures the immediacy of grief as well as the comfort that accrues to believers who are convinced that their deceased loved ones are in a better place, indeed that they have been welcomed to their true and final home, that is, heaven. Throughout African American history and literature, the sentiment that Johnson depicts has been pervasive. For those who were enslaved, overworked, beaten, violated sexually, sold away from relatives, and otherwise generally dehumanized, they could be content in the belief that this world was not their home, that another place, infinitely more congenial and responsive to their conditions, awaited them. That place was a space of transcendent power and beauty, one that the ugliness of enslaved or post-slavery existence could not rival. The spiritual tradition to which Johnson is heir and for which he collected and published two volumes of songs kept that belief vibrant. As early as the 1860s, when the first collectors arrived on the Sea Islands to record spirituals, they noted the explanations that formerly enslaved singers provided for their compositions. If a fellow enslaved person were forced to work harder than his or her energy allowed and was consequently beaten for not meeting a certain quota, a sympathetic enslaved observer might have sung the first words of "Many Thousand Gone":

> No more auction block for me, no more
> No more peck of corn for me
> Many thousand gone.[72]

Those who are "gone," who have made their escape from this troubled world, now reside in the realm of God. The spiritual tradition is rich with expressions of moving from the almost unbearable conditions on earth to a place of welcome and a space of comfort in heaven. Lyrics found in songs such as "Swing Low, Sweet Chariot" specifically employ the trope of going home, as the chariot is "coming for to carry me home." "Deep River" asserts that the singer's "home is over Jordan." "Soona Will be Done With the Troubles of the World" maintains that the singer is "going home to live with God." Other spirituals, including "By an' By," "I Got a Home in-a Dat Rock," "In Dat Great Gittin' Up Mornin'," "When the Saints Go Marchin' In," "Sometimes I Feel Like a Motherless Child," "The Gospel Train is Coming," "Po' Mourner's Got a Home at Las'," "Until I Reach-a Ma Home," and many more also mark the space of heaven as the ultimate home.

Folk narrative tradition joined with the folksong tradition to keep such hopes alive and vibrant through generations of anguished black life on American soil. It is that image of the folk conception of heaven as home that Johnson depicts in "Go Down Death—A Funeral Sermon" and other of the poems in *God's Trombones*. The folk heaven of Johnson's poem is in sharp contrast to earthly existence. Whereas earth has been a place of suffering, heaven will be a place of rest and communion with God. Devaluation on earth will turn into value in heaven. Restriction on earth will give way to freedom in heaven.[73] Specifically in Johnson's poem, it is Sister Caroline who has endured the cares of the world to the point that she can no longer bear such burdens. A sensitive, anthropomorphic God sends Death to earth to take Sister Caroline into his arms and escort her on his flying horse back to heaven, where he lays her "on the loving breast of Jesus."[74] Thus Johnson not only picks up on the folk image of heaven, but he bolsters it with a few other strengthening features. First, God cares about those who are dispossessed and made second class citizens on earth and specifically in the United States. God's eye is on Sister Caroline "tossing on her bed of pain," which means that supplicants can be confident in the fact that God's eye is literally on the sparrow, as the biblical text asserts, and God watches over those who serve God.[75] From the perspective of Sister Caroline and those of the social class and belief system of which she is a part, therefore, they have as much right to a home in heaven as those who are more privileged in the society. That heritage and that home ensure a post-earthly-life equality that provides comfort in the earthly realm even as one is looking forward to that everlasting reward.

Second, Death is not a force that is set loose indiscriminately on the world. Death operates *only* at the command of God; there is nothing for the dying person to fear, for she or he will ultimately arrive into the presence and loving arms of Jesus. Johnson's depiction of a death that does only what God tells him to do thus eliminates the possibility that a believer could just be zapped by a ravaging force that is merely random. In Johnson's portrait, Death is an escort of sorts, almost a courtier, instead of something to be dreaded. For those black folks who may have suffered during Johnson's time from the discrimination and violence of hate groups such as the Ku Klux Klan, or who may have been left to languish and die in jail, or who may have been cramped into diseased northern urban quarters that led to their untimely demises, they can join Sister Caroline in knowing that there is a God who cares about them and who is the ultimate arbiter of their fates. While some might argue that such a view is romantic, it was nonetheless a widespread belief among persons of African descent on United States soil, and it continues to be so.

Third, heaven is the final pausing place. For the work-worn and now fatally ill Sister Caroline, moments to pause have not defined her life. Once Death lays Sister Caroline "on the loving breast of Jesus," He comforts her as a mother would a child.

> And Jesus took his own hand and wiped away her tears,
> And he smoothed the furrows from her face,
> And the angels sang a little song,
> And Jesus rocked her in his arms,
> And kept a-saying: Take your rest,
> Take your rest, take your rest.[76]

Sister Caroline has her reward for faithfulness when Jesus gives her His undivided and personalized attention, when Jesus smooths the furrows from her brow, and when Jesus rocks her into a peace that passes all the confusion and illness that have dominated her life on earth. This depiction of home, therefore, is yet again one in which Jesus cares, one in which Jesus is ever watchful and considerate of those who worship Him, and one in which the burdens, troubles, and hardships of life fade in comparison to the love that one experiences as a result of having arrived in the presence of Jesus.

The anthropomorphism that Johnson identifies as characteristic of God in "Go Down Death—A Funeral Sermon" is also apparent in "The Creation," the second poem in *God's Trombones*. A folk revisionist perspective of the creation story in Genesis, the poem posits that God created man (humans) because God was "lonely." If God thus has needs and expresses them in the value God places on human beings, then even more will God want those human beings to join God in the home that God has created for them, a home that many believe is in the heavens. After having created the heavens and the earth, and all the living beings, God thinks: "I'm lonely still."[77] The emotional void in God thus leads to God's most significant achievement. "The Creation" then documents in minute and loving detail the attention and care that God gave to creating man (humans), the future denizens of God's heavenly space.

> Up from the bed of the river
> God scooped the clay;
> And by the bank of the river
> He kneeled him down;
> And there the great God Almighty
> Who lit the sun and fixed it in the sky,
> Who flung the stars to the most far corner of the night,
> Who rounded the earth in the middle of his hand;
> This great God,
> Like a mammy bending over her baby,
> Kneeled down in the dust
> Toiling over a lump of clay
> Till he shaped it in his own image;
> Then into it he blew the breath of life,
> And man became a living soul.
> Amen. Amen.[78]

Again, the comfort that is implicit in knowing that human beings are the only of God's creations to alleviate God's loneliness adds to the satisfaction believers experience in knowing that they have a home in the heavens.

Johnson's contemporary, Sterling Brown, known especially for his appreciation for black folk traditions, shares with Johnson the folk conception of heaven as home. In poems such as "Sister Lou" and "When de Saints Go Ma'ching Home," Brown depicts heaven as a welcoming and comforting contrast to life on earth.[79] While Johnson mainly uses standard English in his poems, with occasional non-standard features to suggest orality, Brown locates his poems firmly in African American vernacular speech/orality. He thereby combines form and content in the expression of the folk conception of heaven. Unlike Johnson's Sister Caroline, who is work-worn, ill, and generally exhausted, Sister Lou is painted as a capable body whose arrival in heaven is the naturally progressive reward for her life on earth. It is thus unclear if that ending is eminent or something to which Sister Lou can look forward at a later time. What is clear is that a friendly adviser, in a voice that mirrors the world in which Sister Lou resides, provides advice on what Sister Lou should do when her life comes to an end as well as when she arrives in heaven. The tone is casual, comforting, and confident in the speech to Sister Lou. In the conversational manner and calming tone in which it addresses Sister Lou, it may easily be a friend or perhaps even one of her church sisters.

> Honey
> When de man
> Calls out de las' train
> You're gonna ride,
> Tell him howdy.
> Gather up yo' basket
> An' yo' knittin an' yo' things,
> An' go on up an' visit
> Wid frien' Jesus fo' a spell.
> Show Marfa
> How to make yo' greengrape jellies,
> An' give po' Lazarus
> A passel of them Golden Biscuits.
> Scald some meal
> Fo' some rightdown good spoonbread
> Fo' li'l box-plunkin' David.
> An' sit aroun'
> An' tell them Hebrew Chillen
> All yo' stories . . . . [80]

Several things are noteworthy in the advice the friend gives. Most important, the speaker and Sister Lou share the same vision of where they will go after death, and the speaker is offering some friendly advice about how Sister Lou should proceed from earth to heaven, as well as what she should do once she arrives. Worthy of note is the train imagery. As in the song in which "the gospel train is coming," or as other modes of transportation (ships, chariots) get believers to heaven, so one is coming to collect Sister Lou. The last train that Sister Lou is going to ride will have a conductor (not quite as vivid as Johnson's death on a streaking white horse but distinctive nonetheless) who will give his undivided attention to Sister Lou.

As in Johnson's "Go Down Death—A Funeral Sermon," there is no fear of dying here. Death is portrayed as a visit—except that this is a permanent visit to a very special mansion. Implicit in the speaker's advice is the assumption that Sister Lou has earned the right to this outcome and that she will be on par with the other citizens of heaven. Also, what she has done on earth will have value in heaven. Her skills, such as making greengrape jellies and spoonbread, which some might have viewed as less valuable because they were located solidly in the domestic realm, will have special value for Sister Lou in heaven. They will serve as an entrée to her socializing with biblical characters and others about whom she has simply read. This depiction makes Sister Lou more than a begging supplicant; it provides her with social currency in heaven and suggests that she has experiences that will serve her in good stead in offering food and advice to those in heaven. It also places value on her own stories. For years, she has read about the Hebrew children; now, she can showcase her storytelling talents by sharing her narratives with them.

The heaven that the speaker paints for Sister Lou, therefore, is one that shares characteristics of the general black folk depictions of heaven. Sister Lou will be welcomed into the space, and she will be comfortable there. This space is antithetical to what she has known on earth, for she will no longer have to "go 'roun to de back," as she has done on earth; there will be "No mo' dataway/ Not evah no mo'," for, in heaven, she is a first-class citizen with all the rights and privileges thereof.[81] She will have assistance that she has not had on earth, as even the archangel Michael will carry her burdens and her pocketbook, and Gabriel will blow his horn especially for her (particularly worthy of note, given the fact that Gabriel is *the* most important angel in heaven). Sister Lou will then "Go straight on to de Big House," which turns a negative history of enslavement into a positive image, to speak with God without fear and trembling.[82] This reversal of earth, in which Sister Lou can enter freely into spaces from which she might have been excluded on earth, illustrates the constant erasure of previous conditions that the folk conception of heaven allows. Here, Sister Lou can sit and talk with God for a while. But this heaven is not simply a place of idle contentment. It is also a space in which Sister Lou can be useful beyond employing her cooking skills. She is advised to "Give a good talkin' to/ To yo' favorite 'postle Peter,/ An' rub the po' head/ Of mixed-up Judas,/ An' joke awhile wid Jonah."[83] All of these activities suggest the extent to which Sister Lou can feel at home in heaven and bask in the knowledge that she has something to offer instead of being an interloper. Still, she is not in heaven merely to cook or to play psychiatrist. It is also her final resting place, her final homespace.

The speaker makes clear that the resting place is special, for Jesus will show Sister Lou to her bed once she indicates that she is a "mite tired."[84] It is a task that Jesus will not designate to an angel, not even to Michael or Gabriel. And it is certainly not one that Jesus will place in the hands of a "servant" (echoing earth again).[85] The personalized touch reiterates the one that Sister Caroline receives in Johnson's "Go Down Death—A Funeral Sermon." Like Sister Caroline, Sister Lou is favored and positioned in a room with windows from which she can look out upon blooming cherry and plum trees forever. This will be her "everlasting" reward for the life she has lived and the good works she has done. Once she is in that heavenly room, there will be no need for more work, rushing, or anything beyond what Jesus has provided for her. In that space, she will be able to take her "bressed time."[86] For one who has probably been on a schedule, at the beck and call for her entire life of those for whom she has worked, Sister Lou can now pause and enjoy the rewards of having served God well enough to have earned a place in heaven.[87]

The same folksy and vernacular spirit informs Brown's "When de Saints Go Ma'ching Home." The poem, designed to evoke the famed Big Boy Davis with whom Brown established a relationship during his collecting of folk materials among black Americans, features a speaker who, during a musical performance, listens to the performer catalogue the revered and elderly of his community, as well as his mother, who have made or are making the transition from earth to heaven.[88] From his vantage point, the performer observes those "marching into heaven" who have worked long and hard on earth. Evoking the spiritual, "When the Saints Go Marchin' In," Brown extends what is implicit in that song to make it clear that the saints are on their way to heaven, their final home and resting place. In the setting of a secular performance, therefore, the speaker observes that the performer ends each of his appearances with his "chant of saints," after he positions the chant as his "mother's favorite."[89] In an intriguing mix of the secular and the sacred that defines so much of African American cultural expression, the performer moves from singing the blues to the chant of saints and ends his performance by moving from this space to a dance hall or a bawdy house.

His imaginary march of saints into heaven is a caravan of hardworking, ordinary men, women, and children similar to those who make up the majority of African American communities. Among those whom the performer includes in his chant of saints, which the persona describes as a dream, are "Ole Deacon Zachary," who "puffs" and "wheezes" up the "golden stair" and whose chest reveals a lifetime of badges in recognition of his lodge work. There is also "Sis Joe," "Elder Peter Johnson," "little brown-skinned chillen," "Ole Maumee Annie," and "Grandpa Eli."[90] These deserving folks from African American communities will make the cut for heaven because of their service and suffering. However, it is doubtful that whites who were oppressors will be admitted, though whites who have been helpful to blacks might—grudgingly—be allowed in (remember, this is the performer's judgment, not that of God or St. Peter). Perhaps, the performer maintains, there is a smaller mansion for them. Just as he leaves out certain whites, so he leaves out violent blacks and bootleggers, along with voluptuous, bawdy black women. After all, if Sophie, a known beauty, were admitted to heaven, there might be trouble in that peaceful place. Thus governed by a sense of fairness in admitting some whites as well as a sense of morality in keeping out sinning blacks, the performer turns to perhaps the most deserving of all: his own mother. She is "Mammy/ With deep religion defeating the grief/ Life piled so closely about her," who marches along to heaven and finds "The best chair set apart for her worn out body/ In that restful place . . . ."[91] The performer then terminates his performance with: "*I pray to de Lawd I'll meet her/ When de saints go ma'chin' home*" (italics in original).⁹² While the performer may not yet have attained the state of grace that he believes defines those who are on their way to heaven—and his departure for possibly more sinful venues reiterates that—he is nonetheless in the tradition of those who recognize and can articulate the cultural and religious traditions that enable folk characters to enter heaven as their final resting place. He therefore shares kinship with the speaker in "Sister Lou."

In both of these poems that envision a folk heaven, Brown shows awareness of what tradition has meant and means in African American history and culture. When black folks were pressed down, they turned to the blues and to religion as outlets for their oppression. The close kinship between the two forms sometimes made it difficult to tell them apart, for both are soulful expressions for dealing with the troubles of the world. Beyond the earthly realm, though, is solely in the purview of religious belief, and both poems reiterate how vital such belief has been and is in African American communities. In that religious tradition, painting heaven as a final home enabled many to endure the troubles of the world. In literature, it is a tradition that extends from 1920s poetry to novels such as Langston Hughes's *Not Without Laughter* (1930) in the character of Aunt Hagar, through James Baldwin's portrayal of Gabriel and Florence's mother in *Go Tell It on the Mountain* (1953), into perhaps its most memorable literary treatment in Lorraine Hansberry's representation of Mama Lena Younger in *A Raisin in the Sun* (1959).⁹³ While some cultural observers have argued that looking forward to an anticipated heaven as home amounted at times to a defeatist posture, one that allowed for oppression now in the hope of freedom later, such an argument does little to lessen the potency of the belief that guided those literary and historical lives. In the immediacy of their circumstances, they believed what was most fruitful and strengthening for them, and the consistent documentation of belief in heaven certifies the ongoing vitality of the tradition and the expectation of heaven as the final, restful home.

Admittedly, such literary representations are not a constant in the twenty-first century, as new concerns, especially the otherworldly that informs speculative and science fiction modes, as well as the horror genre, have given characters more of an extra-natural ability to determine their own fates. Worthy of note as well is that at least one African American author, namely Octavia E. Butler, has identified "the stars" as the ultimate home of the people of earth. In *Parable of the Sower* (1993), protagonist Lauren Olamina, who founds a new religion, Earthseed, after environmental and other man-made disasters on earth, posits that "The Destiny of Earthseed/ Is to take root among the stars," and the second novel in the proposed trilogy,

Parable of the Talents (1998), actually has a ship that departs for space with proponents of the religion aboard.[94] Such literary movements, however, have not diminished folk representations of heaven as a final resting place, as that traditional view still informs the majority of African American faith communities. A quick perusal of almost any funeral program conducted in historically black churches will reveal that the belief in heaven as home is intact, functional, and thriving among African Americans of the twenty-first century. This is one instance in which literature has perhaps not kept pace with—or at least has diverged from—the dominant beliefs of the communities from which it derives much of its inspiration.

NOTES

1. Paule Marshall, *Brown Girl, Brownstones* (New York: The Feminist Press, 1981).

2. See Isabel Wilkerson, *The Warmth of Other Suns: The Epic Story of America's Great Migration* (New York: Random House, 2010).

3. Alain Locke, *The New Negro: Voices of the Harlem Renaissance* (1925; New York: Touchstone Books, 1987).

4. James Weldon Johnson, *God's Trombones* (New York: Viking, 1955).

5. J. Lee Greene, *Blacks in Eden: The African American Novel's First Century* (Charlottesville: U P of Virginia, 1996), 154.

6. See "Beyond Sandy Hook," which is the first chapter of Hughes's first autobiography, *The Big Sea* (New York: Hill and Wang, 1940).

7. Hughes, *The Big Sea*, 10.

8. See Arnold Rampersad, *The Life of Langston Hughes; Volume 1: 1902–1941, I Too, Sing America* (New York: Oxford U P, 1986), 73 ff. For additional comments on how Harlem Renaissance writers perceived Africa, see my article, "The Image of Africa in the Literature of the Harlem Renaissance," National Humanities Center Online Resources for high school teachers. www.nationalhumanitiescenter.org.

9. Hughes also treats Africa in "Afro-American Fragment," which appears in *The Collected Poems of Langston Hughes*, ed. Arnold Rampersad (New York: Alfred A. Knopf, 1995), 129.

10. Countee Cullen, "Heritage," in *Black Writers of America: A Comprehensive Anthology*, ed. Richard Barksdale and Keneth Kinnamon (New York: Macmillan, 1972), 531–33.

11. Cullen, "Heritage," 1.

12. Cullen, "Heritage," 13, 17, 51. Cullen's mythologizing is also reflected in his conflation of "forests" and "jungles." Presumably, Africa has expansive forests, not jungles.

13. Cullen, "Heritage," 31–32.

14. Cullen, "Heritage," 64–70.

15. Cullen, "Heritage," 80–82.

16. Cullen, "Heritage," 85–92.

17. Cullen, "Heritage," 93–106.
18. Cullen, "Heritage," 119, 120.
19. Cullen, "Heritage," 126–28.
20. Claude McKay, "Outcast," in *Selected Poems* (New York: Harcourt, Brace & World, Inc., 1953), 41. Another poet who labels Africa as home is Lucille Clifton, in her poem entitled "Africa." See *good woman: poems and a memoir 1969–1980* (Rochester, NY: BOA Editions, Ltd., 1987), 73.
21. Cullen, "Heritage," 4–5.
22. Don L. Lee, "But He Was Cool or: he even stopped for green lights," in *Don't Cry, Scream* (Detroit: Broadside, 1969), 24–25.
23. Marita Golden, *Migrations of the Heart* (New York: Anchor Press/Doubleday, 1983), 65.
24. See Trudier Harris, "Romantic and Romanticized International Journeying: Marita Golden's *Migrations of the Heart,*" *Obsidian II: Literature & Arts in the African Diaspora* 41: 1–2 (Fall 2015): 216.
25. Golden, *Migrations*, 86–87.
26. See Richard Wright, *Black Power: A Record of Reactions in a Land of Pathos* (New York: Harper, 1954) and Maya Angelou, *The Heart of a Woman* (New York: Random House, 1981) for their travels to Africa.
27. Alex Haley, *Roots: The Saga of an American Family* (New York: Doubleday, 1976).
28. Saidiya Hartman, *Lose Your Mother: A Journey Along the Atlantic Slave Route* (New York: Farrar, Straus and Giroux, 2007) and Molefi Kete Asante, *As I Run Toward Africa: A Memoir* (New York: Routledge/Paradigm, 2011).
29. Ann Petry, "Mother Africa," in *Miss Muriel and Other Stories* (Boston: Beacon, 1989), 126–62.
30. Petry, "Mother," 127.
31. Petry, "Mother," 139.
32. Petry, "Mother," 161.
33. Barbara Puschmann-Nalenz, "Ann Petry: 'Mother Africa' (1971)," in *The African American Short Story, 1970–1990: A Collection of Critical Essays*, ed. Woolfgang Karrer and Puschmann-Nalenz (Trier: Wissenschaftlicher Verlag Trier, 1993), 35.
34. Keith Clark, *The Radical Fiction of Ann Petry* (Baton Rouge: LSU P, 2013), 205.
35. Lorraine Hansberry, *A Raisin in the Sun* (New York: Random House, 1959).
36. Hansberry, *Raisin*, 49.
37. Hansberry, *Raisin*, 116.
38. In his commentary on *A Raisin in the Sun*, William Murray takes the idea of home in a different direction. He asserts that Hansberry considers the American South as "an ancestral home" for her characters, adding that Hansberry "offers an alternative to those who divorced their connection to the United States in search of a more accepting homeland abroad." See "The Roof of a Southern Home: A Reimagined and Usable South in Lorraine Hansberry's *A Raisin in the Sun*," *The Mississippi Quarterly* 68, no 1–2 (Winter/Spring 2015): 278, 280.

39. Alice Walker, "Everyday Use," in *In Love and Trouble: Stories of Black Women* (New York: Harcourt/Harvest, 1973), 47–59.

40. Walker, "Use," 59.

41. Alice Walker, *The Color Purple* (New York: Washington Square, 1982); Alice Walker, *Possessing the Secret of Joy* (New York: Harcourt Brace Jovanovich, 1992).

42. Alice Walker and Pratibha Parmar, *Warrior Marks: Female Genital Mutilation and the Sexual Blinding of Women* (New York: Harcourt Brace, 1993).

43. Toni Morrison, *Song of Solomon* (New York: Knopf, 1977).

44. Morrison has commented that she heard such stories when she was growing up and that the myths have been forgotten. She sets the record straight by explaining her use of the "flying myth" in *Song of Solomon*: "If it means Icarus to some readers, fine; I want to take credit for that. But my meaning is specific: it is about black people who could fly. That was always part of the folklore of my life; flying was one of our gifts. I don't care how silly it may seem. It is everywhere—people used to talk about it, it's in the spirituals and gospels." See Thomas LeClair, "The Language Must Not Sweat: A Conversation with Toni Morrison," in *Conversations with Toni Morrison*, ed. Danille Taylor-Guthrie (Jackson: U P of Mississippi, 1994), 122.

45. Morrison, *Solomon*, 328–29. In Milkman's exclaiming that Solomon has "No more cotton! No more bales!," he inadvertently echoes the spiritual "Many Thousand Gone"—"No more auction block for me, no more," as the singer also anticipates going home, in this case to heaven, to escape the tribulations of slavery. For a discussion of Morrison's incorporation of the myth of the Flying Africans, see La Vinia Delois Jennings, *Toni Morrison and the Idea of Africa* (New York: Cambridge U P, 2008), 114–20. Jennings places Morrison's usage in the context of folktales, especially from the Sea Islands, as well as in the context of first-person narratives from individuals who professed, in WPA documented accounts of formerly enslaved persons in the 1930s, to have witnessed personally such flying departures from American soil.

46. Many contemporary African American writers reference or treat Africa or ideas of Africa in their works, not all of which are romanticized portrayals. I think especially of Yusef Komunyakaa's reflection on Elmina Castle in his poem entitled "Cape Coast Castle," in which the persona cannot escape the image of the castle as he travels in Ghana or, on his trip home, the images that he conjures of a black woman in the castle's dungeon being forced into a sexual relationship with one of the white governors, whose power will conquer her and those like her (not unlike Yaa Gyasi's depictions in *Homegoing*).

47. Jill Matus, *Toni Morrison* (Manchester U P, 1998), 72, 74, 78–79.

48. Morrison, *Solomon*, 147.

49. Robert B. Stepto, *A Home Elsewhere: Reading African American Classics in the Age of Obama* (Cambridge: Harvard U P, 2010), 69.

50. Phyllis Alesia Perry, *Stigmata* (New York: Random House, 1998).

51. Perry, *Stigmata*, 7.

52. Perry, *Stigmata*, 97, 109.

53. Perry, *Stigmata*, 7.

54. Perry, *Stigmata*, 33, 34.

55. Perry, *Stigmata*, 93–94.

56. Perry, *Stigmata*, 230.

57. In a poem in which she seems to embrace the circularity that Lizzie posits, Lucille Clifton writes in "the raising of lazarus": "the dead shall rise again/ whoever say/ dust must be dust/ don't see the trees/ smell rain/ remember africa/ everything that goes/ can come/ stand up/ even the dead shall rise." See *good woman*, 102.

58. Perry, *Stigmata*, 176.

59. Perry, *Stigmata*, 221, 222.

60. Perry, *Stigmata*, 197.

61. For additional commentary that I offer on the novel, especially in terms of its incorporation of folklore, see "A Haunting Diary and a Slasher Quilt: Using Dynamic Folk Communities to Combat Terror in Phyllis Alesia Perry's *Stigmata*," in *The Scary Mason-Dixon Line: African American Writers and the South* (Baton Rouge: LSU P, 2009), 133–50.

62. There are exceptions in life narrative recordings. For example, in a measured response to a trip she took to Africa, literary and folklore scholar Daryl Cumber Dance comments: "On a very subjective level, my responses to Africa were a mass of contradictions—of joy and sadness, pleasure and anger, comfort and pain, fulfillment and disappointment, delight and disgust, pride and shame. At times I was the long lost daughter of Africa returning to the embrace of the mythical Mother Land; at other times I was the hot and weary traveler, annoyed by the persistent beggar and frightened of the street criminal. Africa was for me at times an emotional roller coaster, made all the more difficult because of the plethora of restraints that constrained me from an unself-conscious expression of my emotions." See *Here Am I: Miscellaneous Meanderings, Meditations, Memoirs, and Melodramas* (Jacksonville, FL: Adducent, 2020), 133.

63. Yaa Gyasi, *Homegoing* (New York: Alfred A. Knopf, 2016); Gloria Naylor, *Mama Day* (New York: Ticknor & Fields, 1988).

64. Olaudah Equiano, *The Interesting Narrative of the Life of Olaudah Equiano, or, Gustavus Vassa, the African*, in *Classic Slave Narratives*, ed. Henry Louis Gates Jr. (New York: Penguin, 1987); Toni Morrison, *Beloved* (New York: Knopf, 1987).

65. Douglas A. Blackmon, *Slavery By Another Name: The Re-Enslavement of Black Americans from the Civil War to World War II* (New York: Anchor Books, 2008).

66. Gyasi, *Homegoing*, 300.

67. E. Patrick Johnson captures some of the complexities of returning to the South after northern migration in his poem, "Home," in which he asserts that "Going home ain't always easy," especially when one must witness continuing diminished familial financial circumstances, drug use, being with black folks who can sometimes make one "Feel bad about being black in a/ White world that's always telling you/ Go Home." (Poem supplied directly to the author.) I explore the complexities of calling the South home in my memoir, *Summer Snow: Reflections from a Black Daughter of the South* (Boston: Beacon, 2003).

68. Paule Marshall and James Baldwin are two other writers who portray characters who return to Africa in attempts to heal from trauma. See Marshall's *The Chosen Place, The Timeless People* (1969; New York: Vintage, 1984) and Baldwin's *Just Above My Head* (New York: Dial, 1979).

69. Another "Africa-American-Africa" narrative is Lawrence Hill's *The Book of Negroes/Someone Knows My Name* (New York: W.W. Norton & Company, 2007), which recounts the story of a kidnapped African girl who spends forty years in the New World before she can return to Africa. Her desperate desire to see her village again is undermined when, after waiting on the West Coast of Africa for an extended period for someone to guide her to her village, she learns that the persons with whom she is dealing instead have a plot to sell her into slavery—again. The striking thing about the novel is the way that Aminata ("Meena") holds on to an idea of Africa through many decades away from it and how desperately she thinks of it as home.

70. Of earlier writers such as Olaudah Equiano, J. Lee Greene writes that, "from this New World African's vantage point, Africa is Eden, and Virginia, if an Eden at all, is Eden after the Fall." See *Blacks in Eden*, 18.

71. James Weldon Johnson, "Go Down Death—A Funeral Sermon," in *God's Trombones* (New York: Viking, 1955), 27–30; 4–7.

72. These spirituals appear in various collections. See, for example, James Weldon Johnson's two collections combined into one volume as *The Books of American Negro Spirituals* (New York: Viking, 1925, 1926), Langston Hughes and Arna Bontemps, eds., *The Book of Negro Folklore* (New York: Dodd, Mead, & Company, 1958), Patricia Liggins Hill, et. al., *Call and Response: The Riverside Anthology of the African American Literary Tradition* (Boston: Houghton Mifflin, 1998), and Barksdale and Kinnamon, *Black Writers of America*. As Jean Wagner points out, several of the poems in *God's Trombones* are structured on spirituals; see *Black Poets of the United States: From Paul Laurence Dunbar to Langston Hughes* (Urbana: U of Illinois P, 1973), 377–84.

73. For traditional tales in which black folks are depicted as arriving in heaven, acquiring wings, and flying all over the place, in addition to performing other antics, see Daryl Cumber Dance, *Shuckin' and Jivin': Folklore from Contemporary Black Americans* (Bloomington: Indiana U P, 1978), Richard Dorson, *American Negro Folktales* (Greenwich, CT: Fawcett, 1967), and Hughes and Bontemps, *The Book of Negro Folklore*.

74. Johnson, "Death," 70.

75. Johnson, "Death," 12.

76. Johnson, "Death," 71–76.

77. Johnson, "Creation," 69.

78. Johnson, "Creation," 76–91.

79. Sterling Brown, "Sister Lou" and "When de Saints Go Ma'ching Home," in *The Collected Poems of Sterling A. Brown*, ed. Michael S. Harper (New York: Harper & Row, 1989), 54–55, 26–30.

80. Brown, "Sister," 1–19.

81. Brown, "Sister," 22–24.

82. Brown, "Sister," 32.

83. Brown, "Sister," 37–41.

84. Brown, "Sister," 45.

85. Brown, "Sister," 47.

86. Brown, "Sister," 55.

87. The fact that "Sister" is used to apply to the characters in both poems reiterates the church-based folk ties of each of the poems, as this appellation is one that is consistently used with black church women.

88. For a discussion of Brown's relationship to Big Boy Davis, see Joanne V. Gabbin, *Sterling A Brown: Building the Black Aesthetic Tradition* (Westport CT: Greenwood P, 1985). Gabbin also comments on "Sister Lou" and "When de Saints Go Ma'ching Home" in the context of the folk vision that informs both. For commentary on Brown's more critical representations of African Americans and religious belief in his poetry, see Wagner, *Black Poets of the United States*, 490–96.

89. Brown, "Chant," 6–7.

90. Brown, "Chant," 39, 47, 56, 64, 75, and 83.

91. Brown, "Chant," 127–29, 138.

92. Brown, "Chant," 140–41.

93. Langston Hughes, *Not Without Laughter* (New York: A. A. Knopf, 1930); James Baldwin, *Go Tell It on the Mountain* (New York: Dell, 1953); Lorraine Hansberry, *A Raisin in the Sun* (New York: Random House, 1959). It is noteworthy in these representations that the characters holding such beliefs are primarily female. Though Gabriel presumably follows in the path of his mother, his belief system is revealed to be almost anti-Christian, especially in his treatment of his wife Elizabeth and her son John. This emphasis on the feminine echoes the pattern of keepers of family traditions to which I referred earlier.

94. See Octavia E. Butler, *Parable of the Sower* (New York: Four Walls Eight Windows, 1993), 78. In several other of her works, Butler explores post-nuclear disasters that leave humankind at the mercy of alien visitors. Earth as home is lost to most of those characters as they try to find new homespaces among the aliens who have rescued them and, as a result, have begun various processes of transformation of what it means to be human and what it means to call various spaces home, whether those spaces are physically on planets or on spaceships large enough to contain worlds.

Conclusion
While We're in This Place . . .

Even a cursory perusal of the works under consideration here leads to the conclusion that most African American literary representations showcase homes that are unhealthy, tainted, poisonous, and generally not conducive to positive growth and development of the characters who inhabit those spaces. Whether focusing on the physical spaces or the intra-familial activities/dynamics that occur in those spaces, it is clear that there is a great gap between any abstract conceptions of home, any idealized imagined spaces, and the actual manifestations of those spaces. Questions obviously turn to why. Beyond the stereotypical idea that "bliss is boring" and that literature in and of itself necessitates conflict, what reasons might account for these portrayals? Is history the culprit, that is, a heritage of loss, movement, and instability instantiated by the system of slavery? Are such representations more reflective of the aftermath of slavery, when Jim Crow practices reigned? Dare we suggest that there is something inherent in African American life and culture that tends more toward movement and only passingly toward concerns about permanent homespaces? Do attractions for transience thus dominate, as the blues tradition and characters such as Albert Murray's Luzana Cholly in *Train Whistle Guitar* (1974) might suggest?[1] Is it enough to conclude simply that "Papa was a rolling stone," that African American women historically were more concerned about nesting than their male counterparts? What is a reasonable path to pursue in trying to understand the ultimate objective of these psychologically and emotionally violent representations of spaces that ostensibly should be the most nurturing of any that human beings inhabit?

Perhaps we can start with *lacks* and *lack of positive role models*. Slavery was built in part upon what black people lacked, what they did not have. They did not have power. They did not have financial resources. They did not have spatial ownership of the cabins, the "homes," in which they resided. They did not have control of their presents or their futures. Indeed, they did not have themselves. These lacks led some of those formerly enslaved, as represented in Margaret Walker's *Jubilee* (1966), to attempt to eliminate the lack.[2] However, it led others, such as newly emancipated and insecure folks whom Booker T. Washington encountered in *Up From Slavery* (1901) and those who similarly elected to remain on the plantation in Ernest J. Gaines's *The Autobiography of Miss Jane Pittman* (1971), to believe the lack was the norm for existence.[3] In the latter case, the inability to imagine how such lacks could be eliminated may have prevented those without homes from ever imagining what a homespace might be or how to work to create such a space that would be positive for its inhabitants. On the other hand, lack of positive role models, again as in slavery and as Walker portrays in *Jubilee*, could have led to the imperfect creation of such spaces. By most of the actions we witness in him, Vyry Brown's husband Innis is a good man. Unfortunately, he has learned from slavery that the only way to make a recalcitrant individual behave is to beat him. Thus he beats Vyry and Randall Ware's son Jim when Jim fails in taking care of the precious sow that Innis is raising. But . . . in contrast to Innis, there is Vyry, who has similarly grown up under the system of slavery but who has managed to separate herself from some of the violent practices of that institution—even as she has suffered a life-scarring beating at the hands of an overseer. Does this mean that the impact of slavery upon home development is a matter of selective, individualized responses and that some black characters transcend that history while others do not?

The movement of Liza Jane in Charles W. Chesnutt's short story, "The Wife of His Youth" (1899), presents an engaging example.[4] Having endured slavery, Liza Jane spends the next twenty-five years of her life looking for the man, Sam Taylor, to whom she was married during slavery and who managed to escape to Cleveland, Ohio. Liza Jane is less concerned about establishing a physical space and calling it home than locating her first husband. It is unclear if she ever contemplates what home might mean. In her noble quest, and in Mr. Ryder's [Sam Taylor's] response to it, there is similarly no indication that there can ever be a homespace beyond the romanticized conception that Mr. Ryder, imbued with the floweriness of the ladies depicted in nineteenth-century British poetry, attaches to it. The very dark-skinned, uncouth, and illiterate Liza Jane, even as she is taken in by this very prominent member of the Blue Vein Society in Cleveland, Ohio, does not have the social skills or the education to be comfortable in such an environment. On the other hand, she will gain the stability that her quarter century of roaming has prevented. Trade off, then, might be more crucial to her existence than a truly defined sense of home. She will certainly have a stable space, but will that stable space be home? Will Mr. Ryder love her in the same way that he has professed love for the widowed Mrs. Dixon, the nearly-white member of the Blue Vein Society to whom he is engaged when Liza Jane arrives? Again, class and literacy conflict seems to be the projected outcome more so than a happily-ever-after scenario.

Still, the impact of slavery has a measurable number of years post that condition. Or does it? In recent years, there has been much commentary about the lingering effects of the traumatic conditions of slavery, and there is no doubt that the consequences of slavery continue to be relevant to the existence of black people on United States soil. However, it is clear that people of color in the United States have managed to survive and thrive even with that history overshadowing their actions. Slavery, then, might be partly accountable but not completely so. The destinies of black people in America are ultimately as much their responsibility as they are the consequence of forces beyond their control. The question becomes, then, when does the literature reflect that ultimate conclusion and transformation? It certainly does not reflect it in works such as Suzan-Lori Parks's *Topdog/Underdog* (2001) or in such works as Delores Phillips's *The Darkest Child* (2004).[5] After slavery, after the convict lease system, after the Great Migration, after Jim Crow practices, after the Black Arts Movement, after the "Black is Beautiful" movement, after the Civil Rights Movement and heroic figures in the quest for civil rights, after it all, homespaces in African American literature are still mostly polluted, toxic, and often dominated by intrusions of the larger American culture. African American writers have mostly not yet imagined spaces in which black people control fully their own destinies, establish their own communities, write their own laws, and chart their own paths to the future. And when they have attempted such, as in Toni Morrison's *Paradise* (1998), internal and external forces have reduced the efforts to tragic results. There have been other attempts, but such attempts have occurred more in the speculative and science fiction modes than in the realm of realism. I think especially of Lauren Olamina in Octavia E. Butler's Parable series, which consists of *Parable of the Sower* (1993) and *Parable of the Talents* (1998), and her attempts to shape family and community after environmental and man-made disasters.[6] However, the desolate and super-violent world in which Lauren lives is not ultimately conducive to her efforts. When the group Lauren gathers arrives at their destination in northern California, they find a burned-out homestead and quickly come to realize that threats exist all around them. The same lack of healthy possibility in attempting to create a homespace is true of Butler's Lilith in the Xenogenesis series, which begins with the novel *Dawn* (1987) and includes *Adulthood Rites* (1988) and *Imago* (1989).[7] Lilith's attempts to re-create family and stability, to return to earth as home after nuclear disaster and alien salvaging of the remains of humanity, are ultimately not successful enough for Lilith to feel secure in any sense of home. As worlds and communities disintegrate in Butler's novels, notions of home get defined and redefined until they become almost meaningless. Essentials for the creation of stability are uniformly missing, and violence, betrayal, and loss dominate landscapes much more frequently than the creative corporation that is the basis for safe homespaces.

These literary disasters notwithstanding, however, it would be difficult to conclude—and I would be extremely reluctant to do so—that literary African Americans do not value the idea of home or the physical manifestations of homespaces. They do. What the literature makes clear, however, is that the quest and the location for such are ever elusive. Yet, characters search. They have expectations for the solace of a space that they can call their own, as Vyry Brown does in Walker's *Jubilee*, as Lauren Olamina and Lilith desire in Butler's futuristic novels, as Hester desires in Parks's *Fucking A* (2001), as Lincoln and Booth long for in Parks's *Topdog/Underdog*, as Lizzie hopes might be possible in Dolen Perkins-Valdez's *Wench* (2010), and as a host of other characters all wish for in various guises through various limitations in various other texts. From Mama Lena Younger and her family in Lorraine Hansberry's *A Raisin in the Sun* (1959), to Rose and her desire to protect her family in August Wilson's *Fences* (1986), to Neesey's constant efforts to make her surroundings pleasant and livable in A. J. Verdelle's *The Good Negress* (1995), characters exhibit strong desires for the unencumbered space and safety of home.[8]

Nonetheless, home, more often than not, is an abstract concept that seldom finds manifestation in concrete reality.[9] While characters can certainly occupy any number of physical spaces that they may identify as home, that concept is not frequently something that is realistically possible for them. Yet they search and long and wish and hope. If where they are is horrible—or at least psychologically or spiritually unlivable—then somewhere else will surely be better. If the people who are supposed to care about them mistreat them, as Margarete does with Neesey in *The Good Negress*, then some other mothers might make life more tolerable. If husbands and wives cannot achieve a level of peace and comfort between themselves and for their children, as is clear with the Breedloves in Toni Morrison's *The Bluest Eye* (1970), then perhaps there is some other place—such as the white Fisher household for Pauline Breedlove—that will allow them the satisfaction of fulfillment of the imagined image they hold in their minds.[10] If Bigger Thomas in Richard Wright's *Native Son* (1940) wants to blot out his family in their kitchenette building, then perhaps the space beyond the Southside of Chicago—so he imagines—will enable him to do something else.[11] Constantly, repetitively, for each of these characters, realization of home is just one step beyond the horizon of their dreams, just one step beyond their imagined grasps. Indeed, they might be compared to characters in folktales, many of whom are ever-questing but never achieving, ever traveling but never arriving.

It would perhaps be a distortion of the quest to suggest that it is fruitless, that the quester may just as well have remained at his or her point of origin. Questing validates desire and, throughout the literary history, characters exhibit desire for what may never appear before them or what may be more of a challenge than they anticipated if it does appear, as with the Younger family in *A Raisin in the Sun*. Throughout the literature, characters move, migrate, and try to locate or identify something better. If they cannot move physically, then they move psychologically and emotionally, as Bigger Thomas does in *Native Son* and as Hester does in *Fucking A*. They make valiant attempts to cope with the circumstances of the worlds that challenge them at every turn. Despite his mother's and Vera's assertions to the contrary, Bigger probably would like to see his family live decently in a roomy homespace that enables the expansion rather than the constriction of their humanity. If her choices had been different, Hester would like to have her son living with her, in a space that enables safety and caring, one that is not bloody, violent, and created by the external forces in *Fucking A*. Both characters, like so many of their counterparts, desire something better. The fact that "better" is not yet realized in the literature is a testament to the impact of history as well as to the lack of independent resources and the lack of political and social currency within the environments in which they live. While those impacts might diminish humanity, imagination and desire sustain it. The characters travel, as their ancestors did, over stony roads and bloody paths, and though they may stumble and be taken out of the race altogether, the fact that they travel, move, and migrate reiterates desire. They may never see safe and happy homes on United States soil, but their questing re-enforces the idea of the value of home.

There is another progression worthy of note. In the twenty-first century, what home looks like in African American literature takes interesting directions that involve futuristic, otherworldly, and suprahuman manifestations. Home moves outward from specific structures at times to the vast reaches of the universe or to the depths of the sea. Octavia E. Butler anticipated these movements with her Xenogenesis series in which a race of aliens, the Oankali, salvage the remains of humankind after a nuclear disaster and transport them to a space ship the size of a planet. Kept in cryogenesis for hundreds of years, they are awakened to discover that returning home to earth is a process that can only be enabled if they "trade genes" with the Oankali, which means that they become less than human even as they become more than human. Lilith, the central figure in this series, is tasked with persuading her fellow humans to embrace the future the Oankali have in store for them. Butler's early vision of these beings—human and non-human—coming together to create new homespaces anticipates works by such authors as Rivers Solomon, Tomi Adeyemi, Nisi Shawl, and N. K. Jemisin. While Butler moves outward, these latter writers target transformations of home on earth.

Solomon creates a world in *The Deep* (2019) where descendants of Africans thrown overboard during the Middle Passage have survived, thrived, and sustained cultures miles below the surface of the ocean. Having mutated to adapt to their new environment—which means they are more fish-like than traditionally human—they find the surface of earth and surface dwellers as alien as the Oankali and their ship are to Lilith. It is nonetheless their home, and their world has given them special powers. So too with Shawl's reconceptualization of an African continent in *Everfair* (2016) in which persons of color and their allies have impressive technological as well as physical powers as they wage war against their oppressors and try to reclaim their homespaces. The power dynamic is also true for Adeyemi's and Jemisin's characters, all of whom have evolved special, more than human powers. Adeyemi's characters in *Children of Blood and Bone* (2018) draw upon the elements for power as well as for communion with the goddess whom they believe is responsible for their existence. Some of Jemisin's characters in *The Fifth Season* (2015) have the ability to manipulate the earth, so that they can cause or control earthquakes.[12]

For these characters in these futuristic worlds, family is a matter of biological and voluntary associations, and home is as much headspace as it is tangible place and space. For example, Adeyemi's characters have seen their home village destroyed, yet they, like so many of their literary ancestors, know it intimately in their memories. They work hard to bring back the magic that they believe will restore their world to its rightful relationship to their goddess, and that means transporting notions of home throughout their quest. Their desire is comparable to Vyry Brown's desire, with only a matter of intensity and supernatural ability separating the two. So too with Jemisin's primary character who is on a search for her daughter. Although she has supernatural powers, the basic desire for restoration of home and family remains the same.

What these twenty-first century depictions of African American homespaces suggest is that the futuristic subgenre of the literature has turned so far from manifestations of home in the realistic mode that such representations may become the exception in the future instead of the norm. While there are certainly still works that portray realistic representations of African American homespaces, the dominant mode in current representation is futuristic, and that futurism involves powers and actions that would literally have been alien to the likes of Pecola Breedlove and Neesey Palms. Just as the neo-slave narrative became prominent in African American literature several decades ago, so now it seems as if the Afrofuturistic mode is becoming increasingly dominant. With it comes transformed landscapes, planets, spaceships, and other venues for representing African American and African-world homespaces. While coverings may change in dramatic ways, the substance of representation seems to be constant. Characters desire homespaces with their biological, legal, and voluntary family units, and that desire remains paramount over all the surface formulations of its resilience.

NOTES

1. Albert Murray, *Train Whistle Guitar* (New York: McGraw Hill, 1974).
2. Margaret Walker, *Jubilee* (Boston: First Mariner Books, 1999).
3. Booker T. Washington, *Up From Slavery* (New York: W.W. Norton, 1996); Ernest J. Gaines, *The Autobiography of Miss Jane Pittman* (New York: Dial, 1971).
4. Charles W. Chesnutt, "The Wife of His Youth," in *The Wife of His Youth and Other Stories of the Color Line* (Ann Arbor: U of Michigan P, 1968), 1–24.
5. Suzan-Lori Parks, *Topdog/Underdog* (New York: Theatre Communications Group, 2001); Delores Phillips, *The Darkest Child* (New York: Soho, 2018).
6. Octavia E. Butler, *Parable of the Sower* (New York: Four Walls Eight Windows, 1992) and *Parable of the Talents* (New York: Seven Stories P, 1998).
7. Octavia E. Butler, *Dawn* (New York: Warner Communications Company, 1987); *Adulthood Rites* (New York: Warner Communications Company, 1988), *Imago* (New York: Warner Communications Company, 1989).
8. Suzan-Lori Parks, *Fucking A*, in *The Red Letter Plays* (New York: Theatre Communications Group, 2001); Dolen Perkins-Valdez, *Wench* (New York: HarperCollings, 2010); Lorraine Hansberry, *A Raisin in the Sun* (New York: Random House, 1959); August Wilson, *Fences* (New York: Dramatists Play Service, 1986); A. J. Verdelle, *The Good Negress* (Chapel Hill: Algonquin Books, 1995).
9. After her study of home in five novels over a span of forty years, Valerie Sweeny Prince agrees with this inability to locate home successfully and productively in a tangible reality. She concludes in *Burnin' Down the House: Home in African American Literature* (New York: Columbia U P, 2005) "that home is somehow beyond place, beyond life, and even beyond death. It is an un-selfconsciously black place where men and women live alongside the ghosts of their past. We cannot walk away without carrying the bones inherited from our years of struggle" (145). Finally, she comments: "we may be damned to walk beside home in a nether region of shadows and ghosts—lurking near but apart from the place we call home" (146).
10. Toni Morrison, *The Bluest Eye* (1970; New York: Plume, 1994).
11. Richard Wright, *Native Son* (New York: Library of America, 1991).
12. Rivers Solomon, *The Deep* (New York: Saga, 2019); Nisi Shawl, *Everfair* (New York: Tom Doherty Associates, 2016); Tomi Adeyemi, *Children of Blood and Bone* (New York: Henry Holt and Company, 2018); N. K. Jemisin, *The Fifth Season* (New York: Orbit, 2015).

Bibliography

Achilles, Jochen. "Does Reshuffling the Cards Change the Game? Structures of Play in Parks's *Topdog/Underdog*." In *Suzan-Lori Parks: Essays on the Plays and Other Works*. Edited by Philip C. Kolin. Jefferson, N.C.: McFarland, 2010, 103–23.

Adeyemi, Tomi. *Children of Blood and Bone*. New York: Henry Holt and Company, 2018.

Alcott, Louisa May. *Little Men*. Boston: Roberts Brothers, 1871.

———. *Little Women*. 1868; Mineola, New York: Dover, 2000.

An, Jee Hyun. "Migratory Spaces of 'Home,' History and Modernity in Zora Neale Hurston's *Their Eyes Were Watching God*." *English Language and Literature* 62, no. 3 (2016): 377–95.

Angelou, Maya. *The Heart of a Woman*. New York: Random House, 1981.

Asante, Molefi Kete. *As I Run Toward Africa: A Memoir*. New York: Routledge/Paradigm, 2011.

Baker, Jr. Houston A. *Blues, Ideology, and Afro-American Literature: A Vernacular Theory*. Chicago: U of Chicago P, 1984.

Baldwin, James. *Go Tell It on the Mountain*. New York: Dell, 1953; 1980.

———. *Going to Meet the Man*. New York: Vintage, 1995.

———. *If Beale Street Could Talk*. New York: Dial, 1974.

———. *Just Above My Head*. New York: Dial, 1979.

———. *Notes of a Native Son*. New York: Bantam, 1968.

———. "Sweet Lorraine." In *To Be Young, Gifted and Black: Lorraine Hansberry in Her Own Words*, adopted by Robert Nemiroff. New York: Signet, 1969, xi-xv.

Barksdale, Richard and Keneth Kinnamon. *Black Writers of America: A Comprehensive Anthology*. New York: The Macmillan Company, 1972.

Beaulieu, Elizabeth Ann. *Black Women Writers and the American Neo-Slave Narrative: Feminism Unfettered*. Westport, CT: Greenwood, 1999.

Black, Daniel. *Perfect Peace*. New York: St. Martin's, 2010.

Blackmon, Douglas A. *Slavery By Another Name: The Re-Enslavement of Black Americans from the Civil War to World War II*. New York: Anchor Books, 2008.

Bradley, David. *The Chaneysville Incident*. New York: Harper & Row, 1982.
Brooks, Gwendolyn. *Children Coming Home*. In *In Montgomery*. Chicago: Third World P, 2003, 77–103.
———. *Selected Poems*. New York: HarperPerennial, 1963; 2006.
———. *A Street in Bronzeville*. New York: Harper & Brothers, 1945.
Brown, Carolyn J. *Song of My Life: A Biography of Margaret Walker*. Jackson: U P of Mississippi, 2014.
Burrill, Mary Powell. *Aftermath*. In *Strange Fruit: Plays on Lynching by American Women*. Edited by Kathy A. Perkins and Judith L. Stephens. Bloomington: Indiana U P, 1998, 79–91.
Butler, Octavia E. *Adulthood Rites*. New York: Warner Communications Company, 1988.
———. *Dawn*. New York: Warner Communications Company, 1987.
———. *Imago*. New York: Warner Communications Company, 1989.
———. *Kindred*. Boston: Beacon, 1979; 1988.
———. *Parable of the Sower*. New York: Four Walls Eight Windows, 1993.
———. *Parable of the Talents*. New York: Seven Stories P, 1998.
Cannon, Uzzie T. "Tears, Fears, and Queers: Transgendering Black Masculinity in Daniel Black's *Perfect Peace*." *CEA Critic* 78, no. 1 (March 2016): 45–58.
Carmichael, Jacqueline Miller. *Trumpeting a Fiery Sound: History and Folklore in Margaret Walker's Jubilee*. Athens: U of Georgia P, 1998.
Cather, Willa. *O Pioneers*. Boston: Houghton Mifflin, 1913.
Chesnutt, Charles W. *The Conjure Woman*. Boston: Houghton Mifflin, 1899.
———. *The House Behind the Cedars*. 1900. Athens: U of Georgia P, 1988.
———. *The Wife of His Youth and Other Stories of the Color Line*. Boston: Houghton Mifflin, 1899.
Childress, Alice. *A Hero Ain't Nothin' But a Sandwich*. New York: Puffin Books, 1973.
———. *Rainbow Jordan*. New York: Coward, McCann & Geoghegan, Inc., 1981.
Clark, Keith. "Baldwin, Communitas, and the Black Masculinist Tradition." In *New Essays on Go Tell It on the Mountain*, ed. Trudier Harris. New York: Cambridge U P, 1996, 127–56.
———. *The Radical Fiction of Ann Petry*. Baton Rouge: LSU P, 2013.
Cleage, Pearl. *Flyin' West*. New York: Dramatists Play Service, Inc., 1995.
Clifton, Lucille. *good woman: poems and a memoir 1969-1980*. Rochester, NY: BOA Editions, Ltd., 1987.
Colbert, Soyica Diggs. *The African American Theatrical Body: Reception, Performance, and the Stage*. New York: Cambridge U P, 2011.
Conner, Marc C. "From the Sublime to the Beautiful: The Aesthetic Progress of Toni Morrison." In *The Aesthetics of Toni Morrison: Speaking the Unspeakable*, ed. Marc C. Conner. Jackson: U P of Mississippi, 2000, 49–76.
Connolly, Andrew. "Shame, Rage, and Endless Battle: Systemic Pressure and Individual Violence in James Baldwin's *Go Tell It on the Mountain*." *The CEA Critic* 77, no. 1 (March 2015): 120–42.

Conrad, Rachel. "*Children Coming Home*: The Anticipatory Present in Gwendolyn Brooks's Poems of Childhood." *Callaloo* 37, no. 2 (Spring 2014): 369–88.
Crank, James A. "Down N' Dirty." *south: an interdisciplinary journal* 48, no. 2 (Spring 2016): 157–69.
Cromwell, Adelaide M. "Afterword." *The Living Is Easy*. 1948; New York: The Feminist P, 1982.
Csapo, Csaba. "Race, Religion and Sexuality in *Go Tell It on the Mountain*." In *James Baldwin's Go Tell It on the Mountain: Historical and Critical Essays*, edited by Carol E. Henderson. New York: Peter Lang, 2006, 57–74.
Cullen, Countee. "Heritage." In *Black Writers of America: A Comprehensive Anthology*, edited by Richard Barksdale and Keneth Kinnamon, 531-33. New York: Macmillan, 1972.
Dance, Daryl C. "You Can't Go Home Again: James Baldwin and the South." *CLA Journal* 18, no. 1 (September 1974): 81–90.
Dance, Daryl Cumber. *Here Am I: Miscellaneous Meanderings, Meditations, Memoirs, and Melodramas*. Jacksonville, FL: Adducent, 2020.
———. *Shuckin' and Jivin': Folklore from Contemporary Black Americans*. Bloomington: Indiana U P, 1978.
Davis, Amanda J. "Shatterings: Violent Disruptions of Homeplace in *Jubilee* and *The Street*." *MELUS* 30, no. 4 (Winter 2005): 25–51.
Dawkins, Laura. "Family Acts: History, Memory, and Performance in Suzan-Lori Parks's *The America Play* and *Topdog/Underdog*." *South Atlantic Review* 74, no. 3 (Summer 2009): 82–98.
Day, Lisa B. "'I Reach to Where the Freedom Is': The Influence of the Slave Narrative Tradition on A. J. Verdelle's *The Good Negress*." *Critique* 41, no. 4 (Summer 2000): 411–24.
de Sousa, Alcina Pereira and Alda Maria Correia. "Living in Between a House and a Home: Where's the Comfort Zone Anyway? Dislocated Identities in Morrison's *The Bluest Eye* and Cisneros' *The House on Mango Street*." *Oceanide* 12 (2020): 18–27.
Dick and Jane. https://www.penguinrandomhouse.com/series/DNO/dick-and-jane
Dorson, Richard. *American Negro Folktales*. Greenwich, Conn: Fawcett, 1967.
Douglass, Frederick. *Narrative of the Life of Frederick Douglass, An American Slave, Written by Himself*. 1845; Cambridge: Harvard U P, 1960.
Dove, Rita. *Thomas and Beulah*. Pittsburgh: Carnegie-Mellon U P, 1986.
Dudley, Marc. *Understanding James Baldwin*. Columbia: U of South Carolina P, 2019.
Ellison, Ralph. *Invisible Man*. New York: Vintage, 1952.
Equiano, Olaudah. *The Interesting Narrative of the Life of Olaudah Equiano, or, Gustavus Vassa, the African*. In *Classic Slave Narratives*, edited by Henry Louis Gates Jr., 1-182. New York: Penguin, 1789; 1987.
FIRE!! New York: 1926.
Furman, Jan, ed. *Toni Morrison's Song of Solomon: A Casebook*. New York: Oxford U P, 2003.

Gabbin, Joanne V. *Sterling A. Brown: Building the Black Aesthetic Tradition.* Westport, CT: Greenwood P, 1985.

Gaines, Ernest J. *A Gathering of Old Men.* New York: Alfred A. Knopf, 1983.

———. *A Lesson Before Dying.* New York: Alfred A. Knopf, 1994.

———. *The Autobiography of Miss Jane Pittman.* New York: Bantam, 1972.

———. *Bloodline.* New York: Random House, 1968.

———. *Catherine Carmier.* Chatham, New Jersey: The Chatham Bookseller, 1964.

Golden, Marita. *Migrations of the Heart.* New York: Anchor Press/Doubleday, 1983.

Goldsmith, Meredith. "The Wages of Weight: Dorothy West's Corporeal Politics." *Mosaic* 40, no. 4 (December 2007): 35–49.

Graham, Maryemma, ed. *Conversations With Margaret Walker.* Jackson: U P of Mississippi, 2002.

———. *Fields Watered With Blood: Critical Essays on Margaret Walker.* Athens: U of Georgia P, 2001.

———. *How I Wrote Jubilee and Other Essays on Life and Literature.* New York: Feminist P, 1990.

———. *On Being Female, Black, and Free: Essays by Margaret Walker, 1932-1992.* Knoxville: U of Tennessee P, 1997.

Greene, J. Lee. *Blacks in Eden: The African American Novel's First Century.* Charlottesville: U P of Virginia, 1996.

Griffin, Farah Jasmine. "On the Ethical Dimensions of Toni Morrison's *The Bluest Eye*." *College Literature*, 47, no. 4 (Fall 2020): 671–77.

———. *"Who Set You Flowin'?": The African-American Migration Narrative.* New York: Oxford U P, 1995.

Grimke, Angelina Weld. *Rachel.* Hays, Kansas: McGrath Publishing Company, 1920; 1969.

Gundarker, Grey, ed. *Keep Your Head to the Sky: Interpreting African American Home Ground.* Charlottesville: U P of Virginia, 1998.

Gyasi, Yaa. *Homegoing.* New York: Alfred A. Knopf, 2016.

Haley, Alex. *Roots: The Saga of an American Family.* New York: Doubleday, 1976.

Hansberry, Lorraine. *A Raisin in the Sun.* New York: Random House, 1959.

Harper, Frances Ellen Watkins. *Iola Leroy.* 1892; Boston: Beacon, 1987.

Harper, Michael, ed. *The Collected Poems of Sterling A. Brown.* New York: Harper & Row, 1989.

Harris, Trudier. "A Different Image of the Black Woman." *Callaloo*, vol. 16 (October 1982): 146–51.

———. "A Haunting Diary and a Slasher Quilt: Using Dynamic Folk Communities to Combat Terror in Phyllis Alesia Perry's *Stigmata*." In Trudier Harris, *The Scary Mason-Dixon Line: African American Writers and the South.* Baton Rouge: LSU P, 2009, 133–50.

———. *Black Women in the Fiction of James Baldwin.* Knoxville: U of Tennessee P, 1985.

———. "Black Writers in a Changed Landscape, Since 1950." In *The History of Southern Literature*, ed. Louis D. Rubin, Jr., et. al. Baton Rouge: LSU P, 1985, 566–77.

———. "The Image of Africa in the Literature of the Harlem Renaissance." National Humanities Center Online Resources for high school teachers. www.nationalhumanitiescenter.org.

———. "Romantic and Romanticized International Journeying: Marita Golden's *Migrations of the Heart.*" *Obsidian II: Literature & Arts in the African Diaspora*, vol. 41, nos. 1-2, Fall 2015, 209–35.

———. *Summer Snow: Reflections from a Black Daughter of the South*. Boston: Beacon, 2003.

Harris, Trudier, ed. *New Essays on Go Tell It on the Mountain*. New York: Cambridge U P, 1996.

Harris-Lopez, Trudier. "Architecture as Destiny? Women and Survival Strategies in Ann Petry's *The Street.*" In Harris-Lopez's *South of Tradition: Essays on African American Literature*. Athens: U of Georgia P, 2002, 68–90.

Hartman, Saidiya. *Lose Your Mother: A Journey Along the Atlantic Slave Route*. New York: Farrar, Straus and Giroux, 2007.

Heinze, Denise. *The Dilemma of 'Double-Consciousness': Toni Morrison's Novels*. Athens: U of Georgia P, 1993.

Henderson, Carol E., ed. *James Baldwin's Go Tell It on the Mountain: Historical and Critical Essays*. New York: Peter Lang, 2006.

Hill, Lawrence. *The Book of Negroes/Someone Knows My Name*. New York: W.W. Norton & Company, 2007.

Hill, Patricia Liggins, et al. *Call and Response: The Riverside Anthology of the African American Literary Tradition*. Boston: Houghton Mifflin, 1998.

hooks, bell. "Homeplace: A Site of Resistance." In *Yearning: Race, Gender, and Cultural Politics*. Boston: South End P, 1990, 41–49.

Hughes, Langston. *The Big Sea*. New York: Hill and Wang, 1940.

———. *Mulatto*. In *Five Plays*, edited by Webster Smalley. Bloomington: Indiana U P, 1935; 1963.

———. *Not Without Laughter*. New York: A. A. Knopf, 1930.

Hughes, Langston and Arna Bontemps, eds. *The Book of Negro Folklore*. New York: Dodd, Mead, & Company, 1958.

Hurston, Zora Neale. "High John De Conquer." *The Sanctified Church*, 69-78. Berkeley, CA: Turtle Island, 1981.

———. *Jonah's Gourd Vine*. Philadelphia: J. B. Lippincott, 1934.

———. *Spunk: The Selected Stories of Zora Neale Hurston*. Berkeley, CA: Turtle Island Foundation, 1985.

———. *Their Eyes Were Watching God*. New York: Perennial, 1937; 1990.

Iloabugichukwu, Arah. "The Strained Relationship Between Black Mothers And Their Daughters." *Madame Noire*, 29 May 2018.

Jacobs, Harriet. *Incidents in the Life of a Slave Girl*. Cambridge: Harvard U P, 1861; 1987.

James, Marlon. *The Book of Night Women*. New York: Riverhead Books, 2009.

Jelsma, Jess E. "Decay and Symbolic Impotence in Toni Morrison's *The Bluest Eye.*" *The Explicator* 75, no. 3 (2017): 200–02.

Jemisin, N. K. *The Fifth Season*. New York: Orbit, 2015.

Jennings, La Vinia Delois. *Toni Morrison and the Idea of Africa*. New York: Cambridge U P, 2008.

Johnson, Barbara. "Metaphor, Metonymy and Voice in *Their Eyes Were Watching God*." In *Black Literature and Literary Theory*, edited by Henry Louis Gates, Jr. New York: Methuen, 1984, 205–19.

Johnson, Charles. *Middle Passage*. New York: Atheneum, 1990.

———. *Oxherding Tale*. Bloomington: Indiana U P, 1982.

Johnson, Georgia Douglas. *A Sunday Morning in the South*, *Safe*, and *Blue-Eyed Black Boy*. In *Strange Fruit: Plays on Lynching by American Women*, edited by Kathy A. Perkins and Judith L. Stephens, 99-109, 110-15, 111-20. Bloomington: Indiana U P, 1998.

Johnson, James Weldon. *God's Trombones*. New York: Viking, 1927; 1955.

Johnson, James Weldon, ed. *The Book of American Negro Poetry*. 1922; New York: Harvest, 1959.

———. *The Books of American Negro Spirituals*. New York: Viking, 1925, 1926.

Jones, Edward P. *The Known World*. New York: Harper Collins, 2003.

Jones, Gayl. *Corregidora*. New York: Random House, 1975.

Jones, LeRoi (Amiri Baraka). *Dutchman and The Slave*. New York: Morrow, 1964.

Jones Jr., Robert. *The Prophets*. New York: Putnam, 2021.

Jordan, Jennifer. "Feminist Fantasies: Zora Neale Hurston's *Their Eyes Were Watching God*." *Tulsa Studies in Women's Literature* 7, no. 1 (Spring 1988): 105–17.

Kenan, Randall. *A Visitation of Spirits*. New York: Grove, 1989.

King, Lovalerie. *The Cambridge Introduction to Zora Neale Hurston*. New York: Cambridge, 2008.

King, Lovalerie and Lynn Orilla Scott. *James Baldwin and Toni Morrison: Comparative Critical and Theoretical Essays*. New York: Palgrave, 2006.

Kolin, Philip C., ed. *Suzan-Lori Parks: Essays on the Plays and Other Works*. Jefferson, N. C.: McFarland, 2010.

———. *Suzan-Lori Parks in Person: Interviews and Commentaries*. New York: Routledge, 2014.

Komunyakaa, Yusef. "Cape Coast Castle." https://www.poets.org/poetsorg/poem/cape-coast-castle.

Koopman, Emy. "Incestuous Rape, Abjection, and the Colonization of Psychic Space in Toni Morrison's *The Bluest Eye* and Shani Mootoo's *Cereus Blooms at Night*." *Journal of Postcolonial Writing* 49, no. 3 (2013): 303–15.

Larson, Jennifer. *Understanding Suzan-Lori Parks*. Columbia: U of South Carolina P, 2012.

Lawrence, Jacob. "The Migration Series." https://lawrencemigration.phillipscollection.org/

LeClair, Thomas. "The Language Must Not Sweat: A Conversation with Toni Morrison." In *Conversations with Toni Morrison*. Edited by Danille Taylor-Guthrie. Jackson: U P of Mississippi, 1994, 119–28.

Lee, Don L. *Don't Cry, Scream*. Detroit: Broadside P, 1969.

Lee, Harper. *To Kill a Mockingbird*. New York: Harper & Row, 1960.

LeMahieu, Michael. "The Theater of Hustle and the Hustle of Theater: Play, Player, and Played in Suzan-Lori Parks's *Topdog/Underdog*." *African American Review* 45, nos. 1,2 (Spring/Summer 2012): 33–47.
Lester, Julius. "People Who Could Fly." In *Toni Morrison's Song of Solomon: A Casebook*, edited by Jan Furman. New York: Oxford U P, 2003, 21–23.
Locke, Alain, ed. *The New Negro: Voices of the Harlem Renaissance*. New York: Touchstone Books/Simon & Schuster, 1925; 1987.
Long, Lisa. "A New Midwesternism in Toni Morrison's *The Bluest Eye*." *Twentieth Century Literature* 59, no. 1 (Spring 2013): 104–25.
Lowe, John. *Critical Approaches to Teaching Hurston's Their Eyes Were Watching God and Other Works*. New York: The Modern Language Association of America, 2009.
Marshall, Paule. *The Chosen Place, The Timeless People*. 1969; New York: Vintage, 1984.
———. *Brown Girl, Brownstones*. 1959; New York: The Feminist P, 1981.
———. *Praisesong for the Widow*. New York: E. P. Dutton, 1983.
Matus, Jill. *Toni Morrison*. Manchester U P, 1998.
McKay, Claude. *Selected Poems of Claude McKay*. New York: Harcourt, 1953.
Mobley, Marilyn. *Toni Morrison's Geopoetics of Place, Race and Belonging: Re-imagining Spaces for the Reader*. Forthcoming from Temple University Press.
Morrison, Toni. *A Mercy*. New York: Knopf, 2008.
———. *Beloved*. New York: Knopf, 1987.
———. *The Bluest Eye*. New York: Plume, 1970; 1994.
———. *God Help the Child*. New York: Knopf, 2015.
———. "Home." In *The House that Race Built: Black Americans, U.S. Terrain*, edited by Wahneema Lubiano. New York: Pantheon Books, 1997, 3–12.
———. *Home*. New York: Knopf, 2012.
———. "'Intimate Things in Place': A Conversation with Toni Morrison." In *Chant of Saints: A Gathering of Afro-American Literature, Art, and Scholarship*. Edited by Michael S. Harper and Robert G. Stepto. Urbana: U of Illinois P, 1979, 213–29.
———. *Paradise*. New York: Knopf, 1998.
———. "Recitatif." In *Confirmation: An Anthology of African American Women*. Edited by Amiri Baraka (LeRoi Jones) & Amina Baraka. New York: Quill, 1983, 243–61.
———. *Song of Solomon*. New York: Knopf, 1977.
———. *Sula*. New York: Knopf, 1973.
———. "Unspeakable Things Unspoken: The Afro-American Presence in American Literature." *Michigan Quarterly Review* 28, no. 1 (Winter 1989): 1–34.
Moynihan, Daniel Patrick. https://www.blackpast.org/african-american-history/moynihan-report-1965/
Murray, Albert. *Train Whistle Guitar*. New York: McGraw Hill, 1974.
Murray, William. "The Roof of a Southern Home: A Reimagined and Usable South in Lorraine Hansberry's *A Raisin in the Sun*." *The Mississippi Quarterly* 68, no. 1-2 (Winter/Spring 2015): 277–93.
Naylor, Gloria. *Mama Day*. New York: Ticknor & Fields, 1988.

Norment Jr., Nathaniel. Review of *Perfect Peace*, by Daniel Black. *CLA Journal* 53, no.1 (September 2009). 113–17.

Obama, Barack. *Dreams from My Father: A Story of Race and Inheritance*. New York: Three Rivers Press, 1995.

Ogunyemi, Chikwenye Okonjo. "Order and Disorder in Toni Morrison's *The Bluest Eye*." *Critique: Studies in Modern Fiction* 19 (1977): 112–20.

Painter, Nell Irvin. *Exodusters: Black Migration to Kansas after Reconstruction*. New York: Alfred A. Knopf, Inc., 1977.

Parks, Suzan-Lori. *The Red Letter Plays*. New York: Theatre Communications Group, 2001.

———. *Topdog/Underdog*. New York: Theatre Communications Group, 2001.

Perkins-Valdez, Dolen. *Wench*. New York: HarperCollins, 2010.

Perry, Phyllis Alesia. *Stigmata*. New York: Random House, 1998.

Petry, Ann. "Mother Africa." In *Miss Muriel and Other Stories*. Boston: Beacon, 1989, 126–62.

———. *The Street*. Boston: Houghton Mifflin, 1946.

Phillips, Caryl. *Crossing the River*. New York: Knopf, 1994.

Phillips, Delores. *The Darkest Child*. New York: Soho, 2004; 2018.

Prince, Valerie Sweeney. *Burnin' Down the House: Home in African American Literature*. New York: Columbia U P, 2005.

Puschmann-Nalenz, Barbara. "Ann Petry: 'Mother Africa' (1971)." In *The African American Short Story, 1970-1990: A Collection of Critical Essays*. Edited by Woolfgang Karrer and Puschman-Nalenz. Trier: Wissenschaftlicher Verlag Trier, 1993, 29–39.

Rampersad, Arnold. *The Life of Langston Hughes; Volume 1: 1902–1941, I Too, Sing America*. New York: Oxford U P, 1986.

Rampersad, Arnold, ed. *The Collected Poems of Langston Hughes*. New York: Alfred A. Knopf, 1995.

Reed, Ishmael. *Flight to Canada*. New York: Random House, 1976.

Reid, Shelley E. "Beyond Morrison and Walker: Looking Good and Looking Forward in Contemporary Black Women's Stories." *African American Review* 34, no. 2 (Summer 2000): 313–28.

Rockwell, Norman. Paintings at https://www.nrm.org/collections-2/art-norman-rockwell/

Roman, Elda Maria. "Mortgaged Status: Literary Representations of Black Home Ownership and Social Mobility." *Contemporary Literature* 55, no. 4 (Winter 2014): 726–59.

Roye, Susmita. "Toni Morrison's Disrupted Girls and Their Disturbed Girlhoods: *The Bluest Eye* and *A Mercy*." *Callaloo* 35, no. 1 (2012): 212–27.

Ruas, Charles. "Toni Morrison." In *Conversations with Toni Morrison*. Edited by Danille Taylor-Guthrie. Jackson: U P of Mississippi, 1994, 93–118.

Sanders, Pamela Peden. "The Feminism of Dorothy West's *The Living Is Easy*: A Critique of the Limitations of the Female Sphere through Performative Gender Roles." *African American Review* 36, no. 3 (2002): 435–46.

Sato, Hiroko. "The Uses of Space in Margaret Walker's *Jubilee*." In *Fields Watered With Blood: Critical Essays on Margaret Walker*. Athens: U of Georgia P, 2001, 269–82.

Scott, Lynn Orilla. "At Home on the South Side: Chicago in Gwendolyn Brooks's *Maud Martha* and *Report from Part One*," *Midwestern Miscellany*, vol 43 (Spring/Fall 2015): 34–51.

———. "Revising the Incest Story: Toni Morrison's *The Bluest Eye* and James Baldwin's *Just Above my Head*." In *James Baldwin and Toni Morrison: Comparative Critical and Theoretical Essays*. Edited by Lovalerie King and Lynn Orilla Scott. New York: Palgrave, 2006, 83–102.

Shawl, Nisi. *Everfair*. New York: Tom Doherty Associates, 2016.

Sherrard-Johnson, Cherene. "'This plague of their own locusts': Space, Property, and Identity in Dorothy West's *The Living is Easy*." *African American Review* 38, no. 4 (2004): 609–24.

Solomon, Rivers. *The Deep*. New York: Saga, 2019.

Souljah, Sistah. *The Coldest Winter Ever*. New York: Washington Square P, 1999.

Standley, Fred L. and Nancy V. Burt. *Critical Essays on James Baldwin*. Boston: G. K. Hall & Co., 1988.

Stepto, Robert B. *A Home Elsewhere: Reading African American Classics in the Age of Obama*. Cambridge: Harvard U P, 2010.

Taylor, Christin Marie. "Feeling Rejected: National Denial of Black Working Mothers in Sarah E. Wright's *This Child's Gonna Live*." In *Labor Pains: New Deal Fictions of Race, Work, and Sex in the South*. Jackson: U P of Mississippi, 2019.

Taylor-Guthrie, Danille, ed. *Conversations with Toni Morrison*. Jackson: U P of Mississippi, 1994.

Thurman, Wallace. *The Blacker the Berry: A Novel of Negro Life*. Macaulay Company, 1929.

Truffin, Sherry R. "'Terrors of the Night': Salvation, Gender, and the Gothic in *Go Tell It on the Mountain*." In *James Baldwin's Go Tell It on the Mountain: Historical and Critical Essays*, edited by Carol E. Henderson. New York: Peter Lang, 2006, 123–37.

Van Der Zee, James. http://100photos.time.com/photos/james-vanderzee-couple-in-raccoon-coats.

Verdelle, A. J. *The Good Negress*. Chapel Hill, NC: Algonquin Books, 1995.

Wagner, Jean. *Black Poets of the United States: From Paul Laurence Dunbar to Langston Hughes*, trans. Kenneth Douglas. Urbana: U of Illinois P, 1973.

Wagner-Martin, Linda. *Toni Morrison and the Maternal: From The Bluest Eye to Home*. New York: Peter Lang, 2014.

Walker, Alice. *The Color Purple*. New York: Washington Square, 1982.

———. *In Love and Trouble: Stories of Black Women*. New York: Harcourt/Harvest, 1973.

———. *Possessing the Secret of Joy*. New York: Harcourt Brace Jovanovich, 1992.

———. *The Third Life of Grange Copeland*. New York: Harcourt Brace Jovanovich, 1970.

Walker, Alice and Pratibha Parmar. *Warrior Marks: Female Genital Mutilation and the Sexual Blinding of Women.* New York: Harcourt Brace, 1993.

Walker, Margaret. *How I Wrote Jubilee.* Chicago: Third World P, 1972.

———. *Jubilee.* Boston: First Mariner Books, 1966;1999.

Washington, Booker T. *Up From Slavery.* New York: W. W. Norton, 1901; 1996.

West, Dorothy. *The Living Is Easy.* New York: The Feminist P, 1948; 1982.

Wideman, John Edgar. *The Cattle Killing.* Boston: Houghton Mifflin, 1996.

Wilder, Laura Ingalls. *Little House on the Prairie.* New York: Harper & Brothers, 1953.

Wilder, Thornton. *Our Town.* New York: Coward-McCann, 1939.

Wilentz, Gay. "Civilizations Underneath: African Heritage as Cultural Discourse in Toni Morrison's *Song of Solomon.*" In *Toni Morrison's Song of Solomon: A Casebook.* Edited by Jan Furman. New York: Oxford U P, 2003, 137–63.

———. "If You Surrender to the Air: Folk Legends of Flight and Resistance in African American Literature." *MELUS* 16, no. 1 (1989-1990): 21–32.

Wilkerson, Isabel. *The Warmth of Other Suns: The Epic Story of America's Great Migration.* New York: Random House, 2010.

Williams, Sherley Anne. *Dessa Rose.* New York: William Morrow and Company, 1986.

Willis, Susan. "Eruptions of Funk: Historicizing Toni Morrison." *Black American Literature Forum* 16, no.1 (Spring 1982): 34–42.

Wilson, August. *Fences.* New York: Dramatists Play Service, Plume/New American Library, 1986.

———. *The Piano Lesson.* New York: Dutton, 1990.

Wilson, Harriet E. *Our Nig.* New York: Vintage, 1859; 2002.

Wolfe, Andrea. "The Narrative Power of the Black Maternal Body: Resisting and Exceeding Visual Economics of Discipline in Margaret Walker's *Jubilee.*" *Interdisciplinary Literary Studies* 20, no. 4 (2018), 409–28.

Woodworth, Christine. "Parks and the Traumas of Childhood." In *Suzan-Lori Parks: Essays on the Plays and Other Works.* Edited by Philip C. Kolin. Jefferson, N.C. McFarland, 140–55.

Wright, Richard. *12 Million Black Voices: A Folk History of the Negro in the United States.* 1941; Brattleboro, VT: Echo Point Books & Media, 2019.

———. *Black Boy.* New York: Harper and Row, 1945.

———. *Black Power: A Record of Reactions in a Land of Pathos.* New York: Harper, 1954.

———. *Native Son.* New York: Library of America, 1940; 1991.

———. "Big Boy Leaves Home." In *Uncle Tom's Children.* New York: HarperPerennial, 1938; 1993, 17–61.

Wright, Sarah E. *This Child's Gonna Live.* New York: Dell, 1969.

Credits

"Go Down Death - A Funeral Sermon" from GOD'S TROMBONES by James Weldon Johnson, copyright 1927 by Penguin Random House LLC, renewed 1955 by Grace Nail Johnson. Used by permission of Viking Books, an imprint of Penguin Publishing Group, a division of Penguin Random House LLC. All rights reserved.

"The Creation" from GOD'S TROMBONES by James Weldon Johnson, copyright 1927 by Penguin Random House LLC, renewed 1955 by Grace Nail Johnson. Used by permission of Viking Books, an imprint of Penguin Publishing Group, a division of Penguin Random House LLC. All rights reserved.

"Sister Lou" from "THE COLLECTED POEMS OF STERLING A. BROWN," edited by MICHAEL S. HARPER. Copyright © 1980 by Sterling A. Brown. Reprinted by permission of Jacqueline M. Combs.

"When de Saints Go Ma'ching Home" from "THE COLLECTED POEMS OF STERLING A. BROWN," edited by MICHAEL S. HARPER. Copyright © 1980 by Sterling A. Brown. Reprinted by permission of Jacqueline M. Combs.

Dorothy West, excerpts from *The Living is Easy*. Copyright 1948, © 1975 by Dorothy West. Reprinted with the permission of The Permissions Company, LLC on behalf of The Feminist Press at the City University of New York, www.feministpress.org.

Quotations from *The Good Negress* by A. J. Verdelle, copyright 1995 by A. J. Verdelle. Used by permission of A. J. Verdelle. All rights reserved.

Quotations from *Perfect Peace* by Daniel Black, copyright 2010 by Daniel Black. Used by permission of Daniel Black. All rights reserved.

Index

The letter *f* following a page locator denotes a figure.

Achilles, Jochen, 63
Africa:
    life writings about, 156–58;
    a realistic approach to the mother
        land, 167–172
Africa as home:
    appeal of, 15, 16;
    escaping to, 164;
    imagination in creating,
        10–11, 162–63;
    mythologizing the ancestral home,
        16, 153–166
African fever, 156–57
African identity, transformation to, 160
Aftermath (Burrill), 6
American Dream, 1
American nuclear family, myth of the,
    6–7, 50–51
Angelou, Maya, 158
architecture, potential to determine
    destiny, 15
art, African American, 152
Asante, Molefi Kete, 158

Baker, Houston A., 12

Baldwin, James, 9, 47, 60, 96,
    179. *See also Go Tell It on the
    Mountain* (Baldwin)
Barksdale, Richard, 7
beauty culture in America, blackness
    devalued, 51, 96–101, 107,
    116–19, 121–22
Beloved (Morrison), 2–3, 9, 24, 33, 169
Bennett, Gwendolyn, 10
"Big Boy Leaves Home" (Wright), 4
black adolescent female in *The Good
    Negress* (Verdelle):
    adolescence removed, 73–74;
    competing for a life, education vs.
        expectations in, 86–91;
    enslaved, training to be, 75–78;
    roles assigned to, 79–80, 86–87;
    servitude, forced and
        voluntary, 73–74;
    subservience, escaping, 91;
    use value of, 78–83, 86, 128
The Blacker the Berry (Thurman), 96
Blackmon, Douglas A., 169
*Black Writers of America: A
    Comprehensive Anthology* (Barksdale
    & Kinnamon), 7
Blue-Eyed Black Boy (Johnson), 6

the blues, 12
Blues, Ideology, and Afro-American Literature: A Vernacular Theory (Baker), 12
The Bluest Eye (Morrison), 12
　beauty culture in America, blackness devalued, 96–97;
　girlhoods disrupted, 53–54;
　migrants cementing disconnection from the South, 56–57;
　migration, successes and failures of, 40, 49–51;
　myth of American nuclear family deconstructed, 6–7;
　nigger, use of the term, 57;
　race and religion, detrimental effects illustrated, 7;
　scholarship on, 12
The Bluest Eye (Morrison), home in:
　alternatives, 56–58;
　dysfunctional, 56;
　external values and racist formulations entering, 51–52;
　healthy, the caring parents in, 55–56;
　migration and Christianity in creating, 39, 49;
　northern geography, impact on the creation of, 15;
　pretty vs. poisonous, creation of a, 56–58;
　the prostitutes,' 55–56;
　as a safespace, 52;
　ugliness of, 51–53, 57–58;
　white, creating a, 57
The Bluest Eye (Morrison), physical space inhabited:
　abandoning for white spaces, 53–54, 57;
　alienation from the, 49–50;
　escaping the, 51–52, 55–56;
　as a homespace, 52;
　imprisoned in the, 49;
　memories in the, 51–52;
　as a safespace, 53–55;
　ugliness of, 49, 51

The Bluest Eye (Morrison), relationships in:
　abandonment within, 54;
　a father's rape, 53–55;
　a mother's rejection, 53–54;
　physical violence in, 53–55;
　protecting the vulnerable, 54;
　ugliness and unhealthiness of, 51–53, 57–58
The Book of American Negro Poetry (Johnson), 22–23
Brooks, Gwendolyn, 8, 14, 96
Brown, Sterling A., 11, 175–79
Brown Girl, Brownstones (Marshall), 151–52
Burnin' Down the House: Home in African American Literature (Prince), 12–13
Burrill, Mary Powell, 6
"But He Was Cool or: he even stopped for green lights" (Lee), 156
Butler, Octavia E., 3–4, 11, 179–180

"Cape Coast Castle" (Komunyakaa), 11
Carmichael, Jacqueline Miller, 22, 24
Chesnutt, Charles W., 4, 96
Christianity-homespace connection, 7, 34–36, 39, 43–49
Civil Rights movement, 23
Clark, Keith, 159
colonization societies, 152
colored people, presentation of, 57
colorism and colorphobia:
　in *The Living is Easy* (West), 127–28, 131, 135, 142;
　in *Perfect Peace* (Black), 95–99, 101, 129.
　See also skin color
The Color Purple (Walker), 161
The Conjure Woman (Chesnutt), 4
conversion, Christian, 42–43
convict lease system, 169
Corregidora (Jones), 12
Correia, Alda Maria, 52

"Couple in Racoon Coats" (Van Der Zee), 50
Crank, James A., 49
"The Creation" (Johnson), 174–75
Crummell, Alexander, 152
Csapo, Csaba, 43
Cullen, Countee, 10, 11, 153–56, 160, 166

The Darkest Child (Phillips), 3–4, 129
Davis, Amanda J., 28–29
Davis, Big Boy, 178
Day, Lisa B., 87
The Deep (Solomon), 10, 191
dialect poetry, 22–23
Douglas, Aaron, 10, 11, 152
Douglass, Frederick, 13, 33, 74
Dove, Rita, 14
Du Bois, W. E. B., 133
Dudley, Marc, 43
Dunbar, Paul Laurence, 22–23
Dutchman (Jones), 23

Ellison, Ralph, 8, 12
Equiano, Olaudah, 169
escape:
  in *The Bluest Eye* (Morrison), 55–56;
  from a physical space, 55–56;
  from mothers, 122;
  from subservience, 91;
  from the homespace, 45, 47–48, 138, 142;
  in *The Good Negress* (Verdelle), 91;
  in *Go Tell It on the Mountain* (Baldwin), 45, 47–48;
  in *Incidents in the Life of a Slave Girl* (Jacobs), 33;
  in *The Living is Easy* (West), 138, 142;
  in *Perfect Peace* (Black), 122
"Everyday Use" (Walker), 16, 160–61

family:
  myth of the American nuclear, 6–7, 50–51;
  storybook narrative of the American, 1.
  See also relationships
fathers. *See* relationships: fathers:
Fences (Wilson), 9
FIRE!! 10
Flying Africans, 11, 14, 161–62, 164
forgiveness:
  in *Jubilee* (Walker), 21–22, 34–36;
  in *Perfect Peace* (Black), 96, 109–13, 118–19, 121–22
freed blacks, living spaces of, 5–6
Freedom From Want (Rockwell), 1
Fugitive Slave Act, 169

Gaines, Ernest J., 5
geography, impact of northern on the creation of home, 15
Giovanni, Nikki, 23, 24
"Go Down Death—A Funeral Sermon" (Johnson), 172–74, 176, 177
God's Trombones (Johnson), 152, 173–74
Golden, Marita, 156–58
Goldsmith, Meredith, 128, 142
The Good Negress (Verdelle):
  home in, migration of an idea of, 15;
  homespace, violations of a, 83–85;
  memory, making into reality, 15;
  overview, 75;
  relationships, mother-daughter, 15, 73–76, 81–83, 85–86, 91
The Good Negress (Verdelle), the adolescent black female in:
  adolescence removed, 73–74;
  competing for a life, education vs. expectations in, 86–91;
  enslaved, training to be, 75–78;
  roles assigned to, 79–80, 86–87;
  servitude, forced and voluntary, 73–74;
  subservience, escaping, 91;
  use value of, 78–83, 86, 128
Go Tell It on the Mountain (Baldwin):
  lives, ugliness of lived, 40–49;

migration, successes and failures
of, 40–41;
migration patterns, 43;
overview, 39–40;
passing tradition in, 96;
relationships of toxic
masculinity, 43–47
Go Tell It on the Mountain
(Baldwin), home in:
alienation from, Christianity
in, 43–49;
dirtiness of, reflecting character's
lives, 40–49;
escaping the, 45, 47–48;
formation of, Christianity in, 39;
heaven as the ultimate, 179;
is not a home, 9;
northern geography, impact on the
creation of, 15;
violence in, 9, 43–46
Graham, Maryemma, 24
Great Migration, 8, 15, 50–51
Greene, J. Lee, 152
Grimke, Angelina Weld, 6
Gyasi, Yaa, 167–172

Haley, Alex, 158
Hammon, Jupiter, 11
Hansberry, Lorraine, 9–10, 16, 41,
57, 60, 158, 179. *See also specific
works by title*
Harlem, 48–49
Harlem Renaissance, 10, 22, 152
Harper, Frances Ellen Watkins, 7, 96
Hartman, Saidiya, 158, 164
heaven as the ultimate home, 11,
48–49, 172–180
"Heritage" (Cullen), 11, 153–56
"High John de Conquer" (Hurston), 11
home:
for descendents of slaves, 169–170;
for the enslaved,
contingencies of, 3–5;
external forces in
constructions of, 6–7;
ideas central to, 4;
inventing a, 13–14;
leaving to find, 15, 170;
loss of, the ocean as a space of, 169;
physical location as crucial to literary
representations of, 2;
primary factors of, 55–56;
storybook narrative of the
American, 1–2;
transforming a physical
space to a, 10
"Home" (Morrison), 6
home, Africa as:
appeal of, 15, 16;
escaping to, 164;
imagination in creating,
10–11, 162–63;
mythologizing, 16, 153–166
home, memories of:
The Deep (Solomon), 10, 191
home, memory and imagination in
constructing a:
Africa as home, 10–11, 162–63;
in *Jubilee* (Walker), 7, 27, 28–29;
in *Kindred* (Butler), 10;
in *The Living is Easy* (West), 140,
143–44, 146;
in *A Raisin in the Sun*
(Hansberry), 7–8;
in *Song of Solomon* (Morrison),
11, 162–63;
in *Topdog/Underdog* (Parks), 62
home as not a home:
Beloved (Morrison), 9;
Perfect Peace (Black), 96;
Topdog/Underdog (Parks), 58–66
*A Home Elsewhere: Reading African
American Classics in the Age of
Obama* (Stepto), 12, 13
Homegoing (Gyasi), 167–172
home in African American literature:
Christianity-homespace connection,
7, 34–36, 39, 43–49;
contradictions and complexities
shaping, 3–4;

creation of, features of the, 8–10;
defined, 2–3, 5, 11–12;
descendant of slavery
  reflected in, 4–5;
disappeared, the nature of
  enslavement, 168–69;
elusiveness of, 12–13;
familiarity as precedent in, 2–3;
heaven as the ultimate, 11,
  48–49, 172–180;
ideal spaces evoked by, 1–2;
ideas central to, 4;
the intangible concept of, 167–69;
inventing a, 13–14;
keeping inviolate against
  societally inspired violence,
  challenge of, 32;
the place of, 2–3;
race, impact on, 6;
religion, influence on the
  creation of, 6–7;
representations of, 3–10;
scholarship on, 12–14;
slavery's claims upon the
  construction of, 2–4;
the space of, 2, 171;
a violent disruption of prejudice and
  hostility, 28.
*See also under specific works by
  title* homelessness, 25–27, 45,
  48–49, 169
homosexuality, 109–16, 119
hooks, bell, 29
Horton, George Moses, 11
The House Behind the Cedars
  (Chesnutt), 96
a house is not a home:
  Beloved (Morrison), 9;
  Douglass, Frederick, 33;
  Go Tell It on the Mountain
    (Baldwin), 9;
  Perfect Peace (Black), 96;
  A Raisin in the Sun
    (Hansberry), 8–10

Hughes, Langston, 6, 8, 10, 153,
  160, 163, 179
Hurston, Zora Neale, 8, 10, 11

Incidents in the Life of a Slave Girl
  (Jacobs), 26, 33–34
Invisible Man (Ellison), 8, 12
Iola Leroy (Harper), 96
As I Run Toward Africa: A Memoir
  (Asante), 158

Jacobs, Harriet E., 26, 33–34
"Jessie Mitchell's Mother" (Brooks), 14
Johnson, Avey, 11
Johnson, Charles, 24
Johnson, Georgia Douglas, 6
Johnson, James Weldon, 11, 22, 152,
  172–74, 176–77
Jonah's Gourd Vine (Hurston), 8
Jones, Gayl, 12
Jones, LeRoi (Amiri Baraka), 23
Jubilee (Walker):
  aboutness, 21–22;
  African American literary history,
    significance in, 21–25;
  Christianity-homespace connection,
    34–36, 39;
  colored, presentation of, 29–30;
  education in, 32–33;
  emotional cruelty found in, 25–27;
  the enslaved in, 26–28;
  faithfulness in, 34–36;
  forgiveness's centrality in,
    21–22, 34–36;
  historical patterns underlying, 32–34;
  mothers, loss of, 25, 34;
  post-emancipation, choices
    made, 27–28;
  power dynamic of the political
    system, 26;
  questing narratives, similarity
    to, 28–29;
  reactions to, 22–24;
  scholarship on, 22, 24, 128;
  setting, 23;

time span, 25;
violence in, 21, 25–26;
white helpers and hinderers, 29–30;
will to triumph over adversity, 17, 21
Jubilee (Walker), home in:
boundaries of, violence against, 28, 31–32;
constructing a, 7;
dedication to the objective of, 34–35;
desire for, 25–27;
homelessness, emotional cruelty of, 25–27;
an idea shaped in reaction to slavery, 14–15;
imagining a, 7, 27, 28–29;
is elsewhere, 33–34;
issues relevant for later conceptions of, 31–35;
place and space constituting, 27;
quest for, successful/happy ending of, 36;
white helpers in obtaining a, 29–30, 32

To Kill a Mockingbird (Lee), 1–2
Kindred (Butler), 3–4, 10
King, Martin Luther Jr., 23
Kinnamon, Keneth, 7
Komunyakaa, Yusef, 11
Ku Klux Klan, 28, 31

Lawrence, Jacob, 83
Lee, Don L., 156, 160
Lee, Harper, 1–2
literature, African American:
Great Migration in, 8;
passing tradition in, 96;
Protest Tradition established, 128;
themes underlying, 7;
violence portrayed in, 23.
See also home in African American literature
The Living is Easy (West):
the black female character, creating the, 147;

colorism in, 127–138, 142;
nigger, use of the term, 137, 141, 142;
patterns of migration and attempted integration, 151–52;
racial politics, 133;
scholarship on, 128–29
The Living is Easy (West), home in:
class desires as a factor of the, 127, 131, 138, 139, 143–44, 146;
class values in the, 127–28;
collapse of the, 144–48;
escaping the, 138, 142;
external forces shaping, 127–28;
imaginary, creating the, 140, 143–44, 146;
lies as basis of, 131–34, 136, 140–48;
summary overview, 148;
toxicity of the, 129, 134–35, 138;
ugliness defining, 127;
violence, physical, 142;
women controlling, 15–16
The Living is Easy (West), marital relationships:
financial lies and manipulations, 131–34, 136, 141, 143–47;
imaginary, creating the, 140;
intimacy denied, love unrequited, 130–31, 135;
of self-esteem sacrificed, 129–135;
values of colorism affecting, 131, 135
The Living is Easy (West), relationships:
mother-daughter, 128, 131, 135–38;
sisters, 128, 139–148;
skin color as element in, 127, 128, 131, 135–38, 142;
summarized, 148;
use value dominating, 128
Locke, Alain, 10, 152
loneliness and alienation as homelessness, 45
Lose Your Mother: A Journey Along the Atlantic Slave Route (Hartman), 158

Index

lynching plays, 6

Mama Day (Naylor), 167
marriage. *See* relationships: marital:
Marshall, Paule, 11, 151–52
masculinity, toxic, 32, 43–47
McKay, Claude, 10–11, 11, 155–56
Middle Passage, 164, 166, 169
migration:
 and attempted integration, 151–52;
 in *The Bluest Eye* (Morrison), 39–40, 49, 56–57;
 forced, psychological violence of, 25;
 in *Go Tell It on the Mountain* (Baldwin), 39–41;
 and home in African American literature, 7–9;
 in *Jubilee* (Walker), 25, 27–29;
 successes and failures of, 40–41, 49–51;
 in *Topdog/Underdog* (Parks), 40;
 to transform a previous existence, 151–52;
 urban spaces of, 50–51
migration patterns:
 in *Go Tell It on the Mountain* (Baldwin), 43;
 in *The Living is Easy* (West), 151–52
"Migration Series" (Lawrence), 83
Migrations of the Heart: A Personal Odyssey (Golden), 156–58
Miss Muriel and Other Stories (Petry), 158–59
Morrison, Toni, 2–3, 6, 9, 24, 33, 56, 111, 169. *See also* works by title; *specific works by title*
Mother Africa, 158–59, 165
"Mother Africa" (Petry), 16
mothers:
 abandonment by, 34, 54, 74–76, 165, 167–68;
 escaping, 122;
 loss through childbirth, 13;
 reclaiming, 166;
 reuniting with, 165, 166;
 in slavery, loss of, 4, 25, 34, 158;
 surrogate, 79–80, 86–87.
 See also relationships: mother-daughter
Mulatto (Hughes), 6
Murray, Albert, 8

Narrative (Equiano), 169
Narrative of the Life of Frederick Douglass (Douglass), 13
Native Son (Wright), 9, 12, 40, 57, 128
Naylor, Gloria, 167
neo-slave narrative, the, 2–3, 24
The New Negro (Locke), 10, 152
nigga, use of the word, 99, 104, 118
nigger, use of the term, 57, 137, 141, 142
Not Without Laughter (Hughes), 179
Nugent, Bruce, 10

Obama, Barack, 13
"One-Way Ticket" (Hughes), 8
"Outcast" (McKay), 10–11, 155–56

Parable of the Sower (Butler), 11, 179
Parable of the Talents (Butler), 180
parent-child relationships:
 abandoning daughters to the South, 74–79;
 in *Jubilee* (Walker), 31–35;
 love despite destructive, 101;
 replicating dynamics of societal violence and domination, 31–35;
 self-definition within, 44, 114–16;
 violence in, 43–46, 53–55.
 See also relationships
parents, compensating for absent, 13, 63
Parmar, Pratibha, 161
passing tradition, 96
Perfect Peace (Black):
 blackness devalued, 96–101, 107, 116–19, 121–22;
 colorism and colorphobia in, 95–99, 101, 129;
 homosexuality in, 111–16, 119;

human kindness and forgiveness in, 96, 109–15, 118–19, 121–22;
nigga, use of the word, 99, 104, 118;
overview, 95;
perfect peace in, 121–23;
pigmentocracy, origin of, 95;
religion in, 7;
values, color-defined system of, 129
Perfect Peace (Black), home in:
church house as the, 7;
external forces impact on the, 111–14;
female control of, 15–16;
a house is not a, 96;
ugliness defining, 127
Perfect Peace (Black), relationships:
brothers, 115–16;
color politics shaping, 99, 127;
father/daughter-son, 109–13;
marital, 102–4;
mother-daughter, 97–99, 101, 104–8, 121, 122;
sisters, 100;
violence in, 98
Perry, Phyllis Alesia, 164–66
Petry, Ann, 11, 16, 158–59
Phillips, Delores, 3–4, 129
The Piano Lesson (Wilson), 4
pigmentocracy, 95–99
poetry, dialect, 22–23
Possessing the Secret of Joy (Walker), 161
Praisesong for the Widow (Marshall), 11
primitivism, 152
Prince, Valerie Sweeney, 12–13
Puschmann-Nalenz, Barbara, 159

Rachel (Grimke), 6
The Radical Fiction of Ann Petry (Clark), 159
A Raisin in the Sun (Hansberry):
African identity in, 160;
home in, 7–10, 16, 41, 57, 60, 179;
religion in, 7
Rampersad, Arnold, 153

"Recitatif" (Morrison), 6
Reed, Ishmael, 24
relationships:
of love, violence, and forgiveness, 109–15;
use value in, 78–83, 86, 128;
violence in, 53–55
relationships, brothers:
of hypermasculine competition, 64, 66;
imagined, 62;
in *Perfect Peace* (Black), 115–16;
potential for violence in, 60–61;
in *Topdog/Underdog* (Parks), 58–66
relationships, color's role in:
in *The Living is Easy* (West), 127–135, 142;
marital, 129–135;
mother-daughter, 97–99, 128, 135–38;
in *Perfect Peace* (Black), 97–99, 127;
sisters, 100
relationships, fathers:
in *The Bluest Eye* (Morrison), 53–55;
a father's rape, 53–55;
in *Go Tell It on the Mountain* (Baldwin), 43–47;
in *Perfect Peace* (Black), 109–13;
of toxic masculinity, 32, 43–47;
violence in, 31–32, 110–13
relationships, marital:
color and class dynamics, 96, 102–4, 129–135;
financial lies and manipulations, 131–34, 136, 141, 143–47;
gender expectations, 102–3;
in *Go Tell It on the Mountain* (Baldwin), 40–43;
imaginary, creating the, 140;
intimacy denied, love unrequited, 130–31, 135;
intimacy vs. expectations in, 103;
in *The Living is Easy* (West), 129–136, 140–41, 143–45, 146–47;

Index 215

in *Perfect Peace* (Black), 102–4;
self-esteem sacrificed, 129–135;
slaveholders, 26
relationships, mother-daughter:
adolescence removed, 73–74;
in *The Bluest Eye* (Morrison), 53–54;
color and class dynamics, 97–99, 128, 135–38;
desperation for a, 104–9, 116–18;
destroying potential for a healthy homespace, 128;
escaping, 122;
father figure, influence on, 73;
The Good Negress (Verdelle), 15, 73–76, 81–83, 85–86, 91;
impact of space on, 73;
in *The Living is Easy* (West), 128, 131, 135–38;
a mother's abandonment, 54;
a mother's rejection, 53–54, 96–99, 106;
in *Perfect Peace* (Black), 97–99, 101, 105–8, 121, 122;
power and resentment in the, 82–83, 85–86, 91;
respect in the, 81–82;
rewriting, 105–8;
self-definition within, 137–38;
toxic, 15, 73;
violence in, 98
relationships, parent-child:
abandoning daughters to the South, 74–79;
the absent parent in, 13, 61–63;
in *Go Tell It on the Mountain* (Baldwin), 43–45;
imagined, 62–63;
in *Jubilee* (Walker), 31–35;
love despite destructive, 101;
replicating dynamics of societal violence and domination, 31–35;
self-definition within, 44, 114–16;
in *Topdog/Underdog* (Parks), 58–59;
violence in, 43–46, 53–55
relationships, sisters:

colorphobia within, 100;
lies as basis of, 139–145;
in *The Living is Easy* (West), 128, 133, 135, 139–148;
in *Perfect Peace* (Black), 99–100;
use value in, 128
Rockwell, Norman, 1
Roots (Haley), 158
Rosewood Massacre, 16–17
Roye, Susmita, 54–55

"Sadie and Maud" (Brooks), 14
Safe (Johnson), 6
Sanchez, Sonia, 23
sharecropping/sharecroppers, 4–5
"Sister Lou" (Brown), 175–78
sisters. *See* relationships: sisters:
skin color:
devaluing and dismissal based on, 95–101, 116–19, 121–22;
light skin advantage, 135;
in *The Living is Easy* (West), 127–138;
relationships, effects on, 127, 128, 131, 135–38, 142;
sexual stereotyping dimension of, 100;
social segregation within the family and, 99;
spatial segregation in a public space, 99;
to wield control and domination, 127, 129–135.
See also colorism and colorphobia
Slavery By Another Name: The Re-Enslavement of Black Americans from the Civil War to World War II (Blackmon), 169
Solomon, Rivers, 10, 191
Song of Solomon (Morrison), 2, 11–14, 161–63
"Sonny's Blues" (Baldwin), 47
Sousa, Alcina Pereia de, 52
spaces, physical:
alienation from the, 49–50;

escaping the, 51–52, 55–56;
as homespaces, 52;
memories in the, 2, 52;
as a safespace, 53–55;
transforming to a home, 9–10;
urban, dirtiness of the, 40–42, 50–51
spiritual tradition, 172–73
Stepto, Robert B., 12, 13
Steverson, Delia, 129
Stigmata (Perry), 164–66
A Street in Bronzeville (Brooks), 8
suicide, perfect peace in, 122–23
Sula (Morrison), 56, 111
A Sunday Morning in the South (Johnson), 6

"Taking in Wash" (Dove), 14
Their Eyes Were Watching God (Hurston), 8
The Third Life of Grange Copeland (Walker), 5, 32
Thomas and Beulah (Dove), 14
Thurman, Wallace, 10, 96
Topdog/Underdog (Parks):
 community, lack of, 65–66;
 of family wounds and healing, 58–66;
 migration, successes and failures of, 40;
 a vacuum of existence, 65–66;
 violence dominating in, 64
Topdog/Underdog (Parks), home in:
 changing, desire for, 59;
 described, 59;
 dreams and fantasies, death of, 59;
 enslavement scenarios acted out in, 66;
 healthy, creating a, 66;
 is not a home, 8–9;
 isolation of the, 66;
 memory and imagination in, 62;
 northern geography, impact on the creation of, 15;
 potential for disaster, 60–61, 64;
 spaces labeled as, 9;
 toxicity of the, 32;
 unrealistic expectations within the, 59
Topdog/Underdog (Parks), the brothers' relationship:
 external world's influence on, 66;
 of hypermasculine competition, 64;
 hypermasculine competition, 66;
 lack of, 65–66;
 memory and portability in, 58–59, 61–63;
 ritual in, 63;
 shared history unglued, 62–64;
 spatial configuration, influence on, 39–40
Train Whistle Guitar (Murray), 8
Truffin, Sherry R., 47
Tulsa Race Massacre, 16–17
12 Million Black Voices: A Folk History of the Negro in the United States (Wright), 1

use value in relationships, 78–83, 86, 128

Van Der Zee, James, 50
violence:
 emotional, 64;
 of rape, 21, 25, 40, 53–55, 115, 120;
 white, against black characters, 6
violence, physical:
 in *The Bluest Eye* (Morrison), 53–55;
 forgiveness for, 22;
 forgiveness of, 21–22, 34–36;
 in *Go Tell It on the Mountain* (Baldwin), 43–46;
 homes disrupted by, 6;
 in *Jubilee* (Walker), 21, 25–26, 28, 31–32;
 in *Kindred* (Butler), 2–3;
 in *The Living is Easy* (West), 142;
 in parent-child relationships, 43–46, 53–55, 110–13;
 in *Perfect Peace* (Black), 110–13;
 in *Topdog/Underdog* (Parks), 64

violence, psychological:
    of forced migration, 25;
    in *Go Tell It on the Mountain* (Baldwin), 43–46;
    in *Jubilee* (Walker), 21, 25–26;
    in *Kindred* (Butler), 2–3;
    in *Topdog/Underdog* (Parks), 64

Walker, Alice, 5, 11, 16, 32, 158, 160–61
Walker, Margaret. *See* also *Jubilee* (Walker), 24, 24–25
The Warmth of Other Suns (Wilkerson), 152
Warrior Marks: Female Genital Mutilation and the Sexual Blinding of Women (Walker & Parmar), 161

Washington, Sondra, 129
West, Dorothy. *See The Living is Easy* (West):
Wheatley, Phillis, 7
"When de Saints Go Ma'ching' Home" (Brown), 175, 178–79
"When the Saints Go Marchin' In" (spiritual), 178
Wilkerson, Isabel, 152
Wilson, August, 4, 9
Wolfe, Andrea, 28, 35
Woodworth, Christine, 65
Wright, Richard, 1, 4, 9, 12, 24, 40, 50, 57, 128, 158

About the Author

Trudier Harris graduated Magna Cum Laude from Stillman College with a B.A. degree in English and Social Studies in 1969; she received her degree in three years. She earned her M.A. from The Ohio State University in 1972 and her Ph.D. from Ohio State in 1973. She is now University Distinguished Research Professor in the Department of English at the University of Alabama and formerly J. Carlyle Sitterson Distinguished Professor of English at the University of North Carolina at Chapel Hill, where she taught courses in African American literature and folklore. In addition to lecturing throughout the United States, as well as in Jamaica, Canada, France, Germany, Poland, Spain, Italy, England, Northern Ireland, and South Africa, Harris has written and edited twenty-six books, including *Exorcising Blackness: Historical and Literary Lynching and Burning Rituals* (1984), *Fiction and Folklore: The Novels of Toni Morrison* (1991), *The Scary Mason-Dixon Line: African American Writers and the South* (2009), *Martin Luther King Jr., Heroism, and African American Literature* (2014), and a memoir, *Summer Snow: Reflections from a Black Daughter of the South* (2003), which was chosen by the Orange County, North Carolina, Commission on Human Relations to inaugurate its One-Book, One-Community Reading Program for 2003–2004. Harris has received numerous teaching awards, including, in 2005, the Board of Governors Award for Excellence in Teaching at the University of North Carolina at Chapel Hill. She has also received several awards for lifetime achievement in literary studies, including the Eugene Current-Garcia Award for selection as Alabama's Distinguished Literary Scholar (2002). During the fall semester of 2006, she was Faculty Director of an Honors Study Abroad Seminar in Cape Town, South Africa.

Her alma mater, Stillman College, has recognized Harris for several achievements. In 2010, Stillman College awarded Harris an Honorary Doctor of Letters Degree. In 2013, she was inducted into the Stillman College Educator Hall of Fame. And, in 2018, Stillman bestowed a Distinguished Alumni Recognition upon Harris.

In March of 2014, the University of North Carolina at Chapel Hill created the "Trudier Harris Distinguished Professorship" in her honor. In 2017, The College of William and Mary honored Harris as its first tenured African American faculty member (in 1979) and presented her with an honorary degree at its 325th Charter Day celebration in 2018. In 2018, she also received the Richard Beale Davis Award for Lifetime Achievement in Southern Literary Studies and was awarded a Resident Fellowship to the National Humanities Center for 2018–2019, where she worked on *Depictions of Home in African American Literature*. Harris was named the recipient of the 2018 Clarence E. Cason Award in Nonfiction Writing, and won the 2018 SEC Faculty Achievement Award at the University of Alabama (which is a "Professor of Year" designation for the University of Alabama).

Harris is a Zeta DOVE and a member of the Beta Eta Zeta Graduate Chapter of Zeta Phi Beta Sorority, Incorporated. She is also a founding member of the Wintergreen Women Writers' Collective, which celebrated its 34th anniversary in 2021.

www.ingramcontent.com/pod-product-compliance
Lightning Source LLC
Chambersburg PA
CBHW020117010526
44115CB00008B/870